NORMAN COLLIE

A LIFE IN TWO WORLDS

Other AUP titles

HALDANE
the life and work of J B S Haldane, with special reference to India
Krishna R Dronamraju
Foreword by Naomi Mitchison

GEORGE WASHINGTON WILSON
artist and photographer 1823–93
Roger Taylor

COBBETT'S TOUR IN SCOTLAND
edited and introduced by Daniel Green
Foreword by Lord Grimond

SPEAK TO THE HILLS
an anthology of twentieth century British and Irish mountain poetry
selected by Hamish Brown & Martyn Berry

POEMS OF THE SCOTTISH HILLS
an Anthology *selected by Hamish Brown*
Foreword by Norman MacCaig

THE LIVING MOUNTAIN
a celebration of the Cairngorm Mountains
Nan Shepherd

NORMAN COLLIE
A LIFE IN TWO WORLDS

Mountain Explorer and Scientist
1859–1942

Christine Mill

ABERDEEN UNIVERSITY PRESS

First published 1987
Aberdeen University Press
A member of the Pergamon Group

The publisher acknowledges subsidy from the Scottish Arts Council towards the publication of this volume.

British Library Cataloguing in Publication Data

Mill, Christine
Norman Collie: a life in two worlds:
mountain explorer and scientist 1859–1942.
1. Collie, Norman 2. Mountaineers—
Scotland—Biography
I. Title
796.5′22′0924 GV199.92.C6/

ISBN 0-08-032456-8

Printed in Great Britain
The University Press
Aberdeen

Dedicated to the memory of
Donald Mill 1931–1981

Contents

Illustrations

Collie's own maps have, on the whole, been used throughout, both because they indicate how little was known about the mountain areas he set out to explore and also because they show how modern maps have developed from them. Collie's spelling of place names has also been used to coincide with the maps, although nowadays variations have occurred and in Canada some names have actually been replaced. For the same reasons heights of mountains and passes are occasionally given Collie's measurements in order to prevent confusions between maps and text:

Maps

Acknowledgements

I would like to thank Collie's niece, Mrs Susan Benstead, for her invaluable help and for the loan of photographs; Professor W C Taylor for photographs and many a helpful letter; Peter Hodgkiss of Ernest Press whose letters provided a constant source of new ideas and whose enthusiasm kept me going; Hamish Brown for putting me on the Collie trail; Professor A E Davies and John Cresswell of the Department of Chemistry, University College London; Martyn Berry for criticism and advice; Dr C W Gibby; Bill Wood and Michael Low who knew Collie in the later years of his life; Dr David Crout of the University of Exeter, and Walt Unsworth for information about Everest publicity. I would also like to thank Bob Grieve, Tom Weir, Robin Campbell, J Logan-Aikman, Alex Harrison, G G Elliot, Gidean MacRae, Noel Odell, Donald Bennett, the late Eric Roberts, Dr J Monroe Thorington, David Cox, Susan Parkinson, C Collie-MacNeill, Jean Valdar and Gillian Lacey. The following publishers, institutions and clubs all helped with information or gave permission for photographs and quotations to be used: Archives of the Canadian Rockies; Alpine Club; The Alpine Club of Canada; British Library; Blackwell Press Ltd; Edward Arnold Ltd; B T Batsford Ltd; Cairngorm Club; Cheltenham Ladies' College; Peter Whyte Foundation, The Royal Society of Chemistry; *The Daily Telegraph*; J M Dent & Sons Ltd; Fell & Rock Climbing Club; Victor Gollancz Ltd; Glenbow Museum; Federation of Mountaineering Clubs of Ireland; Robert Hale Ltd; University of London King's College; King's College Hospital Medical School; Longman Group; John Murray Ltd; Macmillan Ltd; National Library of Scotland; The Royal Society; Royal Geographical Society; Science Museum Library; Scottish Mountaineering Club; *The Times*; University of Bristol School of Chemistry; University College London, libraries; Universities of Liverpool, Glasgow, St Andrews and Sheffield; The Queen's University Belfast; The Wellcome Institute for the History of Medicine; also any publisher, or the executors of any writer, who produced work at the beginning of the century and whom it has been impossible to trace. Finally, my thanks to Mrs Pat Johnson of the Alpine Club library who was indefatigable in tracing information with never a word of complaint.

Chapter 1

The Early Years

> Well do I remember my first ascent of a real mountain. It was many years ago, in 1867, when I climbed the Hill of Fare. ... Since then I have climbed many mountains, higher and more difficult, but the memories of those later climbs are not quite the same, part of the magic of youth is missing, the memory of them is more fleeting, not so vivid, some of the glamour has gone, and, at last, the remembrances become more and more shadowy and are lost. (J N Collie, Independence, *Cairngorm Club Journal*, 15)

Scotland enjoyed a long, hot summer in 1886. So perfect was the weather that two brothers, one a chemistry teacher the other a soldier, decided to spend their summer holiday together. Since their close childhood days they had had a love of fishing and swimming and these pleasures took them to the Island of Skye. The rivers were low so the fishing poor and the bathing was little better due to a heavy concentration of jellyfish in the sea lochs. Consequently the brothers walked and bemoaned the loss of their holiday.

Early in their holiday they watched with amazement two men climbing the rocks of a magnificent mountain near the small, island hotel where they were staying. They were impressed and could talk of little else; it took them back to their boyish days of tree climbing. That activity was a family joke and many was the time they had been reprimanded for taking unsuspecting cousins into high trees after birds' eggs. They decided to send to the mainland for a rope and try the climb themselves but they were soon to discover that climbing up rocks was quite a different thing from climbing up trees. Try as they might they could make little progress, constantly being stopped by seemingly impregnable walls. Even worse, one of them was quite obviously nervous and only continued on the insistence of the other. For two days they persisted, trying to work out a route to the summit, but each evening returned completely baffled to the hotel. On the third day they enquired of a local gillie how they could climb it. They took his advice and later that day met with success climbing an easy route to the summit of Sgurr nan Gillean.

The two brothers were Norman and Harry Collie, the gillie was John Mackenzie. It was the first time they had met, and it was the beginning of a unique friendship between Norman and John; a friendship based on a mutual love of Skye and deep admiration for the qualities of each other. Their social backgrounds were very different but on such a level of understanding were the two men that often there was no need for words between them. Legend has it that when Mackenzie died in 1933, Collie walked alone to the summit of Am Basteir declaring it his last mountain climb—which possibly it was.

1 Norman Collie. Date unknown. *Photo from University College archives.*

Norman Collie was a man with an extraordinary personality, great presence and high intellect yet he provoked diverse feelings amongst those who knew him. He was deeply loved, almost revered by many, intensely disliked by others. There was no artificiality about him and, therefore, he could not pretend to like people or to see quality in others where there was none. Fools he could not tolerate; small talk found him turning away. Many preferred to avoid him, others to dismiss him as cold and disdainful, yet to those he favoured with friendship he gave an unswerving loyalty and love which was a great source of strength to many and was always reciprocated. He was very unpredictable in his reactions to people—'When he became interested in a man, his penetrating eyes flashed suddenly into an observant personal sympathy; when he was not, he was incapable of the pretence, even, of awareness of him.'[1] The mosaic of his personality was summed up by one close friend when he wrote: 'His benign look could turn to one of rallying amusement or to a meditative and pipe-puffing remoteness, or if he saw or heard something offending his sense of decency out came the pipe, the mouth compressed and there was a moment's fixed and scowling glare followed by a stoney aloofness, again it would change to courteous interest or to a vivacity of pleasure and quick utterance at something really new or striking.'[2]

John Norman Collie, known always to his family as Nor, was born on 10 September 1859 at Ferns Cottage, Alderley Edge, Cheshire, a suburb of Manchester. He was the second son of John and Selina Collie.

His mother was one of the five daughters of Henry Winkworth, a silk manufacturer with mills in Manchester. There were also two sons, William and Stephen. The Winkworths were a prominent, middle-class family, of the type thrown up by the Industrial Revolution. Wealthy, highly privileged but with a united social and moral conscience. They were well-known liberals, supporters of Richard Cobden and John Bright's Anti-Corn Law League and deeply committed to the improvement of social conditions. They were lively commentators on the religious issues of the day ranging from the Oxford Movement to the Darwinian controversy. The letters of Selina's sister Catherine read like a Who's Who of the literary, religious and political figures of the day. One moment she is corresponding with Harriet Martineau, then with Mrs Gaskell, Charlotte Brontë or F D Maurice. Mazzini, the architect of Italian republicanism, was favoured by the entire family and went from one sister to another for hospitality and financial support.

Catherine Winkworth was committed to the education of women and helped to set up a Working Women's College in Manchester on the model of the Working Men's College in London. Unlike many, however, she thought the poor should be educated and that the church should not be in charge of it. She did not see education, as so many did, as a threat to the social hierarchy.

The striking thing about the family was their total lack of stuffiness. They were able to comment, with intelligence and humour, on the issues of their time without lapsing into moral outrage or narrow-mindedness. It is not difficult to see where much of Norman Collie's character came from. He saw a great deal of his aunts and many cousins and it must have been a very stimulating environment in which to grow.

Selina Collie was herself an accomplished woman, a fine artist, pianist and singer who knew an assortment of languages. Her conversation was described as 'lively, pointed and clever'.

Less is known about the Collie side of the family. They originated in Ireland and moved to Aberdeen in the sixteenth century. By the nineteenth century they were involved in the cotton trade and at one time were the largest cotton importers in Britain. John Collie's mother was described by Susannah Winkworth as a very energetic woman full of good works and totally lacking

2 Selina Collie and her sons (Henry standing, Norman sitting). *Photo from Mrs Susan Benstead, with permission.*

in 'scotch narrow-mindedness'. John Collie does not seem to have been involved in the family business to any great extent although his income certainly came from it. He was a very tall, lounging man and Mrs Gaskell for one admired his good looks but he seems to have had little impact on his son Norman.

John and Selina were married on 25 August 1857 and during the same year a crisis began in the silk trade which continued for many years. This was mainly due to the competition from French silk goods and also competition from cotton. Selina's father complained of how the home market kept mistaking the fine quality of his silk garments for French workmanship and refused to buy them. He also wrote about the difficulty of trying to find 'money from week to week for your hands when your capital is locked up in silk machinery and goods that wont sell'.[3] Henry Winkworth was one of the few manufacturers to pay his workers something when they were laid off.

Selina's first son Harry was born on 13 June 1858. John Norman soon followed. His Aunt Emma described him as 'fascinating with deep thoughtful eyes and wall-like brow, more intellectual looking than Harry. . . . Normie is of a much less soft affectionate disposition [than Harry] but very funny and very spirited, goes into tremendous passions sometimes and comes out quite as suddenly sweet and merry again'.[4] In 1861 Selina's only daughter Susan Margaret was born. Susan was thought of as the cleverest of all the children. She was one of the first woman graduates of Bedford College, University of London and later became a very successful headmistress. Arthur Leslie was born in 1862 and Alexander the following year.

In 1862 Selina's parents and her three unmarried sisters, Alice, Susannah and Catherine, left Manchester and went to live in Clifton near Bristol. The move was occasioned by a drastic reduction of the family income. Henry Winkworth had had to give up his business due to the continued silk depression. John and Selina moved into Thornfield, the family home in Alderley.

It may have been about this time that Selina's brother Stephen went into the cotton business and moved to Bolton in Lancashire. Collie's Uncle Stephen played a formative part in his life. Although he died in the year that Collie and Harry made their first rock climb, he may well have laid the foundations for his nephew's obsession with the mountains.

Stephen was elected to the Alpine Club in 1861. He went regularly each season to the Alps, making respectable but not dramatic ascents such as the Aletshorn and the first ascent to the Col d'Argentière. His wife, Emma, often went with him and was the first woman to ascend the Jungfrau in 1863 with the famous Alpine guides Croz and Bennen. It was a long, hot climb of seven hours made all the more difficult by the encumbrance of petticoats and skirt. When she returned to her hotel that night the guests arose and applauded. Stephen knew well some of the big names of that Golden Age of Mountaineering; Professor James (Glacier) Forbes, Leslie Stephen and John Tyndall.

The Collies only stayed at Thornfield for five years before John took his family back to his native Scotland in 1867. He apparently 'retired' from the family cotton firm but it is unclear why he did so. The Collies were certainly beginning to experience financial difficulties themselves and a letter from Catherine to Selina suggests that John's brother Alexander was not behaving exactly as he should have done with regard to the business. Catherine added that she felt it only just that people should know that John 'had left a good business as soon as he found that Alexander was inclined to go crookedly at the sacrifice of a large income'.[5] John, however, did not withdraw his capital from the business.

The family stayed for some months at Bridge of Allan whilst looking for a permanent home. Finally they rented Glassel House on Deeside. It was intended that John Collie should arrange shooting parties all through the season over the land that he also rented. The three years the family spent at Glassel were to have a deep and lasting effect on Norman Collie. It was from Glassel that he climbed his first mountain, the Hill of Fare, and he maintained that his love of mountains began during these boyhood years.

Glassel House was a low, grey stone house with roses and fuchsias growing against it. The gardens sloped down to fields with sheep and ended in a belt of woodland through which a river flowed. Beyond this lay one long ridge after another of purple-brown, heathery hills. It was a lonely spot, ideal for a growing family of five children who seem to have led an idyllic existence. There was no school nearby so they were all tutored at home. When not at their lessons they were out in the countryside. Norman and Harry began their tree-climbing partnership after birds' eggs and nests. They built up a fine collection of both. Then there was fishing, long hours of it; then cricket, or a pony to ride, followed by the excitements of the shoot with men and beaters about the hills and all the boys learning to shoot. Finally came the hot days of haymaking.

It was quite a different thing for Selina Collie, who much as she valued the life for her children, found that she had too much to do and John too little. There was nothing else to occupy him, apart from shooting, on land that was not his own. She complained that in winter they arose by candlelight and were shut in by 4.30 p.m. The financial situation also continued to worry her. She wrote to Catherine: 'I often think, and have thought for years past, how very different my life is, both every day and otherwise, to anything that ever came into your and my joint experience. Some of it perhaps we shall some day talk over, when we are old women; but a great deal will be buried out of sight. I fancy there are not very many people who have to come (to the same extent as I have) to their life being a complete uncertainty and makeshift from day to day, from great plans for their children etc. down to the time of one's dinner ... it would really be an awful thing to be left with these "croupy" children to go through a Scotch winter in these inaccessible wilds. Last winter they were snowed up here three weeks at a time, and at the best we shall be four and a half miles over a cross-roads from doctor, baker, butcher and church ...'[6] It must have been a very different life from the cultivated, social round she was used to. In 1868 she wrote again to Catherine: 'You've no conception of the really constant drive it has been since you left ... late breakfasts, lunches ditto, dinners; all the servants ill one after the other. ... Deer drive yesterday ... to get provisions and cook for 15 men in hall besides three gentlemen in parlour, Duncan storming at us women like a demon in the middle of it. Breakfast for gentlemen at half-past nine; then sandwiches, bread and cheese, whisky, etc., for beaters, and all to prepare; lunch and children's dinner at half-past one; incursion of beaters, etc., three; dinner at six; ... not a drop of water in the house ... so that all has to be carried from the well and men never coming in without wanting a bath.'[7]

She also worried about the children's education and the effect on their manners and behaviour from being so little in company. Selina's sisters worried about her and plans were afoot to persuade the Collies to join the rest of the family at Clifton. John readily acquiesced and the boys' carefree life came to an end. The family moved in December 1870 to 37 Royal York Crescent, Clifton. There is no doubt that Selina was happier and her sisters recalled how popular the Collie family were and how they entered into the Clifton social scene with endless rounds of dinner parties and calls.

When the family arrived in Clifton, Harry was immediately sent to Clifton College as a day boy but for some reason Norman was sent to boarding school in Surrey. He had never been away from home before and the contrast to the previous years must have been enormous. He was very unhappy and recalled in later years how he would walk down to the pond in the school grounds and contemplate drowning himself. The misery lasted until 1873 when his parents moved him to Charterhouse, one of England's most famous public schools. Collie was being given the best possible education for a Victorian gentleman. There is no knowing what would have happened to him if he had continued in this privileged way of life. However, in 1875 after only two years at the school, the Collie cotton firm went bankrupt and John lost his entire fortune.

The cotton for the family firm came from the southern states of America which had been troubled and unsettled since the ending of the American Civil War ten years before. An enormous amount of it was burnt as it was awaiting shipment to England. Alexander tried to redress the situation by raising two loans on the non-existent load of cotton hoping that government compensation would arrive in time. Unfortunately it did not and when the loans were called in the business collapsed taking many smaller concerns with it. Collie heard the news whilst at Charterhouse and wrote to let his mother know that he had read in the papers that his uncle had been committed and then released from Newgate Prison. Alexander later emigrated to America and John Collie, who had left his capital tied up in the business, was to be in financial difficulties for the rest of his life.

The years following this disaster were troubled and unhappy ones for Selina Collie. The small amount of capital that the family possessed was put into a paper mill in Kent. Selina had a small annual allowance of her own. It was now that Selina's brother Stephen took over the financial affairs of the family but it still meant a great reduction in their lifestyle. Norman was now 16 and his uncle withdrew him from Charterhouse and sent him to Clifton College to finish his education.

All the children were told that their future incomes would now depend upon themselves. Harry was sent to Aberdeen to learn banking but he later became a soldier, eventually emigrating to New Zealand where he farmed. Susan, Arthur and Alexander were still too young to leave school.

In the years that the Winkworths had been in Clifton they had immersed themselves, as they had done at Alderley, with the social problems of the day. It was education again that took up most of Catherine's time. In 1868 she had founded a committee to promote the higher education of women. Classes and lectures were begun on various subjects to aid women in preparing for the Higher Cambridge Examination. In 1876, whilst Collie was at Clifton College, the headmaster was Dr Percival, later Bishop of Hereford. He and Catherine decided that what Bristol needed was its own university college. Consequently the two of them, with typical Victorian zeal, set about organizing one. They wanted to ensure that a fund should be opened to raise money for scholarships to be held by women at the college. Bristol was one of the first cities in England to possess a university college open alike to men and women and offering scholarships to both and this it owes to the headmaster of Clifton College and the committee of which Catherine was the mainspring.

Whilst his aunt and headmaster were busy with their plans, Norman Collie was languishing slightly at Clifton College. He was not happy or doing well so in 1878, when he was 18, it was decided to send him to the new University College of Bristol, which had just opened, to train as a chemist. It was only due to his Uncle Stephen's financial help that he was able to do this. At the same time Stephen took Selina, who was now ill, to the South of France to get her away from the depressing financial problems in Clifton. It was whilst they were away that their indomitable sister Catherine died aged 51. Two Catherine Winkworth Memorial Scholarships for the education of women were immediately set up at University College Bristol to perpetuate her memory.

In 1878 the first Chair of Chemistry at Bristol was held by Professor Edmund Letts, a family friend, and a man Collie readily acknowledged as an influence upon his life. Letts thought highly of Collie from the first. 'My attention was drawn to him at once,' he wrote in 1894, 'by his aptitude for chemistry. His progress was remarkably rapid and while still a junior he published a scientific paper.'[8] In fact Collie had only been a student for a year when he published *On the celestine and baryto-celestine of Clifton*. He wrote this paper from observations he had made of his mineral collection. Baryto-celestine he discovered in the rocks of the railway tunnel being cut under the downs which was linking Bristol to Avonmouth. Collie's immediate grasp of his subject must have been very gratifying after his poor showing at Clifton. His ability and progress were rewarded in his second year by a scholarship. This brought more than just financial help—it also carried with it the duties of demonstrator and assistant to the Professor. Here was a fine opportunity to study chemistry, which, together with an easing of the financial worry, enabled Collie to concentrate on a career that was to prove no less successful than his mountaineering one. A close bond developed between the two men, now thrown much into each other's company, and the year 1879 must have convinced Collie of his true vocation.

Letts at this time was travelling in the neighbouring towns giving a series of lectures in chemistry. Collie prepared these lectures and also assisted in practical classes that Letts was giving at Stroud. Collie, as Letts' assistant, worked with him on the action of sodium phosphide with alkyl chlorides and ethers. There is no doubt that, under Letts, Collie gained a mastery of fundamental techniques in chemistry and, later, of analysis and exploration in new fields of research.

At the end of Collie's second year Letts was appointed to the Chair of Chemistry at Queen's College, Belfast. It looked as if they would have to part. However, Letts, no doubt realising the potential and value of his pupil, asked Collie to go with him as his full-time assistant. At the end of 1879 Collie began his third year of tutelage, in the enviable position of paid assistant to an outstanding practical chemist, and was financially independent at last.

During his journey to Belfast to take up his post, Collie travelled through the storm that brought down the Tay Bridge. After spending Christmas at Edinburgh he left there at 5.30 p.m. on 28 December 1879 by train for Glasgow. At the time a violent westerly gale was blowing over central Scotland. It was an awful journey and Collie wrote to his mother;

> I thought every moment the train was going to be blown off the line it rocked to and fro in the most alarming manner and the window of the carriage next to mine was blown in. We got to Glasgow at 7.30 so that while we were going along the Tay Bridge was blown down. What a dreadful accident it was, happily for the people in the train it must all have been over in a moment though. I slept in Glasgow amidst tiles, chimney stacks, pots etc. flying about in wild confusion. I shall never forget the state of the roads and the wind was perfectly awful. On Monday morning I started at a quarter to seven for Stranraer and got on board a small but very powerful mail steamer. As soon as we got outside the headland into the channel the waves were terrific and we were going at such a pace that we literally went through one or two waves while the spray was flying to the mast head. Luckily this only lasted for about an hour for it was much calmer under the lee shore of Ireland. I got here at 1.15 p.m. called on the principal of the college and then went out to look for diggings which I have got I think. They are very nice ones, 15/- a week including gas and fires. The woman said that they were going to have been taken by a Dr Park who tried for the Chemical Chair here but as Letts got it Dr Park did not want them. The house is very substantially built about 40 years old and my bedroom is very nice and airy looking straight out across fields into the country. I have got the drawing room let. It is less than 5 minutes walk from the College and a train starts from the end of the street which will carry me right through the middle of Belfast out to the other end. With love to all, Your affectionate kid Nor. PS I was not sick coming over this morning.[9]

Collie spent three years at Belfast, working so closely with Letts that in 1882 and 1883 two papers were published in their joint names. Letts at that time was investigating the action of heat on ammonium and phosphonium salts, and it was in this area that Collie began his first independent investigations. During the period at Belfast Collie also taught the basics of chemistry to the students, and Letts found him 'zealous and efficient as a teacher and a most enthusiastic worker at research'.[10]

Collie enjoyed his time at Belfast. His letters to his mother were full of the exciting social life he was leading. He describes the most wonderful musical evenings, where he was learning to appreciate 'only the most classical of music', and he tells her everything in great detail adding that he wishes she were there to hear for herself. He also explains his love of Italian sculpture and of his desires to go to Italy and see for himself all the wonderful things of which he only has picture postcards. All his letters are trying to take her out of herself and he recommends books for her to read, in particular anything she can get about the life and teaching of Buddha. In return her letters to him tell very little which annoys him and he begs for news of the family and his dog Tod whilst also trying to persuade her to have a happy time. She was in fact ill, constantly plagued by headaches, always worried about money and now concerned about the younger members of the family. Susan was no problem and was training as a teacher but Di, as Arthur was called, was being particularly difficult. He was studying law with the financial help of Uncle Stephen and it was not his idea of a good life. He was artistic and his dislike of the career he felt was being chosen for him made him rebellious and inattentive towards his exams, which he kept failing, much to Collie's annoyance. Di was also unable to come to terms with his reduced standard of life and bothered his mother constantly for money. Alexander was trying to get into Cambridge but having to compete against '34 fellows including the 2nd boy at Harrow and heads of five other public schools'.[11] He failed to win the classical scholarship he was after but eventually went to Oxford. Alexander later became a teacher in India but died in middle-age when his houseboat home caught fire.

During 1882 Letts thought Collie should obtain an academic qualification if he was to further his career. Though loath to part with him he advised him to take a Doctor of Philosophy degree at a German university. Germany had for years led the field in scientific education. Her universities were issuing degrees long before their British counterparts had stopped arguing about the superiority of a classical education. Although London had instituted degrees in science in 1861 there were no PhD degrees and the teaching side was in a moribund state. Letts helped Collie find a place at Würzburg University, and to this town, and to the famous Dr Johannes Wislicenus, Collie went in the summer of 1882.

With the loss of his salary, however, Collie once more had to be helped by Uncle Stephen. The letters passing between mother and son indicate constant worry about this. It was particularly difficult for Collie to ask his mother for help, as he was obliged to on one occasion,because he had been able to assist her a little during his time at Belfast. Germany, however, was a lot more expensive than Ireland. He wrote to his mother:

> Dear Mamma, I got your letter and I am awfully sorry to hear how hard up you are. I am still worse or I never should have asked you for money. I have got nothing at all and Richardson has only 8 shillings and I owe him some money. So in 4 days we shall starve. So I hope you will be able to beg, borrow or steal some money. I find things over here not so cheap after all and screwing at every point not having any beer never having a fire etc that £5 a month is the very lowest I can do it on. I pay here 25 for rooms, 12 for breakfast, about 7 for fire, 2 to slavery, 3 for light, 4 for washing = 53 and about 46 for dinner and supper probably more which is £5 a month. Then the fees are more than I expected so that is why I am so short. I don't know how we shall get on when Richardson's 8 shillings are gone. It is a nice disgrace to the family Di not passing his exam, what is going to be done with him. Has Uncle Stephen said anything; why not pack him off at once to some place on £80 a year. I am doing my living out here on less. Today I feel dreadfully tired hence the letter written with a pencil in front of the stove, which I am having today as I can't stand 35° of frost again in my room. All the water was frozen and my sponge was like a brick.[12]

Uncle Stephen came to the rescue on this occasion. Collie was very lonely in Germany and wanted to come home. He only spent one year at Würzburg and was awarded his degree in 1883. He dedicated his thesis, written on the action of ammonia on ethyl acetoacetate, to 'My Dear Friend Professor Letts'.

Now he had qualified, Dr Collie searched for full-time employment and made a somewhat curious choice. He went to Cheltenham Ladies' College, Cheltenham, founded in 1853 to further women's education, then in a deplorable state. Its headmistress was the redoubtable Miss Beale. She was a remarkable woman, who, together with her friend Miss Buss, was a pioneer of women's education. Collie's aunts, Catherine and Susannah, had both been governors of the College and all the family knew Miss Beale. It is most likely that it was to help his mother with the family finances that he took this unsuitable post. At first his mother was not at all keen on the idea. While Collie was in Würzburg Miss Beale had visited her to enquire whether Collie would take up the vacancy she had for a chemistry teacher. His mother wrote to him: 'I don't think myself it is at all the sort of thing. She would probably not give much and talked about taking pupils in the town which seems to mean that she does not intend to pay as much as she thinks he is worth. It would not be a pleasant place. She would bully frightfully for she has never been accustomed to having gentlemen as regular masters.'[13]

At the same time, Miss Beale was trying to engage Collie's sister Sue, who had just qualified first-class from Miss Buss's Bedford College. She had been a pupil at Cheltenham. A few days later, however, Mrs Collie wrote to her son in quite a different vein. This may have been due to the fact that Miss Beale had offered £200 per annum, the top salary for a teacher in those days, as well as the offer of private pupils at two guineas a term. Just before Collie qualified she wrote to him again: 'A night's rest and cogitation has made me feel much more strongly than before that Miss Beale's proposal is a very desirable one in a pecuniary point of view. Better than you would get elsewhere. If you by any misfortune miss your degree a salary as that would help you to go back and take it.'[14]

Collie accepted the offer but his sister, who according to their mother, 'was not over fond of Miss Beale', and resented the peremptory letters arriving with every post, insisting that she come, decided to go elsewhere. Miss Beale must have thought very highly of Collie because there was a tremendous prejudice at this time against men teaching girls—they were even chaperoned at university lectures. She would have had to justify his appointment on academic grounds. In September 1883 Collie took up his post at Cheltenham, where apart from one other male companion, J Eadie Reid, who was art master and became well-known as a painter of church murals, the entire establishment was female.

Little is recorded of the three years Collie spent at Cheltenham. That he disliked it is apparent from many comments he made in later life. His niece wrote many years later: 'Uncle Nor's dislike of Cheltenham Ladies' College probably arose from his intense dislike of Miss Beale also he was far from being a ladies' man and probably found that schoolgirls in bulk were rather more than he could stomach.'[15] It may also have been the unsuitability of a girls' school for research which contributed to his dislike, although Collie did manage to publish three papers while he was there.

He was certainly glad of his high salary for at this time his father was having a great deal of worry over his paper mill. The mill was not a success and there were few orders. John Collie was engaged in working a patent for a new invention for paper making but he was coming up against machine breaking because the new machines could be worked by semi-skilled men. On several occasions when the machines were started the pulp flew out due to the removal of tiny screws. Collie does not seem to have had much to do with his father; it was his mother who claimed all his attention, and Susan Collie does not seem to have even liked their father. Mrs Collie was very unwell during Collie's years at Cheltenham and her pathetic letters to Norman tell of the unpleasant treatment she was having for cancer 'whilst I have a house to be ill in'. After her death in 1883, followed rapidly by that of her sister Susannah and brother Stephen, Collie was never able to forgive Di for what he regarded as his selfish behaviour towards their mother, to whom Collie himself was devoted.

Although Collie felt that Cheltenham was a scientific backwater, there were, nevertheless, two events that occurred during his time there which were to have a great influence on his later life. The first of these was his holiday on Skye with Harry, which was the start of his involvement with mountaineering; the other was his meeting with William Ramsay.

When Letts went to Belfast, the Chair of Chemistry at University College Bristol went to Professor William Ramsay. Ramsay, who was an extraordinarily energetic worker, was to become a famous chemist and Nobel Prize winner. His years at Bristol laid the foundations for his biggest scientific coup—the discovery of the noble or inert gases of the atmosphere.

This prominent chemist knew the Winkworth family and had a very high opinion of Norman Collie, foretelling a great future for him as a chemist. Collie must have confided in Ramsay about his unhappiness with his position at Cheltenham.

In 1887 Ramsey was appointed Professor of Chemistry at University College, London, and Collie tried, unsuccessfully to get Ramsay's Bristol

3 Collie, 1896. *Photo from Professor Taylor, with permission.*

Chair. His failure may have been due to his youth—he was only 28—and lack of experience. Ramsay knew of Collie's attempt, and he asked him, as Letts had done seven years before, to become his assistant. Although it meant taking a drop in salary of £50 a year, Collie nevertheless accepted. Ramsay sang, at a laboratory dinner the following year,

> When first I came to London town
> As Williamson's successor
> And donned his figurative gown
> As Chemical Professor
> With Plimpton and with Rideal too
> I felt uncommon jolly
> But in my eye I had in view
> Our friend—J Norman Collie.
>
> In Cheltenham his mission lay
> To train the girls in science
> And demonstrate to them each day
> Some chemical appliance.
> But weariness on him did press
> And deep set melancholy
> Right glad was he to come to me
> Our friend—J Norman Collie.[16]

When Collie left Cheltenham he had already acquired that somewhat enigmatic and aloof personality that aged into eccentricity. Many already thought him unfriendly and humourless; those who knew him appreciated his shyness and his sardonic and impish sense of humour that one was never quite sure of. Ramsay thought him a 'jewel' and Collie, after spending that first summer in Skye, went with much enthusiasm to the antiquated chemistry department of London University which first Ramsay and then Collie were to build into a great school.

Chapter 2

Island of Cloud

> Many are the memories one can bring back from the mountains, some of peace and some of stern fights with the elements, but they are all memories of freedom. The restraint of ordinary life no longer holds us down, we are in touch with nature. The sky, the winds, the waters, and the earth, surely these ancient elements of life can teach us secrets that a more protected existence hides from us. In the old Gaelic lore that deals with a people whose daily world lay close to the earth, one sees how their passion for freedom is told in their poetry. It came from their intimate relation with nature. May we not also find contentment and a larger interest in life from friendly communion with the hills and the wide open spaces of our Highland land? (J N Collie, Independence, *Cairngorm Club Journal*, 15)

For over 400 years the Norsemen held Skuy-ö, the Island of Cloud. Much evidence of their occupation survives today, both on the surface of the land and in the names of many of its features.

Skye, island of mountains, mist and moorland indented by numerous sea lochs, is a place whose mysterious qualities appeal strongly to anyone with powers of imagination as highly developed as Collie's.

On the western side, swept by Atlantic gales, moors of peat, treeless and desolate, end abruptly in sea cliffs fringed with scattered stacks and skerries crowded with seabirds. On the eastern side, in the few sheltered places the vegetation is surprisingly lush, for the winters are mild; even on the mountains snow falls less frequently, and vanishes more rapidly, that on the mainland hills.

In the south-west corner are the Black Cuillin, geologically young mountains of bare gabbro, sharp jagged ridges and summits riven by gullies often white with water and buttressed lower down by great glacier-worn boiler-plate slabs which, at the southern extremity, plunge straight into the sea.

In clear weather there are stupendous views to be had from the summits across deep corries to the islands, Eigg, Rhum, Canna and far out to the

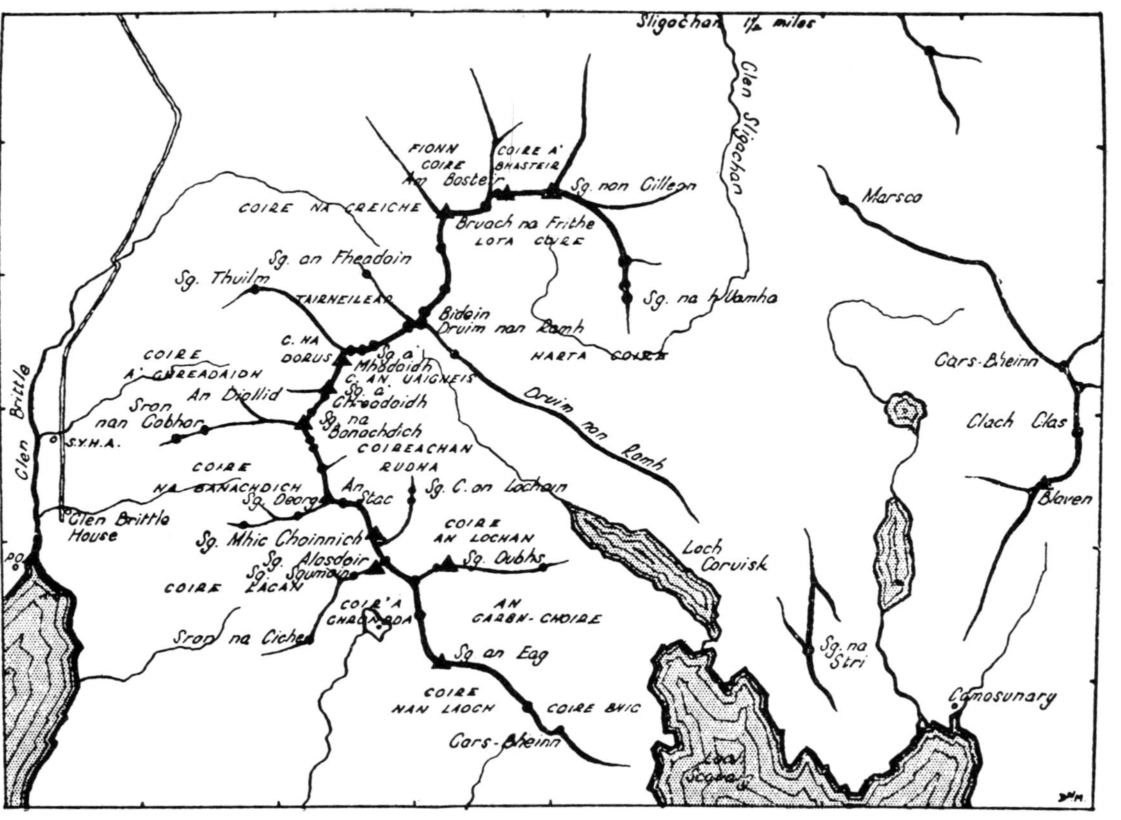

Map 1 The Black Cuillin. *From* Climbers Guide to Cuillin of Skye SMC. *Permission for use given by SMC.*

Outer Hebrides, the Long Island, almost on the western horizon. In the cloudy weather, which is more common, the climber may spend a whole day scrambling along the ridges to be rewarded, if he or she is lucky, with a ten-second glimpse of the black waters of Loch Coruisk, 3,000 feet below.

For Collie, autumn was the best time of all. Then, 'the moors rioting in all the marvellously rich colours of decay, will serve as a splendid contrast to the dark purple of the corries that seem as if they were hung with royal velvet'.[1] It is a land 'where the rains weep and the plovers cry, and the wild west winds sweep in straight from the outer ocean—a lonely land, where one can wander far from the haunts of men, following the streams as they flow seaward through the quiet valleys'.[2]

As Skye settled back into an uneasy peace in the decades following the 'Forty-five', or the Jacobite Rebellion, it was visited by few travellers. Dr Samuel Johnson spent a short time there in 1773 but he left rapidly, beset by storms, like many since, declaring that 'a walk upon ploughed fields in England is a dance upon carpets, compared to the toilsome drudgery of wandering in Skye'.[3] How many tourists he managed to put off we do not know, but the very qualities that repel the tourist attract the true mountain lover, and Collie, for one, may have had reason to be grateful to him. Sir Walter Scott was one of the first to appreciate the wild beauty of Skye but it had not, in Collie's time at least, acquired the 'gross paraphernalia of tourism' which so appalled him on his first visit to the Alps, in 1892.

Collie's love affair with Skye falls into three periods. During his vacations from 1886 until 1891 he was hardly seen anywhere else. Then from 1891 to 1904 he became gradually more aware of other mountain areas throughout the British Isles and further afield, and he travelled extensively, visiting Skye less frequently. From 1904 he became re-united with the island and visited it frequently until he died there in 1942.

In 1886, at the time of his first visit to Skye, the climbing of British mountains was a novel activity. Mountaineering as a sport, an invention of the Victorian British, had confined itself mostly to the Swiss and French Alps. It was fashionable to admire the beauty of British hills, but the average Alpine mountaineer did not regard them as worthy of his attention, and the average walker was not inclined to attempt the very few mainland summits which demanded the use of hands as well as feet. In the Black Cuillin, however, only a few of the summits could be reached without taking one's hands out of one's pockets, and consequently many were rarely visited and some of the more remote and difficult were still virgin.

During the 1860s and 1870s, a native of Skye Sheriff Alexander Nicholson, had been very active, wandering, like Collie after him, all over the island; and in 1873 he had climbed what later turned out to be the highest peak in the Cuillin, which was named Sgurr Alasdair, the Gaelic equivalent of his Christian name, in his honour.

By the 1880s, a very few members of the Alpine Club were beginning to visit Skye, often during the shorter Easter vacation since it was recognized that the quality of the rock provided excellent training for their summer seasons in the Alps. However, sections of the main ridges of the Cuillin had not yet been traversed, and the faces were virtually untouched. Furthermore, the Ordnance Survey map was grossly inaccurate. There was ample scope still for exploration and Collie was the right man at the right time.

He was to become more deeply involved with the Cuillin than any other, before or since. Though he was to explore and become almost familiar with other more remote mountain regions of the world, none was ever to rival Skye in his affections. From that very first visit in 1886 until he died, lonely and withdrawn, in the Sligachan Inn nearly 60 years later, he regarded the island, and in particular the Cuillin, as his home.

No account of Collie's obsession with the island would be complete without a description of John Mackenzie. Mackenzie was a native who spent his entire life on the island. Living in the village of Sconser just a few miles down the Broadford road from the Sligachan Inn, he started by offering his services

4 Mackenzie in Scotland. *Photo by Collie, permission of the Alpine Club.*

5 Mackenzie with catch, 1919. *Photo by Collie from his slide collection, permission of the Alpine Club.*

as a guide to the few walkers who ventured across from the mainland. In the Alps, a highly organised system of officially recognised guides had already been developed but in Britain no such system existed. Nevertheless it was not uncommon for a tourist to engage a native to show him the way to one of the local beauty spots or viewpoints.

Mackenzie progressed from this to become, by the standards of the day, a first-rate climber, initially with the Pilkington brothers—early rock climbers who made the first ascent of the Inaccessible Pinnacle of Sgurr Dearg—and later with Norman Collie, whose most constant companion he became for almost half a century. Mackenzie was the first British rock-climbing guide, and many of those who made significant contributions to the development of British climbing went on their first expeditions with him.

Mackenzie was held in such esteem by the mountaineering establishment for his contribution to the sport that the Alpine Club, in later years, always sent him a complimentary copy of *The Alpine Journal*—a rare privilege.

When they first met, Collie was 28, Mackenzie 31. In their seventies, when they became too old to climb, they continued to fish together and to enjoy their mutual companionship. In Collie's words, 'he was a lovable, charming and delightful companion ... a great lover of beauty with a deep feel for the wild lochs and moors. As a companion on a long summer day he was perfect. Those who knew him will remember him as a perfect gentleman, one who never offended by word or deed. There was only one John, simple minded, most lovable and without guile'.[4]

Within four years of his acquaintance with the Cuillin, Collie was the acknowledged expert on their topography. His gift for solving the problems of uncharted country, or of an unclimbed mountain face, made him stand out from his contemporaries. From the very beginnings Collie was making his own maps and estimating the heights of the summits he passed over. Unravelling the mysteries of the Ordnance Survey maps was, he said, the hardest part of climbing in Skye. The one-inch map, published in May 1885, was wildly inaccurate: 'One must possess that faith which is said to be able to remove mountains before a proper understanding of this map can be obtained which harmonizes with the environment.'[5] The six-inch maps which followed were little better, showing, not with particular accuracy, the heights of only 11 of the 30 or so main peaks. Skye weather was of course largely to blame for the inability of the official surveyors to make a first-rate job of it within their allotted time. The deficiency in what was after all one of the tools of their trade had already driven other climbers, such as Charles Pilkington, to produce their own very useful sketch maps.

When Collie started to check the heights of summits by means of an aneroid barometer he was astonished by the results, for not only did they differ from the Ordnance Survey results, as he had expected, but they did not even correspond with his own readings taken a few days later. There were two possible sources of error—inaccuracy in the instrument and rapidly changing atmospheric pressure. For the first he designed and constructed his own portable mercurial barometer, while for the second he devised a system for using the OS map as a base and keeping to a minimum the time which elapsed between readings. His survey of the Cuillin established that at least 13 mountains were over 3,000 feet and, more significantly, that the highest point of the Cuillin was in fact Sgurr Alasdair and not, as had been thought, the Inaccessible Pinnacle on Sgurr Dearg.

This interest in mountain heights in general and the 3,000-foot contour in particular, which followed the publication of the OS maps, was not confined to Collie. In 1891 the third president of the Scottish Mountaineering Club (SMC), Sir Hugh Munro, produced a list of all the mountains in Scotland over 3,000 feet. Known as the 'Munro Tables', this consisted of 283 separate mountains and 255 subsidiary 'tops'. Hugh Munro did not himself quite manage to climb every one of these separate mountains, or 'Munros' as they soon came to be known, but by 1901 another SMC member, the Reverend A E Robertson, became the first person to do so. These two stalwarts could not have realised the far-reaching consequences of their actions: collecting these mountains, or 'Munro-bagging', is nowadays a highly popular obsession amongst hill-walkers. In 1976 Hamish Brown set a record by bagging all the Munros in one continuous 1,639-mile walk, taking 112 days.

Another outcome of this sudden interest in heights was the appointment in 1895 of Dr Alfred Harker to the Geological Survey of Scotland with a special responsibility for mapping the Cuillins.

The name Cuillin in fact embraces two ranges, quite distinct both in form and in colour. The Red Cuillin are relatively smooth, rounded hills composed of granite mainly in the form of scree and holding little interest for the climber, though the persevering walker may be rewarded by fine views of their more impressive neighbours, the Black Cuillin, by whom they are most definitely upstaged. From Sgurr na h-Uamha in the north-east to Gars-Bheinn in the south-east, the main chain of the Black Cuillin takes the form of a six-mile horseshoe, either side of which project many secondary ridges 'between which are numerous wild corries, including the huge hollow of Coruisk the bed of which is 200 feet below the level of the sea. Neither in the corries nor on the mountain sides is there much vegetation, for the gabbro when disintegrated does not readily form a soil suitable for plants. The summits are of naked rock, blue-black or purple in colour, while the corries contain the debris torn off from the peaks above, and tossed into a state of inconceivable chaos.'[6] To the south-east of the horseshoe lie Blaven and Clach Glas, also distinctly black in character, but merging off north and eastwards into the softer outlines of the Red Cuillin.

In 1886 when Norman and Harry had gone to Skye they had no thoughts of mountaineering. Collie described his first sight of the rock-climbers on the face of Sgurr nan Gillean;

> I saw two mountaineers, A H Stocker and a friend, climbing on the rock face of one of the pinnacles. Hundreds of feet above me, on what appeared to me to be rocks as steep as the walls of a house, they moved slowly backwards and forwards, but always getting higher till they finally reached the summit. In

> those days I knew nothing about climbing, and it seemed to me perfectly marvellous that human beings should be able to do such things. That evening I got as much information as I could from them, and, having asked many questions about mountaineering, I telegraphed to Buckingham for an Alpine rope, for I was told that without it rock-climbing was dangerous. A few days later my brother and I started out with our new rope, also with the intention of climbing Sgurr nan Gillean. We went straight for our peak, up into the Bhasteir Coire and on to the ridge. We never got to the summit; the narrow ridge and the tooth of Sgurr nan Gillean proved too much for us, and after climbing for hours on the face we gave up the attempt. Next day we returned to the mountain, again spending many hours trying, first to surmount the pinnacles of Sgurr nan Gillean, and finally the peak itself, but we were unsuccessful, and the end of the story is, we had to inquire from John Mackenzie, one of the guides at Sligachan, how people usually ascended the mountain. Following his advice on our third attempt, we conquered the peak by the ordinary route. That was my introduction to mountaineering. The temptation was too great, and for the next twenty-five years, mountain-climbing became more important to me than fishing . . . .[7]

Gillean always had a special place in Collie's affections. Not only is it a very fine mountain, the first of the Black Cuillin to meet the eye of the traveller arriving at the Sligachan Inn, but also because it was the scene of his first climb. Ashley Abraham, one of the next wave of rock-climbing pioneers, shared his enthusiasm:

> Sgurr nan Gillean takes high rank amongst the mountains of Great Britain for beauty of form and commanding situation. Seen from Sligachan, it rises full 3,000 feet from its pedestal of dark moorland, broad of base and massive in mould, but delicately poised and graceful to a degree. As the eye wanders upward over wild corrie, dark ravine, and shattered precipice to its summit, one cannot but be struck by its arresting presence, nor help feeling proud that there belongs to our homeland such a fine mountain as this. For mountain it is, in the most exacting sense of the word. True, it possesses no glacier, and is comparatively insignificant in mere size; but it boasts a feature that many a peak four times its height cannot—there is no way of reaching its summit without actual hand-to-hand climbing.[8]

This peak dominated the view from the smoking room window at Sligachan Inn. Its north ridge, the Pinnacle Ridge, is seen in profile, five pinnacles separated by deep gaps and increasing in size to the Fifth Pinnacle which is the summit of Gillean itself. It was on the Fourth Pinnacle that Stocker and Parker were making a route when they caught the attention of the Collie brothers. They climbed Gillean by the south-east ridge, the 'tourist route', the easiest way up, and approximately the route of the first recorded ascent by Professor Forbes in 1836. However, Collie was to overcome his initial rebuff. He later climbed Gillean by many routes, some of them first ascents including the steep north-east face of the First Pinnacle.

On reaching the summit of Gillean in clear weather (it is necessary always to make this qualification when describing views in the Cuillin), the climber sees spread out before him or her the whole of the Black Cuillin, the more distant peaks silhouetted against the sea, and there can be little doubt that this tremendous sight contributed to Collie's instant conversion. Along this chain curving round to distant Gars-Bheinn can be seen the various landmarks of Collie's climbing career in Skye. The main ridge runs west from Gillean, narrow and shattered at first with a 'gendarme' barring the way, to Am Basteir, 'The Executioner'. Reaching the top by an easy scramble up a ridge with a sensational drop on the right one looks down an 80-foot step to the broad top of the Bhasteir Tooth, a striking semi-detached pinnacle, with a formidable western prow avoided on the south side by Collie and Mackenzie when they made the first ascent of the Tooth in 1889, by a route which is still used today because, though circuitous, it is the easiest way to the top.

Passing easily over Sgurr a Fionn Choire and Bruach na Frithe, the most accessible of the Black Cuillin tops, the elegant triple peaks of Bidean Druim nan Ramh bring back the climber's attention from more distant views. Next comes Sgurr a Mhadaidh with four summits, each with a sharp little drop on its far side. When Collie and Mackenzie approached Mhadaidh from Coire na Creiche in 1888, the view of the north-west face came as 'a revelation'. Ashley Abraham was also impressed by 'two massive rock towers connected by a wild cordon of shattered precipice, jumbled crags as a whole, but beautifully sculptured in detail, falling a full thousand feet to the huge glacier worn, boulder strewn slabs at their base'.[9] To make a first ascent of a great rock face such as this, as Collie and Mackenzie did when they climbed the North West Buttress in 1896, is a rare experience for which today's mountaineer must search hard in the more remote mountain regions of the world.

Continuing now along the knife-edge of Sgurr a'Ghreadaidh one becomes aware of the great sheet of water enclosed by bare glaciated rock which is Loch Coruisk, almost at one's feet. In 1907 Collie climbed from the loch to the summit of Ghreadaidh by the south-east ridge, described in the *Scottish Mountaineering Club Journal* as the 'finest climb' on the mountain and 'the best bit of mountaineering in Skye', comments expressive of the state of the art at that time: the route is a fine mountaineering line, with remoteness and exposure, but because of its limited technical interest it is nowadays rarely repeated.

Next Sgurr na Banachdich, one of whose four tops bears Collie's name—Sgurr Thormaid, or Norman's Peak, probably named by Naismith. Banachdich is not one of the great Cuillin mountains and Thormaid, in particular, lacks character and interest for the mountaineer. Considering Collie's contribution to mountaineering in the Cuillin, the choice was a poor one. Collie perhaps felt the same way, for he never referred in his writings to Sgurr Thormaid. He made several ascents, none of them recorded, on other peaks of Banachdich.

Sgurr Dearg follows. On its north-west flank, facing Banachdich and prominent from Glen Brittle, is Window Buttress, now a popular 'trade route' for the hordes of summer visitors to the Glen. When Collie was living out his old age at Sligachan Inn he was approached by a young climber, Bill Wood, about to attempt his first 'difficult' climb. Knowing of Collie's first ascent in 1906 he asked for details of the route. The old man replied: 'I can't remember anything about it except that I've taken hundreds of women and children up it!' Bill Wood wrote: 'This was the collapse of yours truly and we have always called it the "women and children's climb" ever since.'[10]

Dearg was long believed to be Skye's highest peak, until relegated by Collie. On its rather rounded top stands a magnificent shark's fin of rock—Inaccessible Pinnacle. The name has stuck, though it ceased to be inaccessible in 1880 when the Pilkington brothers climbed its eastern ridge. Collie and Mackenzie found it hard when they climbed it in 1888 from the more difficult

6 Window Buttress, Sgurr Dearg. *Photo by Collie, permission of the Alpine Club.*

western end, Mackenzie having removed his boots and led the climb in stockinged feet to provide better friction on the wet rock. From their windy perch on top Collie noticed that the summit of Sgurr Alasdair, across Coire Lagan to the south, seemed higher, and he decided he must check this at once by means of an aneroid reading, thereby committing the pair of them to a very exhausting day.

> Everything was wrapt in gloom ... one seemed cut off entirely from the outer world and the lonely grandeur of the place and the stillness of the night was a thing I have never forgotten. How many mountains we went over and how many feet we climbed it is impossible to say for in many places we traversed backwards and forwards and up and down in our endeavours to overcome the difficulties that we met with on that extraordinary ridge of the Coolin (sic).[11]

The traverse from Dearg to Alasdair around the head of Coire Lagan is a good day's mountaineering by any standards. Having gingerly lowered

7 Inaccessible Pinnacle. *Photo by Collie, permission of the Alpine Club.*

themselves off the Pinnacle, they had to cross the rocky little peak of An Stac to the neck before the long, narrow and exceedingly steep-sided ridge of Sgurr Mhic Choinnich (Mackenzie's Peak, named, by Charles Pilkington, after John Mackenzie—a very much more worthy peak than Sgurr Thormaid) from whose summit a vertical step in the ridge, a prominent feature of the Coire Lagan skyline, was avoided by a series of exposed ledges on the west face.

A scramble over Sgurr Thearlaich (after Charles Pilkington) and a short vertical descent landed them in the gap at the head of the great Stone Shoot from which the sharp little summit of Alasdair was quickly gained.

Alasdair stands, a graceful mountain, a little apart from the main Cuillin ridge, as if to remind the other summits of its now indisputable position as the highest of them all. The Coire Lagan face is impressive, and contains routes taken by both Collie, in 1896, and Abraham, in 1907.

8 Mackenzie on the Cuillin Ridge. *Photo by Collie, permission of the Alpine Club.*

Continuing for the moment to follow the main ridge southwards, the climber shortly arrives at a formidable cleft separating Thearlaich from Sgurr Dubh, and known as the Thearlaich-Dubh Gap. Collie's crossing of the Gap, in 1891, opened up for the first time the possibility of traversing the entire main ridge in one continuous expedition, a feat not accomplished until 1911 and not until 1965 under winter conditions. This traverse is indisputably the best 'Alpine' expedition in the British Isles.

Though not a difficult route in dry weather, the almost vertical walls of the Gap make it a nasty place in the wet, the rock on both sides being nowadays highly polished and providing little friction for an inexperienced party, who are recommended to ensure that not every member descends into the gap before at least one has climbed up the other side.

The main ridge continues southwards over Sgurr Dubh na Da Bheinn, with Sgurr Dubh Mor and Beag on an important spur running east down to Loch Coruisk, then the fierce and abrasive Caisteal a'Gharbh-Choire, and, more gently now, over Sgurr nan Eag to terminate at last in Gars-Bheinn overlooking the wild and lonely Loch Scavaig.

However, there is a very important subsidiary ridge leading westwards from the summit of Alasdair to complete the enclosure of Coire Lagan, one

9 Collie's slide showing the Cioch shadow. *From R W Clark and E C Pyatt,* Mountaineering in Britain, *permission given by Phoenix House Ltd.*

of the grandest, and certainly the most visited, of the great corries of the Cuillin. To reach the summit of Alasdair's westerly neighbour, Sgurr Sgumain, it is necessary to cross another 'Bad Step', less spectacular but just as serious as the Thearlaich-Dubh Gap. Beyond Sgumain there extends westwards the spur of Sron na Ciche, where in 1899 Collie made a most interesting discovery.

He and his companions, Charlie Bruce and Gurkha Harkbir, had spent a long day on Alasdair, further extended by the rescue of cragbound sheep. By the time they reached the lochan in Coire Lagan the westering sun was slanting across the face of Sron na Ciche. Collie spotted one immense shadow in the middle of the face which puzzled him at first until he realized it could only be caused by a huge projecting tower of rock. He took a photograph, determined to return and investigate, but seven years passed before he had the opportunity to do so. Incredibly, no one else had noticed the phenomenon

10 Mackenzie on the Cioch Slab. *Photo by Collie from his slide collection, permission of the Alpine Club.*

in the meantime. In 1906 he returned. On the magnificent precipice of Sron na Ciche, still completely untouched, he saw this

> interesting tower quite removed from the great rock face, standing out in the most imposing way over the Corrie below. From the top to the bottom is at least 1,000 feet, perpendicular in many places and a narrow knife-edge of rock about 100 feet long runs out from it rather less than half-way down. On each side of the knife-edge are steep clean slabs of rock that at their base overhang the gullies below. At the end of this knife-edge is placed the tower that casts its shadow across the great slab. I do not know of any great mass of rock like it in Great Britain. It is not part of the rock face, but stands away from it and its face has a sheer drop of about 500 feet into the corrie below.[12]

As Collie was alone at the time he wisely bided his time until Mackenzie's arrival that evening before making a serious attempt.

> As it turned out, it was a climb full of excitement, for one never knew what was round the next corner. We traversed slabs, we worked up cracks, and went right away from the Cioch into the gully on the east side, losing sight of the Cioch altogether. Then we fortunately found a queer traverse unlike any traverse I have ever seen, that led out of the gully across the perpendicular face of the cliff, and back in the direction of the Cioch. But the Cioch itself we could not see, until having got round several corners, suddenly it came into view and we found ourselves on the end of the knife-edge. We sat down on that knife-edge, and slowly made our way to the great rock tower at its end, up this we climbed, and John and I were mightily pleased with our climb. After that everyone at Glen Brittle had to climb it and I believe that during that July and August John and I made the first ten ascents of the Cioch.[13]

It was Mackenzie who named the tower the Cioch and Collie who gave the name Sron na Ciche to the great face.

One of the difficulties in researching the early history of rock climbing is the absence of topographical detail concerning the routes. Credit cannot be had for a first ascent unless one member of the party takes the trouble to record the facts, usually in a club journal or, in those days, in the logbook of the hotel.

March 1889 saw the formation of the Scottish Mountaineering Club (SMC). The club's Journal was published the next year and has appeared regularly ever since. Its birth coincided with the beginnings of the development of climbing not only in Scotland but throughout the British Isles. There were one or two mountaineering clubs already in existence, chief of which was the Alpine Club, which did not take British mountains seriously. The SMC, however, was primarily, though by no means exclusively, concerned with mountaineering in Scotland and, as members were encouraged to contribute articles of mountaineering interest and to record details of their expeditions, there exists today a remarkably useful record of their activities.

So far as Collie's achievements are concerned, whereas the 1880s are poorly documented, the SMC Journals of the 1890s are a treasure trove.

11 Ladies and Mackenzie on the Cioch. *Photo by Collie from his slide collection, permission of the Alpine Club.*

Much of the credit is due to William Douglas, the editor, who energetically badgered members for their contributions: not that he got much co-operation from Collie, who pleaded lack of time and left it to Douglas to write up the historic 1894 Meet, when climbing on the Scottish mainland really took off. Collie moreover did not see the point of route descriptions. He wrote to Douglas: 'It would only be a very bald narrative—we went up a snow slope, then we went up a rock, then we went up some snow and ice then some ice and snow and finally got to the top.'[14] The idea of recording routes in sufficient detail to enable other parties to follow exactly the same lines 'like railway timetables', stripping mountains of their mystery and depriving others of the chance to explore for themselves, was against his principles. Nevertheless he gladly contributed articles on his explorations, where his feelings for the mountains and their appeal to his senses could be indulged, but most of the articles he wrote about the British hills lack route details.

Collie was particularly reticent about his doings in Skye, where the number of his recorded routes is remarkably low considering the many active summers he spent there. H B Buckle and G Barlow arrived in Skye in August 1906, a month after Collie and Mackenzie had first climbed the Cioch. They thought they were making a first ascent via the Cioch Gully and East Gully and were surprised to find a cairn on the way. That evening at Glen Brittle they intended to ask Collie what he knew of Sron na Ciche but he was aloof and unapproachable and neither man mentioned their climb. Not until the

12 Ladies on the Cioch. *Photo by Collie, permission of the Alpine Club.*

13 At Glen Brittle. G Solly (*back left*), Collie (*centre front*). *Photo from Collie's slide collection, permission of the Alpine Club.*

14 At Glen Brittle. Mrs Inglis Clark (?) (*far left*), Collie (*centre front*). *Photo from Collie's slide collection, permission of the Alpine Club.*

15 Collie, Mackenzie and Colonel Campbell in Skye, *c.* 1931. *From Collie's slide collection, permission of Mrs Benstead.*

next year did Barlow receive details of Collie's first ascent and not until 1923 did he manage to get the exact date of the climb.

Geoffrey Winthrop Young, outstanding mountaineer, poet and author recalled how, later in life, Collie 'might now and again chuckle grimly over accounts of new climbs on Scottish cliffs, and remark with the familiar saturnine sidelift of his lip: "They'll find a little cairn there—when they get up"!'[15]

Happily, something of his spirit survives today. It is a deliberate policy of the SMC, who are still responsible for producing the definitive guidebooks to the Scottish mountains, not to give a detailed pitch-by-pitch description of the route—in sharp contrast to the English and Welsh guidebooks, as many a visiting climber has discovered to his discomfiture, and to the secret delight of the natives.

One suspects that Collie disliked, furthermore, the idea of publicity of any sort which might endanger those very qualities of remoteness and solitude for which he loved his mountains. For the same reason he resented the advent of the motor car, bringing to these areas unsympathetic tourists and driving the 'new nickel-plated, pneumatic-cushioning, electrically-driven modern mountaineer on his fascinating career'.[16] Fortunately he did not live to see Sligachan on a Bank Holiday weekend in recent times.

From 1904 when Collie once more began to spend long periods in Skye he was appearing less frequently at SMC meets, and though with Mackenzie as his constant companion he was still tackling the rock faces of the Cuillin, he began to leave less and less evidence of his activities. Other names such as Tough, Brown or Raeburn, younger and better technical climbers, were putting up routes of increasing difficulty and filling the pages of the Journal. Collie, however, had started to keep himself to himself, a trend which was to continue throughout his long life.

Chapter 3

Wasdale

> Only last year a celebrated climber of Alpine repute came to Wastdale for the first time. 'Climbing in the Caucasus,' he said, 'was easy and safe; also it was usually easy and safe in the Alps, though sometimes difficult; but climbing as practised at Wastdale Head was both difficult and dangerous.' (J N Collie, Climbing near Wastdale Head, *Scottish Mountaineering Club Journal*, 13; referring to Mummery's one and only visit to the Lakes)

After his introduction to climbing in 1886, Collie devoted the next four summers to Skye. At the end of 1891, however, his attention was diverted and two years were to elapse before he was to return.

In his early youth Collie had been in the Lake District, his father and Uncle Stephen having spent walking holidays at Grasmere. This exquisite area of lakes, dales and fells had, with the help of some promotion by William Wordsworth and others, already become well-known as a holiday paradise. By contrast with Skye, 'The Lakes' are rarely gloomy and the scenery hardly ever harsh, but then neither is the isolation ever quite so complete; and though in those days one rarely met another person on the fells there was none of the wild grandeur which makes the ridges of Glencoe or Skye, even today on all but a few days of the year, very lonely. But, though most of the fells are gentle and a pleasant stroll will take one to their summits, there are many fine crags, some of them quite large, which nowadays offer a great variety of routes on rock of excellent quality.

In 1891 Collie was ignorant of their rock-climbing potential. 'When first I visited Wastdale Head it was at Christmas time. I knew there was a pinnacle of rock on Great Gable, also that another rock climb could be obtained on the Pillar mountain—that was all.'[1]

His ignorance was shared by many members of the Alpine Club (AC), amongst whom, as has been said, recognition of the merits of their homeland hills was slow in coming, though by 1891 the situation was beginning to change. Certainly the Lake District, where the sport of pure rock climbing can be said to have begun, was better known than the Scottish mountains. But Collie was still writing in 1894, to William Douglas, that he would like to open the eyes of some AC members. 'None of them have the faintest idea what can be got in the way of climbing in Scotland and only a very few even know the Lake District.'[2]

For a decade, one man, Walter Parry Haskett Smith, had been quietly exploring the crags of the Lakes. His list of gully climbs for 1882 had marked 'not merely the beginning of a new epoch in the sport but its very foundation.'[3]

But it was his solitary ascent of Napes Needle in 1886 which really caught the attention of mountaineers and laymen alike. Napes Needle is a 70-foot high obelisk perched on a rock ridge on the flanks of Great Gable overlooking Wasdale. Today it is graded 'very difficult' by the easiest route and it is quite hard for that grade. In June 1890 an illustrated article on Haskett Smith's climb had appeared in the *Pall Mall Budget*. Collie read this on the train carrying him back from Skye that autumn. He immediately arranged a visit to Wasdale Head that Christmas, and naturally enough his first climb was the Needle, in un-nailed boots, without a rope. He was very glad of a hand from his companions on the last tricky move.

These companions, on this and many other expeditions, were John Wilson Robinson and Geoffrey Hastings.

Robinson, a local man, became Haskett Smith's climbing partner. Together, they were a considerable force and their achievements far-reaching. Robinson, according to Collie, was 'a very cheery companion—full of enthusiasm and stories and a great sense of humour'.

Hastings became a life-long friend. Quiet and modest, he was the sort of companion valued on an expedition when tension can build up quickly. On his many trips with Collie, Hastings was always first to volunteer for unpleasant tasks or give way to his companions' whims. He was a man of 'great muscular strength and grim determination, whose step cutting was rapid and untiring be the difficulty and danger what they might'. But, if for nothing else, Hastings would be remembered for the sumptuous contents of his rucksack which ranged from luxuries like champagne to fresh milk or bacon. He had been climbing for several years longer than Collie, and while the latter was first getting to grips with gabbro he was engaged on a guideless ascent of the Dru. Hastings also climbed in Skye with the Pilkington brothers. Though history has recorded much of his friends' activities, Hastings still remains on the edge of things.

These three men made their base at the Inn at the head of Wasdale, the wildest and most remote of the dales. The Wasdale Inn was the centre for climbers in the Lakes in those days in the same way as the Sligachan Inn was for climbers in Skye. There were of course no climbing-club huts or youth hostels, and camping was practised only by a few cranks. Haskett Smith's explanation for this was only part of the story: 'Just as bicyclists suffered by the scathing definition "cads on casters", so the enthusiasm of the camper may have received a check when he heard himself described as a "fool in a bag".'[4]

Because the sport of mountaineering had started off in the Alps and then spread back to the British hills, these simple inns were taken over completely by the climbing fraternity as a sort of combination of mountain hut and Alpine village hotel. Collie records how Alpine indulgence in early starts had, in Britain, given way to late arrivals. He wrote that from the comfort of distance he could romanticise on the journey from Dungeon Ghyll to Wasdale at ten o'clock on a wild winter's night, lantern in hand, with an unreasonable Hastings who would be energetic at the worst possible times.

After his ascent of the Needle, Collie decided that the Lakes deserved more of his time. He spent the rest of the holiday 'persuading' Hastings and Robinson to accompany him 'up and down rock, snow and ice'. He was very keen to pay a visit to Pillar Rock because of the stories he had heard from Haskett Smith.

Above Ennerdale, a remote and even today relatively inaccessible valley, there lies a huge crag detached from the mass of its parent mountain by a vertical gap vaguely reminiscent of the Thearlaich-Dubh Gap. Long before the Alpine Club had ever been thought of, Pillar Rock had attracted considerable local interest, and after many attempts the first successful ascent was made in 1826. By 1891 routes had been made on all sides except the north, and in July of that year, after several previous attempts, Haskett Smith, with Hastings and with William Cecil Slingsby, of whom we shall hear more, had made the first ascent of the North Climb. However, they had avoided the crucial 'Nose' by a detour which came to be known as the Westerly Variation and Savage Gully Exit. It was in an attempt to eliminate this long-winded detour that Collie made for Pillar Rock that Christmas.

The day was bitter but the men climbed without difficulty up the first 300 feet via slabs, grooves and twisting chimneys, until a ledge was reached near the top of the climb. From the right-hand end of the ledge it was necessary to ascend a steep wall for about 10 feet until the sharp edge of a flake could be grasped. A traverse was then made leftwards to the top of the Nose gripping the flake with the hands. It was during this part of the climb that Robinson, whose hands had become frozen, had a spectacular fall. Although he was only a short distance along the traverse he could neither advance nor retreat. Calling out that he could hold on no longer, he fell onto the ledge below, bounded out into the air, turned a backwards somersault, and then hit a grassy patch. At that moment the strain came on the rope and he was miraculously held. It was a very narrow escape because none of the party was belayed, in the now traditional fashion, and if he had not been held the whole party would have followed him.

Collie thought the climb dangerous and had no wish to try it again. A short time afterwards he was asked by a party of Alpine Club men to show them the route as far as the traverse, which he was quite willing to do. When they got there, however, one of the party insisted on attempting the move. Collie replied that he had seen 'one man fall from it, and certainly did not wish to repeat the experience. On his insisting, I said, "If we are roped I shall prevent your starting, and if we are not I am going down at once." He replied, "You don't know anything about real rock-climbing, you are not a member of the Alpine Club, and I am etc." But he did not attempt the traverse.'[5] Only a few weeks later, in February 1892, Geoffrey Solly, with a party including Hastings, successfully climbed the Hand Traverse. The following year Joseph Collier and his party climbed the Nose direct.

At this time climbers still preferred the security of gullies to the exposure of open faces. The reasons for this were not entirely psychological, for at that stage in the development of ropes and rope techniques it was arguable that gullies were safer places. North Climb, like Napes Needle, was an exception and marked the beginning of the transition from gully to face climbing. By the end of the 1890s, when most of the Lakeland gullies had been climbed, climbers wishing to break new ground were obliged to venture onto the faces, and the trend reached its full impetus.

Collie was proud of his participation in the early days of this 'second wave'. Geoffrey Winthrop Young recalled that even during the 'heyday of the gully epoch' Collie had pointed out to him how much he was missing of the beautiful mountain world by being stuck in 'blind gullies and viewless cracks'. And yet, Collie's greatest contributions to Lakeland climbing were both firmly in the old gully tradition: Great Gully on the Screes, in Wasdale, and Moss Ghyll, on Scafell.

The first ascent of Great Gully was made during Collie's Christmas visit in 1891. The Screes, as the name implies, is a face of broken rock and scree, possessing a certain bleak grandeur, which descends steeply from a westerly outlier of Scafell to the shores of Wastwater, wildest and deepest of the Lakes, and fully exposed to the gales which blow in from the Irish Sea. While the face itself has nothing to offer the climber, it is intersected by several gullies of which Great Gully is the best.

It was a perfect winter day, the branches of the few windswept trees white with frost, as the party made their approach over the loose scree to the bottom of the gully. This was straightforward at first, but it soon branched. Following the left branch they had some trouble on the first pitch, a cascade of ice, very hard for cutting steps, which forced them out onto the rock buttress between the two branches. Hastings, with considerable difficulty and some assistance from Collie, led leftwards, back into the main gully, where they found themselves in a deep cleft with perpendicular walls. Towering above them, a magnificent sight, was cascade after cascade of ice, up which they proceeded to cut their way, using the rock walls to steady themselves. The exit from the top of the gully was barred by a great overhang fringed with insecure icicles, some of them 30 feet long. To surmount this impasse Robinson securely belayed himself at the back of the cave below the overhang while Collie in the lead, worked himself into a very insecure position, his right foot lodged in a large hole cut in one of the icicles while his left rested delicately on a tiny rock ledge in the gully wall. Braced in this position across the void, Collie allowed Hastings to clamber over him and from a precarious position on his shoulders to pull himself over the top.

Collie, his appetite whetted, returned to the Lakes the following Easter and Christmas. By contrast with their previous visit the weather in December 1892 was mild and the rock dry and free from ice. Conditions were ideal for Moss Ghyll.

High above Wasdale, on the north side of Scafell, stands Scafell Crag, the largest and highest rock face in the Lakes. Just to the right of the great Central Buttress, which was totally impregnable for the climbers of the 1890s, the crag is split from top to bottom by the formidable cleft of Moss Ghyll. Attempts had already been made to climb it but all had failed at a point where the gully was blocked by an enormous jammed boulder, hundreds of tons in weight, which formed a huge cave.

Collie, Hastings and Robinson, having reconnoitred the upper reaches of the gully from above, came to the conclusion that if the boulder could be surmounted there was nothing above which would stop them. On 27 December they set out, ready for battle.

After the short introductory chimney which brought them to the narrow terrace now known as Rake's Progress, a system of ledges led them easily up the rocks on the right and into the bed of the gully about 100 feet up. After another excursion up the right wall, difficult and strenuous this time, they were able to work their way up into the great cave roofed by the overhanging boulder. A debate then took place on how further progress might be made. In Collie's view the only chance of success would be to bypass the obstruction on the left wall, by traversing out from just under the roof at a point where the angle of the wall eased slightly. Though the rock offered nothing adequate in the way of holds Collie thought he would just be able to balance on a sloping knob which projected a quarter of an inch from the face. He carefully placed the toe of his boot on the sloping hold but as soon as he transferred his weight onto it his boot nails skidded off. Just as he began to fall a mighty heave on the rope from Hastings jerked him back into the security of the cave. Collie, his blood now well and truly up, grabbed Hastings' axe and after several blows, which fortunately did no damage to the famous implement, the projection had been excised, leaving a neat little square-cut hold.

Collie traversed out and back onto the flat bed of the gully above the block. The party completed the climb by working up slabs on the left wall, a finish now known as 'Collie's Exit'. A few days later Joseph Collier, under the impression that he was following the original line, made the more difficult direct finish.

'Collie's Step' is now part of climbing lore, though all traces have long since been erased by the tens of thousands of nailed, and nowadays cleated rubber, boots which have travelled up this most classic of all Lakeland climbs.

Contrary to popular, lay, belief, ice axes are not, and never have been, carried by climbers in order to hack holds in rock. On the occasion in question it was logical that at least one axe should be carried by a party engaged on a gully climb at a level of 3,000 feet at the end of December as ice might easily have been present in these circumstances. Ice axes were frequently, and legitimately, used for carving holds in frozen turf or jammed into cracks to provide artificial holds, but the line has always been drawn at disfiguring the rock in any permanent way. By his action, therefore, Collie knowingly courted censure by the mountaineering establishment.

He wrote afterwards, 'Peccavi!'—I have sinned—to emphasise his breaking of the rules and though he did not show any sign of contrition he recognised that what they did might well be 'severely criticized by more orthodox mountaineers than ourselves'.[6] If he was anticipating with relish the sort of shocked controversy which might ensue, he was to be disappointed, for his action does not seem to have attracted criticism, in print at least.

Though Collie was to return to the Lakes sporadically through the years, none of his later visits resulted in any significant first ascents.

Chapter 4

Argon and Helium

> Collie was a man of remarkable versatility. In my days as a young student at University College he gave me what he called the education of a gentleman. At a series of dinners in his rooms in Campden Grove he discoursed at length on the beauty of early printing and incunabula, the perfection of Japanese carving and the knowledge and appreciation of vintage clarets. One evening his friend Sir Herbert Jackson remarked, 'Collie, it seems to me that you are a chemist only in your spare time.' (*Obituaries of Fellows of the Royal Society*, 4, 1942–4)

The years of Collie's first exploratory work in the mountains were also the years when he was beginning to explore more surely the intricacies of the world of chemistry. The later years of the nineteenth century have been described as 'the age of chemistry' which indicates how new a science it was. Britain was a highly industrialised society and the developing science of chemistry had tied itself closely to industry in order to further technological progress. Many commercially important materials such as dyes and pharmaceuticals, which had hitherto been obtainable only from natural sources, became available from the laboratories cheaply and in large quantities for the first time. It would not be long before the chemical laboratories produced synthetic materials like plastic. Not only did science and industry reinforce one another but scientists, like Mendeléeff with his Periodic Table, gave a theoretical structure to chemistry which could make order out of chaos and provide the foundation for further industrial advance. Organic chemistry in particular made rapid developments during the 1880s and 1890s, and it was during this exciting period, in September 1887, that Collie and Ramsay arrived in London.

Although the Department of Chemistry at University College had been founded in 1828, at the same time as the College, it had over the years lost its impetus towards research. Ramsay found the teaching side disorganised and no research taking place at all. There was a new laboratory but it had been constructed on the same lines as the original one built over 60 years before. The arrangements were primitive compared to the modern and well-equipped laboratory Ramsay had left behind at Bristol. Down in the basements the débris of the past 40 years was stacked in dusty abandon. In those days most chemicals were made in the labs. The residues had been stored in hundreds of bottles and jars, mostly unlabelled. There was no time for analysing them and Collie supervised their clearance by the cartload. Somehow he managed to overlook a mummy that had been lying in the cellars for years. When some unsuspecting student found it lurking in a corner a man from the British Museum was called in to unroll it, watched with relish by the entire department.

Apart from Collie, Ramsay also had three men and a boy as assistants. The total sum available for salaries was £1,200. Salaries were paid out of Ramsay's fees. As a result his salary depended on how much, or how little, he had to pay his staff. Since neither Ramsay nor his assistants had grants to pay for research, all research expenses had to come from their yearly earnings. It was the days before government support of the universities.

Ramsay, when engaging staff, had written in June 1887, 'I want to replace Morley with Collie, nephew of *the* Collie [a reference to Alexander]. He is a delightful fellow with a genius for research and would come for £150. He is also a gentleman (which Morley is not) and a very good teacher.'[1] It was not only Ramsay who thought highly of Collie. From the first his students were impressed by him and he was able to keep perfect order in his classes. This in itself was a feat, for medical students in particular were notoriously unruly, due, in part, to the laxity of the Medical Board examinations in chemistry. During the first term Collie met some of his students at Windsor racecourse. He greeted them with a smile and a tip that proved successful. From then on he had no trouble with his classes. However, it was not just his knowledge of the turf that contributed to the friendly atmosphere between them. Many students recorded their indebtedness to him. E C C Baly, later a professor at University College, was one of Collie's first students. He wrote,

> I first met Collie when I entered University College in January 1889. In the previous December my father had taken me to see Ramsay and suggested my studying for a university degree. Ramsay did not agree with this and strongly recommended my working for the Institute of Chemistry examination. Having advised me to take a number of lecture courses he put me in the hands of Collie to learn practical chemistry. My fellow-students and I found in Collie a born teacher, gifted with a salutary sarcasm which was tempered with a real understanding of the difficulties presented by a hitherto unknown field of study. ... Collie was very human in his understanding of students. He was ever ready with encouragement when any one of us found difficulty in learning a new technique and on occasion would take endless trouble to help us on our way.[2]

There was certainly a heavy teaching commitment. Collie gave courses of lectures to junior students and engineers, and also to medical students preparing for the first Medical Board examinations in organic chemistry. There were lectures for senior students on recent advances in organic chemistry as well as practical classes in qualitative and organic analysis. Collie also bore a large share of the lab teaching, having sole charge of those students engaged in research.

All these commitments had to be seen to before Collie could concentrate on his own work. If Ramsay wanted to build up a successful department from slender beginnings it was essential that his staff contributed to the progress of their science. It was going to be a year or so before the department began to gain international distinction, and this was as well for Collie, who was able to devote his energies to the mountains before chemistry began to encroach so drastically upon his time.

During his first year at University College, Collie had three papers published, one in association with Letts, on the action of heat on tetramethylphosphonium salts. An incidental discovery from this work on the phosphines and their derivatives was the isolation of methyl fluoride. During this research Collie devised a new piece of apparatus, a mercury circulator, which cut down the time involved in making methyl fluoride—'a good dodge', according to Ramsay. This apparatus was used extensively during the discovery of the noble gases, and then spent many years on its own shelf above Collie's bench.

Collie made most of his own apparatus, some examples of which are now in the care of the Science Museum in London. E C C Baly described Collie at this task: 'It happened that my bench in the laboratory was opposite to those on which Collie carried out his work. It was to me a fascinating sight to see him blowing glass and making the apparatus he used in studying the action of heat on the ammonium and phosphonium compounds in which he was interested at that time. He frequently asked me to watch him and I was very intrigued by the fact that he invariably did his glass-blowing with his lighted pipe in his mouth. He strongly advised me to take lessons in glass-blowing, saying that it was an invaluable accomplishment to a chemist.'[3] Nearly all the apparatus used in the discovery of helium was blown by Collie. A visiting professor was very impressed one weekend when, on the breakage of glass apparatus during an experiment, Collie promptly blew some more. There was no need for the experiment to be held up until the Monday when a professional blower would be available.

By 1899 Collie's reputation had begun to grow. He was known to chemists throughout Europe as a worker of the 'first order'. During that year he was appointed to the Council of the Chemical Society, a post he held for five years. More papers were published, all of them in the *Journal of the Chemical Society*. One continued his work on methyl fluoride and another completed his research on minerals begun at Cheltenham. His structure for dehydracetic acid was regarded as greatly superior to that of the famous German chemist Feist.

In recognition of his work, the Council of University College made him an Assistant Professor, a title held by only a few and conferred only after a searching enquiry into the claims of the candidate—an enquiry conducted with practically the same formalities as the election to a Chair. Collie was only 31 when this honour was bestowed upon him.

Ramsay was convinced that Collie's unusual power of work was due to his excellent health and vigour attained through his outdoor life, but nevertheless Ramsay was often put out by the way he 'bolted when the session was done'. Ramsay felt that part of every holiday should be devoted to research in the college. However, in the days before the motor car, climbing could only really be indulged in during the holidays, and Collie's enthusiastic flight is very understandable. Even though he was now an Assistant Professor, nothing would keep him in the lab when the north was calling.

During the summer of 1892 Collie visited the Alps for the first time. When he returned that September it was to an atmosphere of change. Work had begun in the labs that was to culminate in the discovery of the first noble gas, argon. With the discovery of argon at University College the world was suddenly told that the composition of the atmosphere was different from that which had been believed for years. Its discovery also involved Collie in many years of work.

The real search for argon began when Lord Rayleigh, a distinguished chemist, found that the density of nitrogen prepared by removal of oxygen and carbon dioxide from the atmosphere was greater than that prepared by chemical reaction. This puzzled him. He wrote to the scientific paper *Nature* to ask if anyone could supply the answer. Ramsay replied with the explanation that there was probably some other gas mixed with this nitrogen. As a result Ramsay and Rayleigh joined forces to isolate the unknown gas. Ramsay was right, for the abnormal density of atmospheric nitrogen was due to the presence in the atmosphere of 1 per cent of the heavier gas argon.

Most of the work was carried out at University College by Ramsay's team, including Collie. Work in the labs was not at this time easy; the fact that the noble gases were discovered there at all is even more surprising given the conditions under which the scientists worked. There was no money for even basic materials unless paid for by the staff. At one point work threatened to stop due to lack of money for a liquid air plant. Even glass tubing had to be paid for privately.

Collie wrote that he collaborated closely with Ramsay on much of the early work on argon, but it was two years before the gas was isolated in August 1894. With its isolation the work was really only beginning, for the properties of argon had to be determined. Collie and Ramsay ascertained that the gas refused to enter into combination or to exhibit any chemical change when heated. It was in fact largely inert, the chief characteristic of all the noble gases. Collie always referred to them as the inactive gases. Early in March Ramsay tried to find evidence of the formation of a compound by the gas. He heated clèveite, a form of the uranium ore pitchblende, to see if that contained argon and was astounded to discover, in the gas obtained from this mineral, the characteristic sprectra not only of argon but also of helium.

During an eclipse of the sun in 1868, the presence of a brilliant yellow line was first noted in the spectrum of the chromosphere, the layer of incandescent gas surrounding the sun. It was realised that this could not be ascribed to any known element and the new element was given the name helium, derived from the Greek word for the sun. Until Ramsay's experiment there was no evidence to suggest that this supposed element existed on earth.

Ramsay, beside himself with excitement, telegraphed to the Paris Institute and asked them to carry out an identical experiment to confirm his results. Collie was with him in the darkroom when a student rushed in with the reply. Tearing open the telegram Ramsay found the answer he wanted. Collie believed that no other chemist but Ramsay was capable of such a discovery at this time.

The department erupted in a frenzy of excitement. No one was capable of doing any work that day. Chemistry students were seen rushing off to the mineral dealers trying to purchase cléveite, and even Collie's medical students suddenly became interested in chemistry. It was one thing, however, to recognise a new gas but quite another to obtain sufficient quantities of it for study. Ramsay asked Collie and two other members of staff, Alexander Kellas and Morris Travers, to assist him in building up a stock of the gas and then to determine its properties. The work involved great care and patience, and eventually Ramsay was to entrust the work only to Collie and Travers. Kellas, according to Travers, was rather too slow to work with Ramsay.

The Easter holidays were, however, fast approaching. Ramsay asked the three men to return early to the college so that the work could be got under way. This was agreed and Collie took his two colleagues off to Scotland for three weeks.

Kellas and Collie had been drawn together from the first by their mutual love for the mountains. Kellas, like John Collie, was from Aberdeen and had spent his early years wandering over the Scottish hills. Collie later introduced him to the possibilities of the Himalayas and he became an expert on the medical problems caused by high altitude. By 1895 Kellas had been on the staff as a demonstrator for three years.

Morris Travers became a student assistant in 1894, eventually joining the staff. Collie probably introduced him to the mountains on this holiday. Travers did not take to mountaineering quite as Collie and Kellas did, although he went to the Alps on one occasion. There is some evidence to suggest that he and Collie did not really get on. Perhaps this is not so surprising when one finds Collie writing in 1898: 'Now I am hacking my way through a cornice apparently hundreds of feet high, on Aonach Mhor, my companion Travers meanwhile slowly freezing on the brink of an absolutely perpendicular ice slope, the daylight waning, and our retreat cut off.'[4]

As requested, the three men cut short their holiday and were back working on the new gas before the students arrived. Collie and Travers found that helium, like argon, did not combine with any other element and also that like argon it was nearly insoluble in water. It was non-inflammable and had a very low density. (It was destined for use in the new airships when they came into vogue.) It is found in certain natural gases, and chiefly in minerals that contain the rare element uranium, which is now indispensable to the nuclear industry.

According to Professor Sir William Tilden, the novel characteristics of the new gases led to great activity in the scientific world. The learned journals were full of speculations 'as to their origin, their atomic constitution, their recognition in the earth's atmosphere and their position in the scheme of known elements. The excitement extended beyond scientific circles, and all sorts of amateur physicists plunged into extravagant hypotheses as to the functions of argon in nature. Even young students were infected with the epidemic, and the answers to examination questions showed that oxygen as a constituent of our air was almost forgotten in the anxiety of the candidate to show that he or she knew all about argon.'[5]

The conclusion of this part of the work on argon and helium was their incorporation into the Periodic Table of the Elements—the final seal of approval.

Collie lived long enough to see the noble gases become a cornerstone of the theories of atomic structure and chemical bonding—theories which, because of their basic simplicity, wide application and capacity for prediction, probably appealed to Collie's philosophy. As a former pupil wrote: 'The essential feature of his later work was a desire to bring together in one comprehensive scheme the manifold products of organised matter.'[6]

Chapter 5

Undiscovered Scotland

> In thinking of Collie and his era it is like seeing a particular line of peaks, belonging to one of the great mountain ranges. All the summits are remarkable for shape, colour and form, but here and there stands an isolated 'needle' severe yet accessible, rather bleak to the eye, but after some time of watching, there is seen to be a light playing in the shadow and even a welcome friendliness in the approach. This particular peak seems detached from the main body yet is absolutely an essential part of the whole. So I think was Collie to his world—unapproachable at times to his acquaintances, yet to those who knew him well a fascinating companion and a devoted friend, standing apart from ordinary society and yet a host in himself when the company was to his liking. (E Winthrop Young, *Fell and Rock Journal*, 13, p 311)

Just as, during the 1890s, Collie was successfully establishing his reputation as a scientist, so too was he establishing his reputation as a mountaineer.

During these years he participated in a minor way in the transition from gully to face climbing in the Lake District; in the Alps he and his friends dominated the guideless climbing scene; while on the Scottish mainland, as well as on Skye, he was to play a leading part in the very beginning of rock climbing.

From its origins in the Alps, the sport of climbing spread to the Lake District and Snowdonia and later to Scotland where, because of the much longer winter season, the emphasis was more on snow and ice, the climbing more Alpine in character. The Scottish Mountaineering Club from the beginning encouraged all types of climbing at its meets. These were gatherings of like-minded enthusiasts who met two or three times a year at one of the Highland centres. The Easter meet was the SMC's most popular. If Easter was late, and spring came early, conditions might favour rock climbing; if the opposite was true, conditions might be ideal for snow and ice climbing. Sometimes it might even be possible to spend one day hacking your way up

16 Loch Maree, Wester Ross, early 1900s. Haskett Smith handing flask to Collie. Slingsby second from left. *Photo from Mrs Benstead, with permission.*

an icy gully in some high northerly corrie and the next basking on the rough sun-warmed rocks of a low-lying crag. Scotland is like that.

Collie, who spent several seasons on the Scottish mainland during the 1890s, was one of the first mountaineers to have served an apprenticeship on British hills before visiting the Alps, which he first did in 1892.

It was in 1894 that Collie really opened the eyes of the Scots to what was on their own doorstep. He had already done a lot of exploring and his name appears regularly in the visitors' book at Clachaig, one of the two inns at either extremity of Glen Coe. In January 1894 Collie had written to the *Journal* editor: 'If I can possibly abuse a few friends I shall be up in Glencoe next Easter. There is a splendid climb straight up Aonach Dubh on Stob Coire an Lochan from Loch Atriochatan about two thousand four hundred feet of precipice which I once did years ago.'[1] The plans were made for the most successful of his campaigns on the Scottish mainland.

The Easter meet of 1894 was officially based at Inveroran, in the Black Mount, but the events for which it has gone down into climbing history took place many miles further north and indeed after the official meet had dispersed.

When he stepped off the train at Tyndrum, Collie was met by two of his Lakeland friends, Geoffrey Solly and Joseph Collier, his guests for the meet. It was Solly's first acquaintance with the SMC, whose President he would one day become. In those days Inveroran was 'ten miles from anywhere', and they set off on foot while the luggage followed by horse and cart. The little inn was so crowded with climbers arriving for the meet that at breakfast the very next day Collie and his two friends decided to move out. The reason for their premature departure was more probably the nature of the Black Mount, which is walking rather than climbing country, and Collie intended to climb.

They went first to Kingshouse, the next lonely inn, eight rough miles to the north, near the head of Glen Coe, now the most popular climbing area in Scotland but at that time almost untouched. Two miles across the moor from the inn stands the symmetrical triangle of Buachaille Etive Mor, the Great Shepherd of Etive, standing guard over the approaches to Glen Coe on the one hand, and Glen Etive on the other.

Collie, Solly and Collier made straight for the 1,000 feet of ridge, gully, buttress and wall facing the inn. Following a route ready-planned by Collie, they made what was in effect the first ascent of that tremendous face, Collie's Climb, a bold breakthrough in its day, though by keeping to the left-hand edge of the face it avoided the real challenge and has nowadays sunk back into obscurity.

While they were thus engaged, three SMC stalwarts, Brown, Thompson and Naismith, the founding father of the Club, were busy on the other side of the Buachaille making what they fondly believed to be the first ascent of Great Gully. Back at the inn they learned from Collie that he had climbed it years before. In today's guidebook, Great Gully is summarily dismissed as 'not in any real sense a rock climb'. This illustrates well the emphasis

17 Inveroran Meet, Easter 1894. From *SMC Journal*.

16 17

12 13 14 15

1 2 3 4 5 7 8 9

10 11

KEY TO PHOTOGRAPH

1 Col. A. G. Wavell.
2 W. R. Lester.
3 Jas. Macklay.
4 D. A. Forbes. (?)
5 G. G. Ramsay.
6 T. Fraser S. Campbell.
7 Charles C. B. Moss.
8 J. Norman Collier.
9 H. C. Boyd.
10 Joseph Coats.
11 W. Ramsay.
12 J. Collier.
13 G. A. Solly.
14 L. W. Hinxman.
15 F. O. Bower.
16 W. Douglas. (?)
17 J. Rennie

modern climbing gives to pure technical quality as distinct from situation, romance and mystery, qualities which meant so much to pioneers like Collie.

Obscurity was not to be the fate of the next climb which Collie's party attempted. Clachaig Gully, which cleaves the south flank of Sgurr nan Fiannaidh at the lower end of Glen Coe, is 1,000 feet long and a classic climb today. The grading, by today's standards, is 'mild severe'. Not surprisingly, they failed to get up, as did generations of climbers until its ascent in 1938 by W H Murray, who wrote an account of the climb while he was a prisoner of war in Germany. (Memories of his climbing in Scotland kept him going during his long years in prison camps. The evening after his ascent of Claichaig Gully stood out clearly in his memory 'as one of life's milestones of sheer happiness'.[2]) To construe Collie's attempt as 'ahead of his time' would in this case be quite wrong: the initial pitches of the gully are deceptively easy and the harder sections are out of sight from below. The climbing starts a few minutes walk from the door of Clachaig Inn, to which they had moved from Kingshouse, and it is only after some 500 feet of scrambling up waterfalls amongst rowan and birch that the climber encounters the first serious obstacle—the Great Cave pitch. No doubt this was Collie's highest point, for according to the Clachaig visitors' book they were forced out of the gully by an 80-foot waterfall and only escaped with difficulty after a traverse to the right.

After another failure, this time on the Church Door Buttress on Bidean nam Bian, the three, perhaps feeling their luck had run out, moved north again to Fort William and Ben Nevis, where they were to succeed, and succeed brilliantly, with the ascent of Tower Ridge.

Until the following year, when the West Highland Railway reached Fort William, the area was remote and access was difficult. In summer many hardy tourists made the ascent of Britain's highest mountain by the well-engineered pony track which zig-zagged up the rounded south-west flanks from the direction of Fort William. The track had been constructed to service an observatory which had been established on the very summit as early as 1883, manned the year round by a heroic crew who cheerfully faced the worst kind of weather in order to make regular readings of their instruments. After the opening of the railway the observatory staff ran a small hostel for the ever-increasing number of visitors. The entrance hall, according to one of the inmates, 'reminded one more of such Alpine climbing centres as Zermatt than a West Highland tourist resort. The umbrella stand was filled with ice-axes and the hat pegs accommodated climbing ropes.'[3]

Before 1895 however, the great precipices on the north-east side of the Ben were seldom visited, but 'one bracing afternoon not long after the observatory had been opened, a member of the staff was more than amazed on looking over a precipice to see about 1,500 feet down, two dark objects laboriously scaling the ice covered and snow clad face of the declivity. That human beings should attempt to reach the top by such an access never crossed his mind . . . to say that the Observors were astonished would be but meagrely to express their feelings for had they not, like the Russians at Port Arthur, deemed these gigantic precipices impregnable'.[4]

18 Tower Ridge in winter. *Photo by Donald Bennett, with permission.*

Tower Ridge, the most distinctive feature of the greatest mountain face in the British Isles, is a classic for all time. There is a vertical interval of 2,000 feet from the lowest rocks to the point where the climber arrives on the summit plateau. The initial steep slabby tower, 700 feet high, now known as the Douglas Boulder (some boulder!), is followed by a long, narrow section of ridge leading to the Little Tower. Shortly after this the Great Tower rears up in an intimidating 100-foot step. Its summit is 4,000 feet above sea level. A short descent leads to Tower Gap, sensational though not difficult in summer, from which a further 300 feet of scrambling leads to the summit plateau.

In good summer conditions the entire ridge can be climbed direct at around 'very difficult' standard, a very worthwhile expedition, memorable more for its atmosphere and situation than for technical difficulty. In winter it is another matter entirely, a serious expedition on which experienced parties have been turned back or, overtaken by darkness, obliged to spend the longest and least comfortable night of their lives huddled in the lee of the ridge.

In March 1894 Tower Ridge was still unnamed and unclimbed, though it had been climbed as far as the base of the Great Tower in summer conditions 18 months previously by three of the brothers Hopkinson, a family from the north of England, who returning the next day along with a fourth member of the clan, descended the whole ridge from the plateau to the foot of the Douglas Boulder. Their expedition went unrecorded until much later but it is probable that Collie's party had heard of it before their own attempt.

Full winter conditions prevailed as Collie, Solly and Collier approached the foot of the climb on 29 March. Turning the Douglas Boulder on its left, or eastern, side, they gained the crest a little above the Douglas Gap. The ascent took five hours, Great Tower being turned on the western side. It is interesting that this was the side followed by the Hopkinsons in their descent in 1892, though the eastern traverse, discovered by Naismith in 1900, is nowadays normally taken in winter.

There was something of a 'magical mystery tour' about the climb, which obviously made a deep impression on Collie. Tower Gap, in particular, is scarcely less awesome under typical winter conditions today than it would have seemed to Collie, whose inspired account of the climb, 'a pseudo Rabelaisian alchemistic attempt' as he wrote to Douglas when commending it to his editorial clemency, is worth quoting at length. Writing under the anagrammatical pseudonym of Orlamon Linecus, he describes the adventures of three travellers who discover the way to 'attain to the Philosophers' heavenly chaos'. In correspondence with his friends he had been in the habit of referring to a prospective route as The Quest which he defines here as the pursuit of 'secret and hidden mysteries of sublime mountains'. The title of the account, originally published in the *SMC Journal*, is 'On the Divine Mysteries of the Oromaniacal Quest'.

> Thus did they fare onward toward the midst of the valley placed between the red Hill and the great Mountain. Then behold before them rose hugeous rocks and bulky stones standing on end facing to the north where the ice and snow

tarry from one winter even until the following; for in those places the sun shines not, neither are found the comfortable, soft, juicy, and foeculent breezes of the South; there the brood of the black Crow and the white smoak or vapour and comprehensive congelations of the Mistus Scotorum are produced. So were the three Brethren sore amazed, but as yet could see not even the first matter of the Work.

'See', said one, 'the way leadeth upward where the Spirit arising like unto a volatisation, a separation or sublimation or wind, has much bewhited the mighty petrolific ridge full of points, towers and pinnacles. There the pursuit may be pursued, there the volatisation which is an ascension may be compleatly demonstrated, and the operation of the great Work may be begun. First must we fashion in the snow and ice great stairs of steps, by the aid of which, through prolongation, extension, reduplication and multiplication shall we be brought on to the Ridge even at the beginning.' So did they enter upon the Work in this lowest period of obscurity, multiplying the steps in a certain mystic manner which had been revealed to them; and it came to pass that they attained at last on to the Ridge whereon might be perceived far above, towers, pinnacles, points, and other pleasant places, suitable and useful for the furtherance of the Quest.

First did they traverse a narrow edge of snow fashioned by the wind. Then said one, 'Follow me, but look not either to the right or to the left, for there lyeth the Abyss.' So they followed him, with the mystic thread fastened to their girdles ... above and beyond lay the summit of the great Mountain, where clouds are concocted in the natural furnace. ... So did they fare onwards; and by inspection were they aware how others had travelled on the same way, for on the stones and rocks were certain petrographical scratchings and curious markings deeply graven and very evident. But presently they came to a great Rock, a majestic Tower. Here were they perforce compelled to depart to the right hand, placing themselves in steep and perilous positions on slopes of ice, which downward seemed to end in empty air, even in the great void. ...

Behind and far below, imprinted in the snow, were the steps by which they had mounted upwards, winding now this way, now that, looking like scarce seen veins in whitest marble. But before them lay the narrow Way, the Ridge, the Cleft, and the White Slope, leading even unto the utmost Height. ...

So at last they came even unto the very topmost Point, and were aware how that Priests from the heavenly Temple, which is placed on the top of that mountain, had come forth to guide them, to the gates of the Temple itself. ... So were they shown by the dwellers in the Temple many and marvellous wonders. ...

Then did they drink the mixed draught, the comfortable potation, joyously, philosophically and with discernment, for at last had they attained to the divine Secrets of the Philosophers, even unto the mystagorical Delight, the great Fulfillment of the Spagyrick Quest of devout Oromaniacs.[5]

The Temple was not a mere figment of Collie's imagination, but the meteorological observatory whose 'potations' no doubt consisted of hot tea liberally reinforced, according to local custom, in a manner appropriate to such an occasion.

Next day, Collier and Solly had to leave, but Collie, determined to wring the last out of his Easter vacation, had invited Hastings to join him. Together they spent four days in Glen Coe before themselves heading south.

Back in London, Collie received a congratulatory note from Naismith, who wrote simultaneously to Douglas:

> The Sassanachs have indeed taken the wind out of our sails maist notoriously I wull say that. However I suppose we must make a virtue of necessity and try to look pleasant about it. These beggars were more wide-awake than we in skimming the cream off Glencoe and Ben Nevis the year *before* the railway opened, while we in our innocence were still planning what we should do *after* that event. ... This is truly a sad day for auld Scotland. Let us hope that the hotel keepers at Fort William took a good few bawbees off the Englishers. Flodden or even Culloden was nothing to this. If their bit hillocks could be detected with the naked eye we might still get Gibson to pull himself together and astonish them on their own ground. Couldn't he do the Houses of Parliament by the Clock Tower or a traverse of Beachy Head?[6]

There is a hint of apology in Collie's letter to Douglas: 'I felt as if I had rather been poaching on your ground on Ben Nevis but I assure you it is many years ago since I made up my mind that on the first possible opportunity when I could get another man I would have a try at the old Ben.'[7]

Another SMC member, Gilbert Thompson, wrote to Douglas the following year that a route he planned to do must be kept secret from the Englishers until he had done it. This spirit of rivalry which developed at such an early stage between the proud Scots and the marauders from the South is still alive. In 1954, for example, Brown and Whillans climbed a magnificently bold line on Carn Dearg Buttress of Ben Nevis. Provocatively, they named it 'Sassenach'.

Next year, 1895, Professor Ramsay had particularly asked that Collie, Kellas and Travers should be back early from their Easter holiday in order to begin the work on helium. Though this meant that they had only three weeks to spend in Scotland, Fort William was now perfectly feasible because the railway had just been opened. By his enthusiastic accounts of the climbing to be had on the Ben, Collie had persuaded the SMC to break from the traditional venue of Inveroran for the Easter meet.

As another SMC member was to write in the *Journal*: 'To those, who like myself, had been accustomed to think of Ben Nevis as a big lumpy hill, vulgarized by a refreshment saloon at the top and pay box at the bottom, between which the summer tourist passes in a continual stream along a well-kept pony path, the first sight of its north-eastern face comes as a revelation.'[8]

Collie and his two colleagues had already spent two weeks based at Corpach, but no record of their doings has survived. On 11 April they were gathered around the mahogany of the Alexandria Hotel in Fort William. It was a very large meet. Newcomers arrived by every train. Most of the big names in the Scottish climbing world were present.

Collie was a mine of information, inspiring them all to action. They had no need to spend time exploring: Collie had done all the groundwork. Parties were soon scurrying off to try routes which he recommended. Tower Ridge was impracticable due to very heavy accumulations of snow, but Collie,

Naismith, Gilbert Thompson and Travers made the first ascent of Castle Ridge, 900 feet in height, a fine climb in such conditions. Two more parties followed them up. The gullies, well filled with snow, were very popular. After an ascent of No 3 Gully, already a trade route, Collie and Travers had to depart.

There was one particular route which Collie was keen to do but as time had run out he generously handed it, on a plate as it were, to Naismith. Naismith took with him Maclay and ironically enough the same Gilbert Thompson who had wanted to keep his routes a secret from the Englishers. This party accompanied Collie on his train south as far as Spean Bridge, whence they set off to find the mighty ridge about which Collie had enthused. Eighty-five years on, it can still be said of the North-East Ridge of Aonach Beag: 'The climber setting out for it does so in a spirit of exploration, knowing that somewhere on the distant side of the mountain, in its remotest corrie, there is an unknown route calling him. Truly it is a climb for those seeking mountain solitude.'[9]

'The credit of the first ascent of the North-East Ridge of Aonoch Beag is undoubtedly due to the absent Collie' was how the *Journal* put it when describing 'the climb of the meet'. Naismith was over the moon, thought that it was the best arête in Scotland and beat anything in the Cuillin, which, though undoubtedly an exaggeration, was significant: climbers were at last realising that Skye did not quite have a monopoly of the best of Scottish climbing.

Chapter 6

The Three Musketeers

> When I look back and think of all the various places where Mummery, Hastings, Slingsby, and I have slept out in the open, far away from the haunts of men, I for one would go back year after year to the Alps if those times could be brought back again. In those days the glass of time, when shaken, ran in golden sands. Now all that is left of them is the memory. (J N Collie 1902, *Climbing on the Himalaya and Other Mountain Ranges*)

During the years that the search for argon was in progress Collie carried out a remarkable campaign in the Alps. In 1892, the year that the argon work commenced, Collie first followed his Uncle Stephen to the Alps. Hastings went with him and both were accompanied by the well-known mountaineer Albert Frederick Mummery.

Mummery was a man of great intellectual as well as climbing ability who had been mountaineering in the Alps since 1871. By 1879 he had ascended the Matterhorn twice, Mont Blanc and many other mountains mostly in the company of guides. The guides recognised that here was no ordinary mountaineer, for Mummery equalled the very best of them in ability and nerve. An ungainly man, tall, thin and bespectacled, who had a poor back which precluded load carrying, as well as bad eyesight that made walking long distances over uneven ground a nightmare, Mummery seemed the most unlikely person to make a mountaineer.

Collie was attracted to this man for whom questions of political economy were of more interest than his tannery business in Dover. Mummery was a swift rock climber and superb iceman, who could enliven any expedition no matter how long by his quick mind and enthusiastic conversation. Hastings and Mummery were old friends. It may have been Hastings who introduced Collie and Mummery. Their holiday in the Alps was probably the first time all three had climbed together, and was certainly the first time they had been together in the Alps; it was the beginning of a brief but quite outstanding partnership.

During the three Alpine seasons which these men spent together their reputations as 'exponents of guideless climbing' were established. Afterwards, guided climbing was never quite the same.

For years it was the norm for a guide to be engaged from one of the mountain centres, like Zermatt or Chamonix, for a more or less standard fee. A mountaineer followed in his guide's footsteps, and if a first ascent was accomplished he received the credit, even if none of the route finding, risks or decision making had been his. Yet only in this way could a beginner learn good icemanship. Many were not, however, interested in developing these skills in order to dispense with guides. Collie's Uncle Stephen is a good example of the gentleman mountaineer who carried out quite respectable expeditions but always with a guide. For example, he climbed the Aletschorn with guides Croz and Bennen. At the other end of the scale were men like Mummery and Geoffrey Winthrop Young, who, despite being outstanding mountaineers in their own right, nevertheless chose the best guides of their day as their companions for long, difficult, unclimbed routes, where in a tight corner the best guide was always better than any amateur.

For Collie, who rapidly learnt techniques and loved the exploration involved in mountaineering, it was anathema to follow where many others had trod before. Collie recognised that a guide's chief value was in cutting steps and doing much of the hard work which enabled the rest of the party to remain fresh and relatively untired for the technical climbing.

Mummery summed up the feelings of the three men when he wrote:

> My main objection to guide-led parties, however, is to be found in the absolute certainty with which the day's proceedings are carried out. Not merely can the guide 'lie in bed and picture every step of the way up'; but he can also, whilst so reposing, tell you to the fraction of a minute the exact time you will get to each point in the ascent, and the very moment at which he will return you, safe and sound, to the smiling landlord of your hotel. ... When I start in the morning I do not want to know exactly what is going to be done. ... I like to feel that our best efforts may be needed, and that even then we may be baffled and beaten.[1]

Mummery certainly 'indoctrinated' the others with his forceful views on the merits of a climb without a guide but his arguments found very fertile soil. Unlike Mummery, Collie had had no apprenticeship with the men from the Alpine valleys. Consequently, he was one of the first Alpinists to make his reputation, from his first climb, without any assistance from a guide.

There was no question of Collie leaning on Mummery and Hastings, both far more experienced and in Mummery's case, with a reputation as one of the foremost mountaineers of the time. From the beginning Collie brought his own gifts. He readily fell in with the suggestion that they climb without guides, and indeed Mummery's skill was never in route finding. It was Collie who took over as guide to the party.

Guideless climbing was not a new idea. Some climbers had made routes without guides before but it was not really regarded by the Alpine Club as quite the thing. The three friends did a lot to change this view and by being the first to carry out hard new routes without guides they made guideless climbing respectable.

Their partnership would have been innovative for this reason alone. However, all three were also splendid climbers on all types of terrain. By pushing up their own standards they contributed in no small way to the development of the sport itself.

Their exploits hit the Alpine world at a time when it needed a shake up. 'The long years of guided work, under the leadership of highly skilled professionals ..., had led to something closely approaching decadence.'[2] The friends began the process which today sees the employment of a guide as the exception rather than the rule.

During this first holiday together the men were their own guides. Collie, in company with one or other of his friends, made ascents of the Wetterhorn, Dent du Géant and the Aiguille du Dru. He also climbed to the Col du Géant, the first ascent of which helped to qualify his Uncle Stephen for admission to the Alpine Club in 1861. But the holiday was particularly remembered for their first traverse of the Grépon, a climb regarded as a classic even today.

High over the valley of Chamonix, infinitely remote, lies Mont Blanc's dome of glittering ice and dazzling snow. Against that magnificent background, and in delightful contrast to it, stretches a great chain of red granite spires. Prominent amongst these are the Charmoz and its slightly higher companion, the Grépon.

Mummery had already made the first ascents of the Charmoz, in 1880, and of the Grépon the following year. By 1892 a few ascents had been made of the Grépon by a shorter and less elegant route from the south-west, now the usual line of descent, but such was the reputation of Mummery's route (by the north ridge) that it had not yet been repeated. It was the aim of the party to ascend by the north ridge and descend by the south-west ridge, instead of coming down the way they went up as Mummery had done previously, thus making a complete traverse of the mountain.

A few days before, a party, including Mummery's friend Charles Pasteur had planted an ice axe with Pasteur's scarf as a flag, upon the Grépon summit. Mummery asked Pasteur if he would like to recover it by joining them in the traverse. Apart from Pasteur none of the party had been on the south-west ridge and Mummery wanted Pasteur to show them the descent.

At 2 a.m. on 18 August they were met with the news that the porters had fled in trepidation. The problem was solved by waking up a one-eyed guide and a herd boy to carry loads. The herd boy led them through the awkward 'Valley of the Stones' with Mummery stumbling alongside to the moraine of the Nantillons Glacier. They began the ascent as dawn was breaking but here the guide began to show signs of disquiet and tried to persuade the party to return, recounting tales of impossible conditions on the route. Deciding that he was probably anxious to avoid carrying a heavy load they continued, leaving the porter at the foot of the Charmoz-Grépon couloir.

19 Grépon from the Charmoz. *Photo by Ian Van Hinsbergh, with permission.*

Mummery had problems recognising his old route and a violent wind did not help. At last he found the cleft in the rock 40 feet high which has been named the 'Mummery Crack', though it was not Mummery but his guide Venetz who led it in 1881. It had not been climbed since and Mummery now had to lead it. Afterwards he declared it the toughest bit of rock climbing he had ever done. Hastings' shoulder provided a convenient launching spot and apart from a slip, which he managed to check, Mummery was soon hauling his companions and their impedimenta up to join him.

Having surmounted the crack they were now fairly confident of successfully storming the Grépon Ridge. They climbed on until they reached the top of a great gap where 100 feet of rope was fixed to assist the party down into it. All went well until Mummery, as last man, suddenly realised that the rope was loose. This led to a moment's hesitation and he wobbled on the insecure foothold he was resting on. They all thought quickly how best to descend undescendable rock with no assistance from the rope. Collie saw a line he thought would go, and with step-by-step instructions where to place his feet, Mummery was eventually hauled into the gap by Hastings. The rope, which had been hitched around a rock for a belay, had slipped off. This highlighted the still rudimentary rope technique of nineteenth-century climbers. It occurred to them that a return this way, if the south side was impracticable, could be a trifle awkward.

They were now nearly at the final summit and hoped to gain its sharp top by lasooing it and hauling themselves up. For this reason Collie had been climbing encumbered by two large stones with which to weigh down the rope. The party's chances of success in the furious gale were, however, declared to be negligible. Mummery's guide Venetz had got up this last pitch with difficulty and Mummery had told the party it was the hardest part. Just as they were to attempt the assault, Pasteur nonchalantly showed them an easy crack which he had taken previously and they quickly gained the summit. Venetz had been further to the left and Mummery tersely remarked that he would never know if they had been fools at the time or whether the mountain had been altered by a rock fall since 1881.

The wind was now screaming across the ridge. The men crouched under a stone for a brief rest before starting down. Hastings had a slight mishap when his foot caught in a crack and resisted all attempts to free it. By curious girations, on a near perpendicular slab, with one foot 12 inches deep in the crack, the boot was removed and pocketed and Hastings thankfully joined his companions.

A short ascent led them by easy ledges to what was known as the CP Step. The party had thought this might prove their undoing but not only was their porter there to assist with the rope but it was also seen that descent was quite possible without extra help. The difficulties over, the party quickly reached the glacier and raced back to the Montenvers Hotel and tea.

After this first successful trip to the Alps Collie had applied for admittance to the Alpine Club. Even though his experience in the Alps was limited, it was far-reaching enough for him to be accepted, in February 1893. His easy acceptance was not the mirror of Mummery's experience. The Alpine Club was an exclusive, often snob-ridden world where a man of low social rank would have no chance at all of entering its portals. One had to be acceptable to the other members which meant coming from the same social background as they did. Collie, with his family connections, had no problems. Mummery, on the other hand, had been refused admittance in 1879, even though he was at that time one of the foremost climbers of his day. Jealousy of his achievements by some members who disliked his pushy and self-confident style, plus rumours that he was not really part-owner of a tannery but of a shoe shop, conspired against him. Many were shocked that he had been excluded. Mummery was so upset by his rejection that it was eight years before he tried again.

In the summer of 1893, after a short holiday in Yorkshire, where he and Hastings made the second descent of a pothole, Alum Pot, Collie was again on his way to Chamonix. This time he was accompanied not only by Mummery and Hastings but also by William Cecil Slingsby.

Slingsby was ten years older than Collie and was to become his closest friend. He was a well-to-do Yorkshire squire and textile manufacturer who combined a deep love of mountaineering and exploration with a corresponding ability in both. By the time he met Collie, in the early 1890s, he was already known as the 'Father of Norwegian Mountaineering'. Norway was his passion and it was a country to which he would introduce Collie. Slingsby had first brought Mummery and Hastings together and had actually initiated Hastings into the climbing scene.

These four men formed a formidable nucleus of British mountaineers that Swiss summer of 1893. The list of their climbs, most of them guideless, established Collie's reputation and enhanced that of the other three.

Most of Collie's Alpine climbing was done in the Mont Blanc area and this is hardly surprising. Nowhere in the whole Alpine chain is there anything quite so spectacular as Mont Blanc and the spikes and towers of the Chamonix aiguilles that rise around her. Collie's Grépon climb had increased his enthusiasm for aiguilles. With hardly time to change their travelling clothes, and after an exhausting 33-hour journey, the party were on their way to the Dent du Requin.

This secluded aiguille, hidden from Chamonix by the Aiguille du Plan, whose summit of fawn and red-coloured granite rises almost out of the seracs of the Glacier du Géant, is now regarded as the 'most classic and frequented summit of the Chamonix Aiguilles'. In July 1893 no one had reached its top and the mountain did not even have a name. Collie called her the Shark's Tooth or Dent du Requin.

The approach is long and the party decided to sleep out that night near the foot of the climb. Well fed, and in the beautiful evening light, the men lay in their sleeping bags, pipes lit, searching the face of the Requin for a feasible route. Mummery was convinced it would go but as Collie pointed out he was rather more used to thousands of feet of granite set at a steep angle than the rest of them. All, however, were agreed that the crucial part of the climb would be the rock tooth that formed its summit. Before sleeping, Collie and Slingsby worked out a route. They decided to attempt the south-west face and climb from it onto the south-east ridge, and from here to descend to a snow patch on the east face about 500 feet below the summit, then to re-ascend onto the north-east ridge and with luck to the top. This complicated line is what they in fact followed. The ordinary route nowadays is rather different, the line of the first ascent having been relegated to the 'Mummery Variant'.

At 3 a.m. on the following morning, after a breakfast of eggs that no one really enjoyed, the men set off with Collie leading the way and muttering about the inferiority of the Alps to Skye—a feeling that may have been engendered by the earliness of the hour. Crossing a glacier, which rose in spikes of blue ice on one side, they were soon at the foot of steeper slopes

20 The Requin. The Mummery Route goes up the glacier to the line of broken rocks tending right, until the final tower, which has to be traversed around. *Photo by C Douglas Milner, with permission.*

which, covered as they were in ice, proved awkward. Reaching more level ground the decision was taken to leave the open glacier. They kept to an apparently easy valley between it and the rocks of the Requin. This was a mistake and much time and effort was lost in cutting back onto the glacier. By 6 a.m. the weary men had struck rock at about 1,500 feet below the summit.

Their lack of training was beginning to show. Another hour of scrambling up rock made them hungry again so another stop was made. At 8.50 a.m. they reached the ridge about 200 feet below the summit but the rocks above looked impenetrable so they decided to keep to their original plan and descended to the snow patch on the east face. The descent proved far from easy and 200 feet took them two hours. From the snow patch two chimneys led up to the eastern arête. Ascent of the left-hand one proved a struggle, with Mummery having to climb on Hastings' shoulders, and the two of them in danger of toppling out of the crack, but the traverse was completed and the arête reached. They then discovered that it was like a knife-edge rising up at an angle of about 40°.

The summit was in sight but the problems of reaching it had not diminished. At the end of the arête there was a block of rock. Getting off the ridge and around this was going to be difficult. Mummery rose to the occasion. First going along the knife edge *à cheval* he then traversed out onto the perpendicular wall thousands of feet above the glacier. He then climbed straight up onto the arête above. Collie thought this was the worst part of the whole climb but now the difficulties were over. By 1 p.m. they were on the summit.

Because they had left ice axes and clothes scattered over the ascent route it was necessary to return the same way. The snow patch was regained by 4 p.m., the south ridge at 5 p.m. Due to the bad condition of the snow on the glacier it was not until 6.30 p.m. that the bergscrund was reached. Soon darkness fell and it was left to Slingsby to perform the difficult task of threading the party through the crevassed glacier below, a task that left Collie speechless with admiration for his route finding. Mummery found the going tough but just before midnight they regained their camping spot after 22 hours of climbing. Collie and Slingsby crawled into their bags but Hastings and Mummery were not quite tired enough. They decided that a first ascent of the smoking room window of the hotel was called for, so continued downwards to accomplish the task and thence to bed at 4.30 a.m.

On 4 August another ascent of the Grépon was made and this time the men were accompanied by Lily Bristow, the celebrated woman Alpinist. She made the first ascent by a lady. The summit was, however, reached late in the day and there was not enough time to haul Collie up the remaining 50 feet.

Now the party were fitter it was decided that another difficult climb should be attempted. They settled on another aiguille, the Plan, second highest of the Chamonix aiguilles. It was climbed by the south-west face via the Route Mummery, from the Col des Deux Aigles, and the north glacier of the Plan. In making the first ascent of the Plan the party also carried out the first ascent of the Col des Deux Aigles, an interesting climb now rarely done.

Mummery had been beaten on the north face of the Plan in 1892 when he spent two memorable days on the mountain with Slingsby and Ellis Carr, another guideless enthusiast. On 7 August 1893 Mummery, Collie and Hastings were successful partly due to Slingsby who persuaded Mummery to abandon the north in favour of the south-west face. The party had little difficulty in good weather on this very beautiful route.

The reaction to these climbs by the mountaineers and guides of Chamonix alike are shown in a letter Lily wrote to her family. 'Fred's exploits here are causing a great deal of enthusiasm. His having taken a lady up the two most

21 Plan North Face. In Collie's era there would have been considerably more ice on the North face than in this 1970s photo. *Photo by Ian Van Hinsbergh, with permission.*

difficult peaks here (Grépon and Dru), without guides, in the course of a week, and having sandwiched between these expeditions a totally new ascent of a very difficult peak (the Plan) is really worthy of some applause.'[3]

After climbing up the Grand Combin, the friends decided to ascend the Matterhorn. It was Collie's first and Mummery's sixth ascent. Mummery liked to repeat climbs. He once wrote that when he had climbed a mountain it became a friend and he wanted to return again and again to it. This was an attitude that appealed strongly to Collie who disliked the 'first ascent only' mountaineer as much as the tourist in the valley busy ticking off the mountains he had seen from the safety of his conveyance. Mummery had a particular love for the Matterhorn and had experienced most types of weather when climbing her. Once he was on the summit with his wife when a lighted match did not even flicker. On this occasion he probably remembered that climb with redoubled pleasure for the summit was struck by lightning. No one was hurt and the incident gave added zest to a famous mountain climb.

Collie was now hooked on the Alps, although there were many aspects of them that he disliked. The mountains had all been explored but hundreds of routes were still to be made and are still being made. The tourist mountaineers, who came in ever increasing numbers, irritated him as did the clutter of tourism from hotels to railways. He even sarcastically foresaw the days when railways would run all over the mountains, the Matterhorn would be illuminated and the avalanches would be timed for a morning and afternoon performance. But while this has not occurred, the machinery of skiing would have appalled him. In 1894, however, he was determined to return and the 'three musketeers' met for the last time at Chamonix.

They began their adventures with the first ascent to the Col des Courtes on 3 August. This achievement showed that a new pass was possible between the Argentière and Trilot glaciers. It is still regarded as a serious and difficult climb. It was but a training walk to get them over to Courmayeur where an ascent of the Old Brenva Route on Mont Blanc was planned.

Mont Blanc, queen of mountains, had been climbed many times but it was the aim of the three men to make the first guideless ascent of the Old Brenva Route, a fine and demanding ice climb that had been described to them by the guide Emile Rey.

Leaving a bivouac at the foot of the rocks at 3.30 a.m. the following morning, Collie led the party through the ice seracs and crevasses of the Brenva glacier. It looked as if it had once been a roaring sea frozen in its fury. Hastings described the route: 'We were making for the lower Brenva snowfield, so as to reach the ridge which rises against and buttresses this face of Mont Blanc, and dams back the upper snowfield of the Brenva glacier. On reaching the lower snowfield ... we were forced by the run of crevasses away to the left. After going for some distance over steep snow ... we reached the foot of the buttress, close to where it "abuts" on the mountain.'[4] They ascended the buttress and reached the ice ridge. One side was soft snow and dangerous and the other side hard ice and equally so. Neither alternative appealed so it was climbed *à cheval*—legs astride the ridge. By 9.50 a.m. they had reached the end of the ice arête where they rested. Huge ice cliffs guard the summit and here lies the crux. When rested, the climbers approached them and Mummery exhibited his skill with the axe. The cliffs were formidable at 60° to 70° according to Hastings. In two hours Mummery had got nowhere near the summit but took some persuading from Collie before he would hear of retreat. If they continued they would certainly have to spend the night on the summit, for it was already 4 p.m. Mummery admitted afterwards that Collie had tried to dissuade him from the line he had taken in the first place but Emile Rey, who had not in fact climbed Mont Blanc by this route, had misled them as to how far left they should keep up the cliffs.

Hastings reported that the friends could not bear to give up the 'expedition we had placed above all others' and it was agreed to bivouac for the night at the top of the rock buttress that they had ascended early that morning.

The night was uncomfortable. They had neither tent, blankets nor fire and none of the modern down equipment that today makes a bivouac bearable if not exactly luxurious. A flattish rock was found on which to sit. They were soaked to the knees. After wringing out their wet stockings and putting them back on they covered their legs with paper food bags and put their feet in the rucksack to prevent frostbite. It proved difficult for all but Collie, in the middle, to keep them there through the long night. Their thirst was quenched by a drink of icy water, their hunger by a bit of Yorkshire bacon, retrieved from a crevasse where it had been thrown that morning. They attempted to pass the night roped to the rocks. At one point, when they thought they saw dawn approaching, they discovered from their watches that it was only 10.30 p.m. An attempt to make tea by holding the brew over two candles ended in failure when the precious liquid was spilt all over Collie.

When the sky at last began to pale, at about 3.45 a.m., they were delighted to rise but the problem of how to unfreeze their boots had to be overcome. Collie burnt paper bags in his, but during this bonfire succeeded in charring the rope. It was not until 6 a.m. that the sun had thawed their boots sufficiently for them to get going.

This time they took a different line up the ice cliffs but it still involved some very hard ice work. At one point Collie, by sticking three axes into the ice and using them as holds, overcame a difficulty that seemed likely to defeat them. The final grind up the summit slope, at over 15,000 feet, was very painful in the thin air. Always the scientist, Collie had been recording in his mind the effects of high altitude on the human frame, and declined the assistance of the rope for this reason. He was able to make many observations, one being that he was so affected by the altitude that he had to crawl onto the summit on hands and knees!

Whilst Collie took his interest in the atmosphere with him on holiday he may have wished that on this occasion he had stayed working in the labs. On the day he stood gasping for lack of oxygen on the summit of Mont Blanc, Ramsay, back at the university, finally isolated argon.

Their climb was described in the *Alpine Journal*: 'No finer exhibition of determination and skill has ever been given by any amateur party.'

Their next accomplishment was a first ascent of the Aiguille Verte by the Moine Ridge, or so they thought. Not until later did they discover it had been climbed 30 years before. They had the satisfaction at least of restoring to the Alpine world a route that had been almost forgotten.

It was fitting that in Mummery's last Alpine season he should once more stand at the summit of the Matterhorn and that he should climb it by the Zmutt Ridge, the route by which he first climbed the mountain 15 years

22 Mont Blanc from the Aiguille Verte with the Requin far below. *Photo by C Douglas Milner, with permission.*

before. After ascents of the Dent Blanche and Ober Gabelhorn the three men teamed up with the Duke of the Abruzzi (remembered today for his ascent of St Elias in Alaska) and made the third ascent of this route. It was the first time it had been climbed for many years and was Mummery's seventh ascent of the mountain.

A year later Mummery would be dead and Collie would return but rarely to the Western Alps. The association of these mountains with his friend made him almost reluctant to return. When Mummery was making the attack up the blue ice walls of Mont Blanc, Collie and Hastings believed that this was the 'kind of place that Mummery loved to find, and that hereafter his wraith will be found constantly going up and down nearly perpendicular ice cliffs and gullies, like unto Woden's huntsmen, who are known to sweep over the frozen plains of the North hunting the were-wolves'.[5]

Chapter 7

Diamir—'King of Mountains'

> The dominant sensation in this strange land is that of fear and abhorrence; and what makes it all the more appalling is that this thing before one is there in all its nakedness; it has no reserve, there is nothing hidden. Its rugged insolence, its brutal savagery, and its utter disregard of all the puny efforts of man, crushes out of the mind any idea that this spot belongs to an ordinary world.
> (J N Collie 1902, *Climbing in the Himalaya and other Mountain Ranges*, writing about the Indus Valley after the death of Mummery)

When Mummery and his two porters died on Nanga Parbat in 1895, they were the first of 31 men to lose their lives on this giant peak before Hermann Buhl crawled to the summit, on all fours and alone, in 1953. Despite the accumulation of nearly 60 years of hard-won experience, and despite great improvements in equipment, the summit was only just reached in a desperate attempt by a man every bit as 'pushy' in his day as Mummery had been in his.

If Collie, Mummery and Hastings had possessed the knowledge of the 1953 German Expedition they would never have gone to a Himalayan peak expecting to climb it like an Alpine one. With hindsight, their decision to attempt an ascent of one of the highest mountains in the world, at a time when so little was known about high-altitude expeditions, was almost bound to end in failure. They failed because they were pioneers. It was their experience, and that of men like them, that enabled the Everests of the future to be conquered.

As early as 1891 Mummery had been planning a visit to India. Originally he intended to accompany Sir Martin Conway, the mountain explorer. Their ambitious programme was to include an assault on K2, the highest mountain in the Karakoram Range, and second only to Everest in height. At 28,250 feet, K2 is almost 2,000 feet higher than Nanga Parbat at 26,660. The plan was abandoned when the two men realised that their aims were not compatible. Conway wanted to explore, which bored Mummery—he only wanted to climb.

During the early 1890s he made other plans to go to India but they always fell through and he found himself year after year in the Alps. From their first meeting, Collie would have been aware of Mummery's desire to visit this land of mighty mountains. It may well have been on one of their lonely bivouacs in the Alps that the three friends decided to take their climbing partnership further afield.

Mummery and Hastings applied in 1894 for permission to travel to Nanga Parbat and climb it. Collie was able to get leave and join them. His delight at going to India was increased by the thought that he was travelling to a land whose mountains were nearly all unclimbed, and where large areas of snow

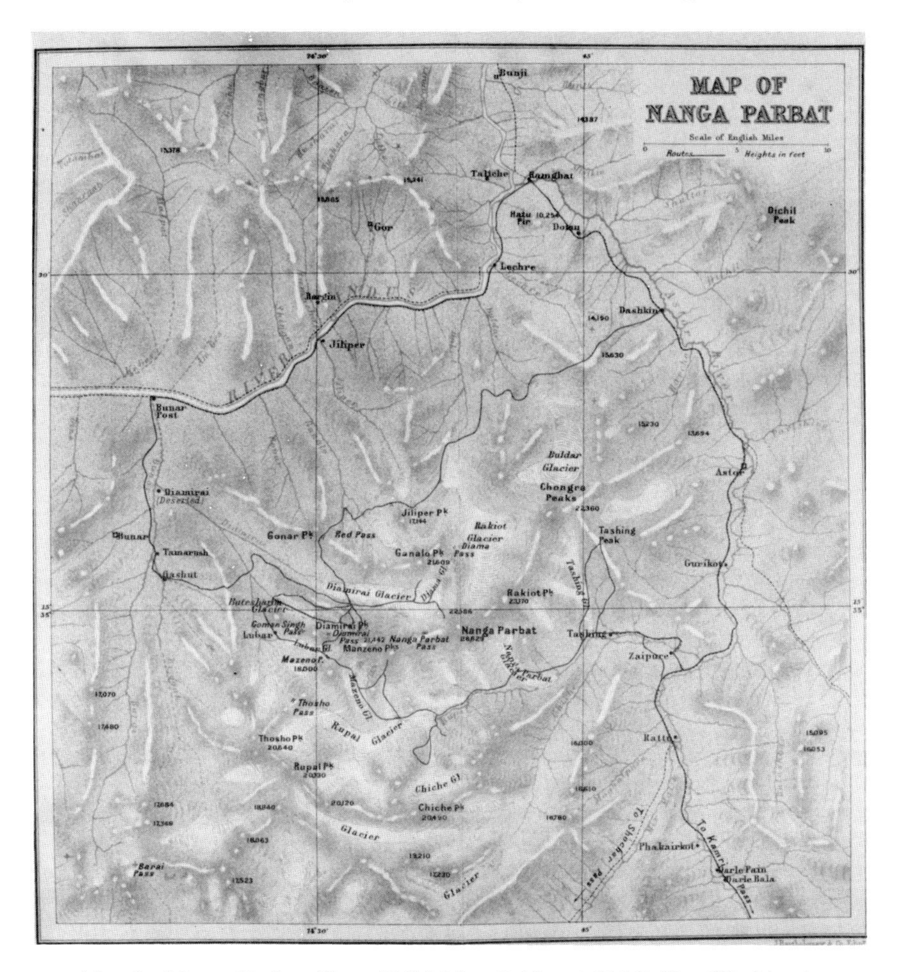

Map 2 Nanga Parbat. From H E M Stutfield and J N Collie, Climbing in the Himalaya and other Mountain Ranges, *permission from Longmans Green and Co.*

and ice were still untrodden. Collie wrote of the Himalayas, awaiting the arrival of the explorer: 'His will be the satisfaction of going where others have feared to tread, his the delight of seeing mighty glaciers and superb snow-clad peaks never gazed upon before by human eyes.'[1]

Scarcely half-a-dozen expeditions had been to the entire Himalaya. Yet Collie was also aware that 'at some future date, how many years hence who can tell? all the wild places of the earth will have been explored ... the vast and trackless fastnesses of that stupendous range of mountains which eclipses all others, and which from time immemorial has served as a barrier to roll back the waves of barbaric invasion from the fertile plains of Hindustan—these Himalaya will have been mapped'.[2] Collie may have written regretfully but he helped this process to begin. It was and indeed still is an occupational hazard of explorers. With high hopes and with very little idea of what awaited them, they left for Bombay on 20 June 1895.

On arrival in India, two weeks later, the party at once headed for the hills. It took two days to reach Rawalpindi whence they had their first glimpse of the Himalayan foothills rising out of the Punjab plains. From Rawalpindi they travelled onwards via Murree, where the monsoon broke, Baramula and Bandapur. They had to ascend one high pass and chose the Kamri, instead of the Burzil, because more fodder was available for their ponies. From the top they saw Nanga Parbat for the first time. Instinctively the men took off their hats in its presence.

23 Nanga Parbat from Kamri Pass 1895. *Photo by Collie, with permission of the Alpine Club.*

Their approach from the south was dictated solely by the political situation in India. West and north of Nanga Parbat the country was unsettled. Only four years before the 'Gilgit Road' had been constructed over the Burzil Pass. This had been used to pacify the wild Hunza tribe, who were later to make excellent porters and were on the first successful Nanga Parbat expedition.

After crossing Wular Lake to Bandapur, they found ponies and provisions left by Charlie Bruce, a young major in the Indian Army. It was to be the first time Collie had met this remarkable man and they were to become firm friends. Bruce had been with Conway on the latter's trip to India, the trip which Mummery had declined to join. Bruce, no stranger to the Himalayan mountains, had done a great deal of climbing in the Khaghan district, south-west of Nanga Parbat. He had trained a few of the men from his 5th Gurhka Regiment in the arts of mountaineering and he was to train many more. Bruce was a large, dynamic man with great personality and physical strength. He was deeply loved by his gurkhas whose language he spoke and they semi-deified him. Bruce became one of the greatest Himalayan soldiers and explorers and gave up a month's leave to support Collie's party, none of whom he had met before.

They made their camp in the Rupal nullah (ravine) about three miles above Tashing. According to Collie's barometer it stood at 10,000 feet. The beautiful camp site, strewn with wild flowers and willow trees, with a trickling stream and plenty of firewood, provided a perfect setting to the mountain they hoped to conquer, high above them. Here Bruce was shortly to join them. Camp life was lazy and warm, with Kashmiri servants to fetch and carry.

The party was anxious to make its attempt on Nanga Parbat from the south because food was readily available and the area friendly. The western, Chilas, side was relatively unknown country. Presumably food supplies would be scarcer there. Nevertheless, before they decided on the Rupal nullah as a base camp they had to see if a route could be made up the south wall of the mountain. From the Chiche glacier the following evening they had a magnificent view of the south face. Diligently they searched every ridge and glacier but nowhere could they find a feasible route. Hanging glaciers and precipices covered the mountain which seemed to rise sheer out of the Rupal nullah for 15,000 feet. The result was not very encouraging. Mummery was enthusiastic about the one possible line but Collie was doubtful.

The route they pointed out to one another involved a climb, via a steep rock buttress, to a pass west of the summit, which they named Nanga Parbat Pass, then onto an ice ridge which they would follow to the top. Collie was not sure that they could even get onto the ridge. If they got that far he believed that its ascent would be even harder and later expeditions found this to be the case. He was also pessimistic about setting up camps on the face—vital to success. Mummery, writing probably to reassure his wife, made light of all these problems: 'We have discovered an absolutely safe way up Nanga.

Easy glacier, up which coolies can carry our camp, and then onward, a broad snow and rock ridge right up to the top.'[3]

When Hastings came up to join them at the Chiche glacier camp a council of war was held. All decided that general unfitness and lack of training at altitude precluded an immediate assault. In order to get fit they decided to walk around to the other side of Nanga to see what that offered in the way of routes. Hastings had typically spent two days organising food to be brought up the glacier and the next day they decamped and headed for the north-west side of the mountain.

24 Major Bruce in the Alps 1899. *Photo from Collie's slide collection, with permission of the Alpine Club.*

To get around to the Chilas side the party had to cross an 18,000 foot pass—the Mazeno La. The pass itself was 3,000 feet higher than anything in the Alps. They were aware that there could be problems when climbing at such an altitude but in 1895 the problems of very high climbing were not really known. They thought they would slow down as they went higher. As it was, Collie crawled to the top of the Mazeno La, feeling very ill. He had been similarly afflicted on the top of Mont Blanc. Mummery made light of this and wrote home that they all felt as 'fresh as daisies' even though they were at heights of 15,000–18,000 feet.

The ascent of the Mazeno La was an unpleasant, interminable grind on loose boulders. None of them would have willingly repeated the experience. Mummery, in particular, hated it. The west side of the pass was steeper, but easier going, down a rock arête to the Lubar glacier below. Here they camped uncomfortably for the night. With the dawn they proceeded down to the valley where they met some Chilas tribesmen. There was no sign of hostility and goats' milk and a sheep were successfully bartered for.

The party intended to make for the Diamirai nullah and, in order to do so, they had to cross two small ridges. Here they first became aware of the enormous distances in the Himalaya. Used to the Alps, they found, as many have done since, that the scale of these mountains makes everything seem nearer than it really is. The two small ridges, which they thought would be finished off in a day, benighted them. They reached the Diamirai nullah the following afternoon.

From their camp, at 12,000 feet, westwards they could see range after range of snow-capped, unclimbed and unknown mountains—a feast for a mountaineer's eye—where no white man had yet been. If they looked eastwards they could see the bulk of Nanga Parbat glowing orange in the setting sun. They marvelled at its magnificence but were momentarily quelled by its vastness. Examining the whole face Mummery was again enthusiastically pointing out a route to the top via some rock ribs.

They only had enough provisions for a day's stay in the nullah but the main objectives of getting fit and of seeing the Diamirai face had been accomplished. Collie went for an exploratory walk up the Diama tributary glacier and next day the camp was packed up. The coolies and servants were sent back to the Rupal nullah by the way they had come but the three friends wanted to find a different way back. The thought of not having to cross the Mazeno La again weighed heavily in favour of this decision. Collie also wanted to see as much as possible of the topography of the area. They intended to cross the ridge on the south side of the valley, sufficiently high up for them to descend either into the Mazeno La or, if they were very lucky, into the head of the Rupal nullah itself.

The decision was in many ways shortsighted for they only had some chocolate left by way of food and carried no camping gear should the trip take longer than a day. One can only assume that they were still thinking in terms of the Alps, for they must have been very sure that they could have reached the Rupal nullah in a day.

25 Ragobir, Bruce and Mummery mending boots. Mummery has two hats on between which was wedged snow for coolness. India 1895. *Photo by Collie, with permission of the Alpine Club.*

They left about midnight. After a tortuous journey they reached the summit of the Diamirai Pass. Great was their disappointment, when looking down the other side, to see neither the Mazeno La nor the Rupal nullah. What they could see was the Lubar glacier where they had camped on their way down from the summit of the Mazeno La. They were on the wrong side of the range, and at least five miles from the Mazeno La, which they would now have to cross in any case. Their nearest food and camp was 20 miles on the other side of it. Mummery suggested a quick ascent of a nearby 21,000-footer to set them onto the Mazeno La but this suggestion was sensibly vetoed. A bivouac at altitude, with no tent or food, would have been extremely foolhardy. There was no alternative but to grind around to the Mazeno La, toil up again to 18,000 feet and then plunge through the interminable stones to their camp.

Twenty hours after they had left the Diamirai valley they began the ascent of the Mazeno La. Collie forged ahead, sustained only by his tobacco, and through the long night they wandered. Fortune smiled briefly in the morning when Collie found one of their camp servants waiting at the foot of the Mazeno glacier with food and drink. He had been instructed to wait there for a week in case they came back that way.

After 40 hours, Collie, in the lead, staggered into the Rupal nullah where Bruce and two gurkhas were awaiting their arrival. Hastings and Mummery straggled in, according to Bruce, 'pretty well done up'.[4]

It was necessary for the party to become acquainted with the two gurkhas, Ragobir and Goman Singh, for they were to act as high-altitude porters and were to stay with the men when Bruce returned in a few days to his army base. Ragobir had only been on a rope twice before but was a good, natural climber. He and Mummery immediately became friends even though they could not speak the same language. Goman Singh was completely inexperienced and had never even seen an ice axe before.

On 27 July the gurkhas were initiated into step-cutting when Collie and Mummery took them on a ridge wander at heights of 15,000 feet. They had intended to climb a peak, but the altitude made them lazy, and they gave up far from the summit.

A decision now had to be made about the route to be taken up Nanga. The time was ripe, they felt, for an attempt on the mountain. They were probably as fit as they were going to be. Collie writes that Mummery had decided that the south side would not really 'go' and he must have been relieved at this decision. The thousands of feet of rock that ran across the south face, were, they felt, too risky an undertaking. Bruce wrote of this side: 'The NW face—one of the most terrifying faces of a mountain I have ever seen—is preferable to the S face.'[5]

On 29 July they packed up camp and made plans to return to the Diamirai nullah and attempt Bruce's terrifying north-west face.

The coolies and baggage were again dispatched over the Mazeno La with Goman Singh, whilst Collie's party, plus Ragobir and Bruce, intended to try again to circumvent that dreadful place. They hoped to cross from the Rupal nullah to the head of the Diamirai nullah by a direct pass. Collie, though, was doubtful whether this could be accomplished, for he alone had seen the head of that nullah on his walk up the Diama glacier a week before. Though he was sure they could reach a pass from the southern side, he had doubts about an ascent on the northern. Nevertheless, they agreed it was worth trying and at least they could explore the area.

In the darkness of 30 July they set off, reckoning to sleep out one night. They took no extra food in case they had underestimated the difficulties. This again seems surprising, for not only were they entering a relatively unknown mountain area, but they were also aware that their way would take them over ground at least 20,000 feet in height, with one member of their party unsure of success.

The route lay over the spur which descends westwards from the summit of Nanga Parbat to the Mazeno La. The first night they spent at 13,000 feet. All the second day they toiled upwards. Bruce was suffering from mumps, and their progress was slow. By 5 p.m. they were still 1,000 feet below the summit of the pass. Collie took a barometrical reading and found they had already exceeded 20,000 feet in height. Mummery now needed no convincing that altitude affected one's performance; from then on he too became gradually more pessimistic about the rarity of the air.

By now it was obvious to the party that they would have to spend a second night out. Collie thought they should retreat to a lower altitude. Bruce and Ragobir accompanied him while Mummery and Hastings attempted to push the route further on. They were hoping for a full moon so they could continue climbing all night!

Darkness soon fell and as descent by candle light was declared unsafe they stopped for the night on a jagged rock arête at 19,000 feet. They were three miles to the east of the Mazeno La. The night was cold and uncomfortable with no extra clothing and no food. Luckily there was no wind and after several hours they heard Mummery and Hastings returning after having reached a height of about 21,000 feet.

The next morning they reviewed their situation. It had a familiar ring. They had no food, their camp and provisions were the other side of the range and the only course open to them was to beat a retreat, descend to the Mazeno La, and cross it yet again.

Once more the ascent was an unpleasant and exhausting boulder plod. Ragobir kept lying down unable to move; it later transpired that he had eaten nothing at all the day before. He and Collie were in the lead and the gravity of the situation was not lost on Collie. It had been his intention to forge ahead to Lubar, with Ragobir, and get provisions sent back up the glacier to the others. Obviously he could not leave the gurkha. He could only wait for the rest of the party to join them. Ragobir was nearly hit by a large boulder that careered down from 3,000 feet above them but he was so exhausted that he made no effort to get out of the way. Although Collie screamed at him to hurry he did not change his pace but collapsed onto the ice groaning from exhaustion. Bruce managed to revive his man a little and the whole party once more set off for Lubar.

As the sun was setting on the third day they reached a shepherd's encampment. Bruce arrived first and when Collie and Mummery staggered into camp he was jovially encouraging the slaughter of a sheep. The four men ate the whole animal washed down by gallons of goats' milk. Wearily they huddled around the fire and slept through the entire night oblivious to the hoar frost that soon enveloped them.

The following morning saw them continuing on to the Diamirai nullah, making the crossing of a new pass—the Butesharon Pass. From here they were able to descend almost straight to their camp of ten days before.

The next two days were spent in organising their camp and resting. Bruce, now very unwell, set off on 5 August to march the 200 miles back to his army camp, a journey that was a nightmare for him. Now the ascent of Nanga Parbat could begin in earnest.

The friends located a second camp, a sort of advanced base, at the head of the Diamirai glacier on the north side at 14,500 feet. Mummery and the two ghurkhas then began a reconnaissance of the north-west face of the mountain.

It was essential that high-altitude camps be set up along the route on the mountain. In any expedition it is this provisioning which calls for the highest commitment of all members of the party. Personal desires to be one of the summit group have to be sacrificed to the general good, for this work is exhausting and exacting and can leave little in reserve for the hardest effort of all—the summit bid. For this reason it is best, if possible, for the summit team to be as rested as they can be and not have to waste their energy carrying heavy loads. This is where high-altitude porters and good team support are indispensable. Mummery believed that if he could get two days provisions and a light silk tent up to 18,000 feet, the summit would be his.

At about 21,000 feet on the Diamirai face lies a snowfield which stretches right up to the ridge connecting the summit of Nanga Parbat with the lower North Peak. The snowfield would have to be attained by about 5,000 feet of climbing up three ribs of rock protruding from a broken ice-fall. To progress from the first to the second rib would involve the crossing of a couloir, down which avalanches thundered. The second rib was composed of steep slabs and towers. It was along these three ribs that the camps must be distributed. When the upper snowfield was gained, a final camp would be established from which the summit bid would be made.

At midnight on 5 August, Mummery and Ragobir started off. During the day, they reached the top of the second rib of rocks at about 17,000 feet. Mummery's enthusiasm was unbounded. He declared the climbing magnificent. A place for a tent had been found at the top of the second rib. Next day, 7 August, the weather, which had been very kind, suddenly turned on them with heavy rains, but the party, now mentally and physically keyed up for its enormous effort, was undaunted. During 8 and 9 August they all joined in a concentrated effort, pushing provisions up the mountain in bad weather. On the second rib they left a waterproof bag of food and lower down at 14,500 feet large quantities of wood.

26 Nanga Parbat taken from the camp at 14,000 ft. The second camp is at the top of the rock rib at 17,000 ft. *Photo by Collie, with permission of the Alpine Club.*

The bad weather persisted and it was decided that the ascent must be delayed for a few days. As they were now very short of food, Hastings as usual, volunteered to make the long journey back to Astor with Goman Singh to bring back sheep, flour and rice. A large supply of luxuries, jam, biscuits and Kashmir wine, had been ordered from Srinagar weeks before: he was also to try to get these sent around to the camp. Already two of their Kashmiri servants had been sent down into the Bunar district on a foraging trip but, as expected, the Chilas side did not yield much in the way of food supplies. During Hastings' absence Collie, Mummery and Ragobir, plus Lor Khan (a Chilas man, completely inexperienced, who had arrived from Gashut determined to climb), would continue to provision the camps.

Collie and Mummery decided that an ascent of nearby Diamirai Peak, about 19,000 feet, on a side spur running to the west of Nanga Parbat, would afford a good day's sport while they waited for the weather to improve. On 11 August the entire party set out by candle light. Hastings and his men soon parted company with the rest. Hastings wanted to make a new pass which would save an unnecessary detour on the way to the Mazeno La. This he managed to do, naming it Goman Singh Pass.

Mummery led the whole way up Diamirai Peak—a splendid achievement. Collie was again and again impressed by his ability as an ice climber. He went as fast as on any Alpine peak, showing no fatigue, even on the final stages. His zest for the climb and exhilaration at the magnificent physical effort were infectious. Collie marvelled at his energy, as he rhythmically cut steps for hours on end. On the summit, Collie and Lor Khan had headaches, but Mummery had no care in the world.

On the ascent they had crossed an ice slope which Collie thought was the steepest he had ever been on. He pictured to himself an involuntary glissade in such a place. The next moment, as they were all strung out along the slope, Collie noticed that the rope between Lor Khan and himself hung in a great loop. Hastily the rope was brought in. Minutes later Lor Khan slipped out of one of the steps, his whole weight coming on Collie and Ragobir, who held him. Collie was mesmerized by the thin coat of snow which had peeled off the face taking with it an enormous mass as it plunged downwards, his one thought being that, if Lor Khan struggled, he too would follow it. But Lor Khan, the inexperienced tribesman who had never climbed a mountain in his life, was superb. He kept his head, did as he was instructed and was soon hauled into a step. It had been a nasty moment.

On the descent they decided to leave the dangerous ice slopes and go down by a rock ridge to the west which they hoped would lead to the Goman Singh Pass. Unfortunately they again miscalculated. Their route kept bending south-west instead of west. Soon their fears were confirmed—the Goman Singh Pass lay 1,000 feet above them. They had descended 1,500 feet on the wrong side of the mountain while their camp was on the other. This necessitated a long detour over Mazeno La-type terrain before camp was reached.

The worry about food had still not been resolved. Hastings was not due back for a week and the Kashmiri servants had not returned from Bunar.

They only had one day's food supply left so there was no alternative but to go and find some in the Bunar nullah. Two days were wasted in this fashion, two days of fine weather. It was very frustrating.

When they returned to camp it was raining again but on 15 August they once more started pushing supplies up the mountain. They all continued up to the second camp on the ribs and it was Mummery's intention to sleep at this camp and push more provisions up to 20,000 feet. Collie made it as far as the second camp but then the familiar headache returned. He was also ill with stomach trouble so regretfully returned to base.

Mummery spent the night out in wind and rain but managed to get one bag of supplies well up the third rib of rock. Not until the evening of 16 August did he return, very wet, but still enthusiastic and full of the superb climbing which he declared to be hard but not impossible. He described, with wonder, the enormity of the avalanches and crevasses. However, to his wife he confides: 'We find Nanga a tough nut to crack'.[6]

On 17 August the weather was very bad again and they were confined to base camp. That night a fierce storm blew up, followed by snow. Next morning they found their beautiful camp covered in snow and the nearby bushes plastered to the ground with ice. By 2 p.m. it had melted and under a cloudless sky they once more set off. Mummery suggested that as the weather was clear, and some supplies were available, he should start at once for the summit. They worried that Hastings might feel left out but decided that as the weather prospects were uncertain, and every snow fall came nearer down the mountain, their chances of success were diminishing rapidly. With Collie's reluctant consent, Mummery and Ragobir set off in high spirits.

The day following, 20 August, Hastings returned with provisions from Astor and late that night Mummery, surprisingly, walked into camp. He had slept out at the top of the second rib of rock and that morning had climbed up to 20,000 feet. Here Ragobir became very ill and quite unfit to spend another night at that altitude. He had forgotten to eat again, or else had eaten all his provisions in one go. With the language problems they never quite discovered what had happened. Mummery was very disappointed for he believed that most of the problems had been overcome and that he would have reached the summit on the 21st.

The two following days were spent in hard discussion and Mummery was finally persuaded to abandon the north-west side. Collie had not been keen on the route from the beginning but now more snow had fallen, Collie was ill, Hastings had a damaged heel, plus a chill and Ragobir, the only other man capable of climbing, had not the experience necessary to give Mummery the support he really needed. Mummery may also have admitted that the difficulties were still formidable and confided to his wife that Collie was not happy. Due to the heavy snowfalls they decided that only a pure snow route would now be feasible. Their last chance therefore lay in the Rakiot nullah, on the north side of the mountain. Here they determined to go. This last choice was to be the choice of many future expeditions and it was from the Rakiot side that the 1953 party reached the summit.

Before they decamped, the two gurkhas were sent up the mountain to collect the provisions from the second rib. The party could not afford to leave much behind. Because Mummery wanted to avoid the long walk to the Rakiot nullah, it was agreed that he would meet Ragobir and Goman Singh at the Diamirai glacier camp, and that all three would then strike up the Diama valley, between Nanga Parbat and Ganalo Peak. The Diama Pass, a 20,350 feet dip in Nanga's north ridge, was all that would separate them from the Rakiot nullah. He left Collie and Hastings on 23 August, joining up with the gurkhas as planned. They were last seen, moving eastwards up the Diama valley, on the morning of 24 August.

Collie and Hastings, with all the paraphernalia of camp life, moved off with their coolies to the Rakiot nullah via the Ganalo nullah. They had to cross two easy passes, just below the snow line, but it took them three hard days to do so. They had arranged to meet Mummery by the side of the Rakiot glacier. Arriving in thunder and rain they found no sign of him. Collie, looking at the face down which they would come, had they reached the Diama Pass, declared it impossible. They both believed that Mummery had turned back and was following in their tracks. Mummery had foreseen that his route could be impossible and had enough food for three days left at the Diamirai glacier camp, should he be forced to return. Believing him far behind them and knowing how he must be hating the long walk, the two men sent back extra provisions and coolies.

It was still raining on 28 and 29 August. Collie and Hastings were getting anxious, not only about the non-return of the men, but also because Collie's leave was nearly up. Any final attempt on the mountain would have to be made at once. On 29 August the coolies returned without having found Mummery. Although worried, the two men were still not overconcerned. Many things could have happened. It was raining and in the mist, Mummery, who was not very good at finding his way, could easily have got lost; perhaps he had sprained an ankle or was ill. The friends, conferring, decided that Hastings would return to the Diamirai nullah to find Mummery while Collie, who had to get to England, would go to Astor and wait there for a telegram from Hastings.

Hastings retraced his steps right the way back to their old camp. He could find no trace of Mummery in the Diamirai nullah. He then went up to the advanced camp on the Diamirai glacier where the extra food had been left. The store was untouched. As there was no other way out, except over the Diama Pass or the way he had gone in, Hastings was certain that the three men must have perished. They may have been engulfed by an avalanche or fallen into a crevasse. Maybe Mummery attempted yet another short cut. Their bodies have never been found and the exact circumstances of their deaths remain a mystery.

Hastings telegraphed to Collie and then went to Astor to meet him. Captain Stewart, political officer of Gilgit, and Captain de Vismes of the Chilas District, ordered men into the Rakiot, Diamirai and surrounding nullahs for an intensive search of the ground, though Collie was convinced

27 Group of Lumbadars and Captain de Vismes co-ordinating the search party for Mummery and the gurkhas at Gashut 21 September 1895. *Photo from Collie's slide collection, with permission of the Alpine Club.*

28 Collie and search party, India 1895. *Photo from Collie's slide collection, with permission of the Alpine Club.*

that Mummery had never got off the mountain. Travelling back from Astor, the two men now found the Indian landscape harsh and forbidding, particularly the stifling Indus Valley. They arrived at the Diamirai nullah to find winter had arrived. The gauntness of the place, where wild roses bloomed no longer, was compatible with their gloomy spirits and in contrast to the sunshine and enthusiasm of two months before. They could not even get up to their camp on the Diamirai glacier for the snow was now low down the mountain and soon they were up to their thighs in it. Very reluctantly they abandoned the mountain. Their last impression of Nanga Parbat was one of fierceness as avalanches poured down her face, forbidding any further search for what the Gods had claimed.

There have been many attempts on Nanga Parbat since 1895 and only a handful have been successful. The Mummery Route, swept by avalanches, is rarely climbed. It was during the 1930s that the ascent of Nanga Parbat was repeatedly attempted, particularly by German expeditions, but the death toll was high. In 1937 alone, seven climbers and nine porters were buried in their camp by an avalanche.

It seems that when the three men began their exploration of Nanga Parbat they encounted many of the problems common to all Himalayan expeditions. Collie's account of the trip in his book *Climbing on the Himalaya and other Mountain Ranges* is straightforward. He makes no adverse comments about Mummery and he remained surprisingly silent about him for the rest of his life. However, it is clear that Collie had become worried about the mountain after he had seen its faces. One can detect his pessimism as a contrast to Mummery's boundless optimism. It was Collie who dissuaded him from tackling the southern side, and applied arguments against continuing the route up the north-west face after the weather had broken. He was aware that Mummery was prepared to take calculated risks and would probably have agreed with the sentiments echoed in the *Alpine Journal*: 'To many of the places to which Mr Mummery went, he went without recklessness but merely with a splendid and justified self-reliance . . . but there were other places—the Col du Lion, for instance—climbed by Mr Mummery with a full sense of the unusual danger thereby involved, a danger uncombatible by any skill. In his opinion the game was worth the candle.'[7]

Collie opened up more in later life and told Bruce that he felt Mummery had taken unjustifiable risks on the mountain, relying too much on his own skill. In 1942 he wrote honestly to his friend Geoffrey Winthrop Young:

> I have always found that people considered Mummery a splendid *rock climber* and that they did not know that he was *by far* the finest *ice climber* amongst *all amateurs*. There have been many rock climbers better than Mummery but no ice climbers who have come anywhere near him. Emile Rey said that he was better than all the Swiss guides.

But Mummery was *not* a good mountaineer. He was not good in knowing what was the best way up a mountain or the safest. Once he was started on a route it was almost impossible to get him to turn back from difficulties and dangers.

Now Slingsby was a *magnificent mountaineer*. It was due to Slingsby that we found the way up the Dent du Requin. It was Slingsby who persuaded Mummery to go up the Aiguille du Plan on the Chamonix side and not go back to the old climb on the other side Mummery had failed on. It was Slingsby who brought us down in the middle of the night through the almost impossible Plan glacier—and to sum things up Slingsby was a *perfectly safe man to climb with* and Mummery was not.[8]

Nanga Parbat lay undisturbed for 37 years after Collie returned to England. There were many more Himalayan peaks to choose from so this is perhaps not so surprising. In 1932 the Germans sent out a large, but unsuccessful expedition, to the Rakiot side which got as far as 23,000 feet. Willy Merkl, its leader, had visited the 72-year-old Collie in 1931. Somehow Collie could not relate to him with his 'all for the summit philosophy'. He possibly resented an enthusiastic, and to his mind brash young German being the first to approach the mountain where Mummery lay. Collie revered Nanga

29 Nanga Parbat. *From Collie's slide collection, with permission of the Alpine Club.*

Parbat and believed that all mountains have some sort of spiritual presence. Maybe it was easier for him to accept Mummery's death if he could rely on this. Perhaps what alienated him was a feeling that Merkl was not approaching the mountain with the right sense of reverence. A mountain was not an object to be attacked but rather to be wooed and won. Mountains were for those who had an affinity for them and 'between the blond and bluff young modernist, efficient and hustling, with his card neatly printed as "leader of the Nanga Parbat Expedition", and the supersensitive "Wandering Scholar artist" out of the Middle Ages, the gap, of time and temperament, proved unbridgeable'.[9]

It was unfortunate for Merkl, because he regarded Mummery as a hero figure and had great respect for this early Himalayan expedition. Collie gave what information he could to Merkl, begging him not to approach from the southern side in the Rupal nullah where Mummery had first so enthusiastically pointed out a route. Merkl was to get nothing more out of Collie, who then withdrew into his own world, and began discussing the optical miracle represented by the first character of the Chinese alphabet!

In 1934 Merkl, three companions and six porters, were to die in particularly harrowing circumstances on the north side of Nanga Parbat.

It was not until 1939, after so many lives had been lost, that the Rakiot side was abandoned in favour of a return to the Diamirai face (now referred to as the Diamir face). During that year a party of Germans, reconnoitring the Mummery ribs, found a log of firewood that had lain for nearly 50 years where the 1895 party had left it. Their reconnaissance showed them how difficult it would be to go up the Mummery Route. Five thousand feet of difficult rock and ice was to be followed by a far from easy looking summit ridge. The whole face was swept by avalanches and the time when a climber would be exposed to them too long.

In 1953 the Germans yet again approached Nanga Parbat. The idea this time was to climb the mountain by way of the Rakiot flank. Their success is an extraordinary story of endurance and courage.

A camp was pushed above 21,000 feet and from here Hermann Buhl made a solo ascent. This involved one night out at about 25,000 feet with no food, drink or spare clothing. When he had crawled to the summit, he descended a short distance, stood on a rock and waited for the dawn. The weather, normally ferocious, was calm. It was a superb, if unorthodox, mountaineering feat: Collie's Gods had been kind.

Many have felt that Buhl's climb had more of the quality of Mummery's than any of the expeditions during the intervening period. At least until Messner's solo ascent in 1978. Certainly Buhl, like Mummery, had an exceptional personality and courage and was every bit as 'pushy'. If Mummery had not had to see the sick ghurkha down the mountain, he too would certainly have pressed on despite the odds. Would he have succeeded? The short answer is no—without a shadow of doubt, and yet. ...

Mummery had intended to make a bid for the summit from a camp at 22,000 feet, a vertical rise of 4,500 feet, a considerable distance at that altitude—but it has been done. Buhl, in 1953, got there from a camp only slightly higher (22,600 feet), but at a very much greater horizontal distance (four miles) from the summit.

In 1907 Longstaff got to the summit of Trisul (23,406 feet, the highest peak climbed by man until Kamet was climbed in 1931) from a camp 6,000 feet below, although this was a lower mountain and an easier one, and he had two Swiss guides to break the trail for him. The other members of this expedition (which was to have been the very first Everest reconnaissance to mark the 50th anniversary of the Alpine Club) were Bruce and Mumm, both close friends of Collie, and it is interesting to speculate that, had things worked out differently in 1895, Collie might have been there with Longstaff on the summit.

In theory, therefore, Mummery would have had a chance, though a very slender one, and if anything had gone wrong he would probably not have returned, leaving the world to debate whether or not he had reached the summit—a more fitting end for such an illustrious mountaineer.

But the chances of success for the 1895 expedition were gradually eroded from the outset. Firstly, the exploration was an expedition's worth in itself, which is probably why Collie was one of the most persistent in demanding that the first Everest reconnaissance sent out by the Alpine Club in 1921 should concentrate solely on exploration and make no bid for the summit. Collie possessed a map that gave the mountain heights in the area and also showed the rivers and nullahs. However, the party had no idea of what lay around the mountain massif itself. Consequently, energy and time was spent in exploring, as in the unfruitful trek up the Diamirai Pass and the first return from the Diamirai nullah. They got badly lost three times, due to lack of maps, though Collie was a first-rate geographer. Then again, Mummery's death was a result of venturing into unexplored country. Subsequent parties recognised how dangerous the avalanche-prone routes to the Diama glacier are. Avalanches, terrifying enough amongst the Swiss peaks, become in the Himalaya 'an overwhelming cataclysm shaking the solid bases of the hills, and capable with their breath alone of sweeping down forests'.[10] It was a fearsome sight to see them pouring off the faces they hoped to climb.

Secondly, food supplies were a constant worry, and much of their remaining time and energy was dissipated in foraging trips. They could not rely on their servants to perform this task, realising at the time that their mountain was being sacrificed. Subsequent expeditions brought all their food with them. The small hill villages produce barely enough for their own needs. They also had no lightweight food for the mountain. When we compare the pre-cooked, freeze-dried meals and camping gas of today it seems astonishing that Collie was labouring up Nanga Parbat with six 2 lb. tins of Huntley and Palmer's biscuits and firewood. They did have some spirits and a stove but these were reserved for the high camps alone.

Thirdly, they had no high-altitude porters simply because in 1895 there were none. It was the days before local tribes like the Sherpas or Hunzas had been trained in this work. Bruce was one of the first to recognise and train local men for mountain work. Collie, Mummery and Hastings had to be their own porters. They tired themselves in load carrying when they should have been saving themselves for the summit. (The 1932 team had 35 high-altitude porters and 500 low-altitude porters and the 1939 expedition declared the Diamirai side as 'unthinkable without Sherpa tigers'.)

Fourthly, through lack of Himalayan experience, they could not come to terms with the scale of the topography and constantly underestimated distances. The long grinds over boulder-strewn hillsides have no equal in the Alps. They had no idea that it would take three long days to go the ten miles from the Diamirai to the Rakiot nullah, and there were many similar instances. They persisted in thinking of the Himalaya as overgrown Alpine peaks and that Nanga Parbat would fall after a two day assault. Mummery was sure the summit could be won in a day from 20,000 feet but we now know that the difficulties do not begin until that height. Gradually the truth dawned and Collie wrote:

> At first we had talked about the 'twenty thousanders' somewhat contemptuously, and not without reason, for our hopes were fixed on Nanga Parbat 26,629; surely if a mountain of that height were possible, those whose summits were 7,000 feet lower ought to be simplicity itself. In fact, we imagined that, as far as difficulties were concerned, they should stand somewhat in the same proportion to each other as an ascent of Mont Blanc to a climb up the Brévent from Chamonix during the springtime before all the snow has melted. Unfortunately they were not quite so easy as we should have liked.'[11]

Fifthly, little was known of the effects of altitude on the human body. They all thought they would slow down the higher they went but they had no conception of what it is really like to climb, without oxygen, to 26,000 feet. Mummery's letters home show how this fact came slowly to dawn upon them. On 26 July he wrote, 'I don't think we are going to be bothered much by the rarity of the air' and on 23 August 'There is no doubt the air affects us when we get beyond eighteen thousand feet.'[12] The lack of oxygen bothered Collie. Being the scientist of the party he was probably more aware than the others of the possible effects. At one point on the trip he informed Mummery of the possibility of paralysis and Mummery, whatever his private fears, laughed at him.

Over the next 60 years there was a gradual increase in the size of expeditions heading for the Himalayan giants, the 8,000-metre peaks as they came to be known. It became commonplace for an expedition to consist of scores of Europeans and Sherpas backed up by armies of coolies to carry the enormous quantities of imported food and equipment. Ironically, and happily, the trend is now in reverse. Developments in lightweight equipment and food, improved climbing techniques which make movement on difficult rock or ice much safer and more rapid, and climbers who are both fitter and more accustomed to survival at high altitudes, have nowadays made it possible to climb big Himalayan peaks with small, light 'Alpine-style' parties.

Of this trend the ultimate manifestation, so far, has been the solo ascent of the Diamirai face of Nanga Parbat, without oxygen, by the South-Tyrolean Reinhold Messner in 1978. Carrying 33 lb. of equipment—food for ten days, tent, sleeping bag and fuel—he left a base camp containing only two people, neither of whom could have rescued him. He made a new route to the right of Mummery's route and after two nights and three days reached the summit. A remarkable achievement. After that one must draw one's own conclusions on the impracticality or otherwise, of the extraordinary climbers of 1895.

Chapter 8

Gower Street, Ghosts and Gases

> The diversity of his deeds however unconnected all express one simple theory of life, consistently practised, consistently pursued; 'always roaming with a hungry heart'. He always sought fineness. Took delight only in the first rate. Yet knowing by the experience of his own gifts that these needed cultivation before they had come to full fruition, he also bestowed kindness and encouragement upon younger and lesser men, if only he saw or thought he saw some small sparks of kindred feeling in them. (J I O Masson, *Donnan Papers*, University College archives)

The last years of the nineteenth century were an exciting period for Collie. At this time he lived in rooms in Campden Grove, Kensington. The new century saw a move to 20 Gower Street, a Georgian house, overlooked by the University of London and only yards from the chemistry department. Here he lived a full and varied life surrounded by a magnificent collection of antiques.

Collie's father had been a collector and Catherine Winkworth had remarked on how well John's 'pretty things and bits of old china' had looked in the family house. Di, whom Collie rarely saw, managed to abandon the law office where he had been placed following the bankruptcy of the Collie cotton empire. At a Bristol auction he recognised a Vermeer going for ten pounds; he bought it and later, in London, managed to sell it for £10,000. With the proceeds he set up an antique business and his affairs prospered. Cecil Rhodes employed him for a short time to furnish Groote Shuur and Di travelled extensively throughout Southern Africa buying up antiques brought by the early white settlers. Although he fell out with Rhodes, Di returned to England and continued to do well until his death, in early middle-age, from tuberculosis.

Collie did not have such a breadth of knowledge as Di but was more of a specialist. His particular interest was in Chinese jade. The collection he

30 Collie with his treasures in Gower Street. Date unknown. *Photo from Mrs Benstead, with permission.*

built up was the envy of the museums who borrowed from it to augment public exhibitions. Such was his knowledge on this subject that he was often consulted as an authority on questions of date and authorship. When Collie died the collection was put up for auction at Sothebys by his niece. She had been advised to sell because 'prices would never be as high again!'

Collie was also a collector of rare books, particularly those concerned with ancient literature and alchemy. His writings, lectures and talks with friends depicted his extensive knowledge on these and other subjects. He was fascinated by colour, collecting precious stones and minerals and Geoffrey Winthrop Young recalled how he would buy jewels on sight at auctions or at the dock sides because he could tell by just looking what their probable value was. Collie would then 'dilate on the multiple glory he could obtain from the colour of jewels, when he bombarded them with rays in his laboratory'.[1] This interest in colour led to Collie being one of the first to take up colour photography. He did his own developing and printing, experimenting in the labs with different qualities of colour. Many of his photographic slides in the Alpine Club archives date from the turn of the century. He carried his fascination with science into many of his other interests and spent a great deal of time analysing the glazes on his collection of oriental ceramics. One of his former pupils, Professor Masson wrote:

> Collie's connoisseurships were based upon a flair which divined intrinsic fineness of design, colour, texture and craftsmanship so penetratingly and with such spontaneous eagerness that his tastes in collecting had no need for the guidance of fashion. In those fields as in mountaineering, as in his chief chemical interests, he pioneered because he always went for the original inner virtue and objective kinships of the thing itself. No jealousy or rivalry or envy of ownership was in him. He collected as he pursued chemical experiments, and as he sought the uncontaminated hills not from pride of capture but simply because to do so enabled him better to admire, to study and learn from things of beauty and to store them in his marvellous visual memory.[2]

Wines of all sorts and, in particular, vintage clarets, were another Collie speciality. On his many expeditions, wine always accompanied him, and during the years of his retirement in Skye he had fine wines sent up periodically from London. With an interest in wine went an interest in cigars and Collie was known to abandon the favoured pipe in order to indulge in one after one of his magnificent dinners.

These dinners became something of a legend. Collie enjoyed food, and often refers to it in his writing. (Even on expeditions friends remarked on the quality of his porridge.) His favourite company was a gathering of two or three friends whose interests were as varied as his own and who could provide an evening's discussion that rivalled the dinner in quality. Collie would borrow the silverware from his friend Robert Cox who had rooms upstairs, then, surrounded by the splendour of a dozen dynasties the night was passed in a cloud of tobacco smoke. Extraordinarily Collie, the lover of the open air, had an aversion to open windows, and every one was tightly sealed.

One would have expected Collie's own rooms to resemble those of a well-ordered museum with his treasures marked and arranged; but everything was jumbled together. Books piled over the floors might rub shoulders with porcelain or bronze objects. Delicate jade bottles and jars peered out of old, and often dusty, cabinets. Yet everything was so placed as to 'pick up and repeat colour and lighting on a scheme designed for his own pleasure'.[3]

Many people have seen in Collie of Gower Street a resemblance to Sherlock Holmes of Baker Street and indeed the similarities are numerous. Holmes was also an aesthetic, a many-sided man with an acute analytical mind who would lose himself in thought for hours on end sucking at his pipe. He too was tall and gaunt, loved the mountains and bore a strict physical resemblance to Collie!

Collie's niece adored visits to her uncle who was also her Godfather. She described how untidy and stifling his rooms were. When Cox died and the silver and glass were no longer available, Collie ceased to bother very much and lived in a delightful clutter. When it was time to eat he would push back the serge tablecloth and deposit everything from the table onto the floor. He sat in a very old armchair with all the stuffing coming out and lived, or so it seemed, on whisky and tobacco. His personal appearance was often shabby, at home a dressing gown, in the mountains incredibly old tweeds and a battered hat. Once during the 1930s, he set sail for New Zealand to visit his brother Harry, taking hardly any clean clothes. One acquaintance was very amused to discover that whenever Collie visited him the clean neatly folded towel in his bathroom always remained in that state.

Collie had diverse friendships. Intellectual quality was not the only thing he sought. His friendships cut across all class barriers, something of a feat in Victorian England. He found a wealth of interest in such simple men as John Mackenzie. In the Canadian Rockies he became a lifelong friend of the outfitter of many of his expeditions, Fred Stephens. He, therefore, had not one circle of friends but dozens. Sometimes, in what was typical of his sense of humour, he would bring such different people together. On one country walk he did this and after a short while one drew him aside and said with frigid politeness, 'Collie what is this person "Y"?' Later the other asked 'Doctor *oo* is this "X"?' You can hear the sardonic staccato 'Ha'! with which he would receive each question and can guess the wilfully mystifying ambiguity of the answers he would give.[4]

There was one trait of Collie's complex personality that was particularly interesting and this was his fascination with the unexplainable. Spirits of the mountains, mysticism, the folk stories of long ago were all subjects that he took seriously. This interest may have been inherited from his mother who, at least on one occasion, claimed to have seen a small, gnome-like, impish figure looking at her from the half-drawn curtains of her four-poster, but it was certainly a strange dichotomy in his character. On the one hand the rational scientist, trying to find satisfactory answers and laws to the workings of the world, and on the other hand, the irrational romantic who often disliked an explanation provided by science, preferring one of his own, even when the rationalist in him knew the scientist was right.

For instance, Collie did not relish the idea that the mountains and valleys he loved so well were the products of natural forces. 'These wonderful geological truths', he wrote, 'how simple how all sufficient they are to explain to the uninitiated the why and wherefore of the ancient mountains.'[5] How all sufficient and how unromantic. Collie was not a religious man and the absence of a Christian God in the makings of the world bothered him not at all, but the geologists destroyed something of the inscrutability of the world with their straightforward reasoning.

His feelings, almost of reverence, for some mountain areas rested on a half belief in a mountain world possessed of spiritual qualities. He wrote:

> Yet a wanderer's dreams are happy dreams. He should sacrifice often at the shrines of the Gods of the Wilds, for they are pleasing Gods when they whisper to one in the dusk. . . . His Gods are those of the open sky and the mighty woods, the lakes, the rivers and the mountains. . . . When the old memories from the dream gardens of our youth return; perchance it is only the Gods sorrowing have relented, and are but giving back some of the gold that they robbed from us in the days of long ago, when we troubled not that the years were slipping silently beneath our feet.[6]

There was undoubtedly a streak of mysticism in Collie which revealed itself on many occasions. When he and Mackenzie had achieved a new and difficult climb, he would be silent for a while and then suddenly proclaim that the good spirit of the mountain must have been their unseen companion on that day.

Someone as involved as Collie with the mountain world would naturally respond to the age-old stories of long ago and in particular the Celtic legends which surround the mountains of Scotland and Ireland. Tales like those of Ossian, the Orpheus of the Gael who married a daughter of the fairy folk and the beautiful legends surrounding Deirdre, fair daughter of Erin who lived in the glens of wild Loch Etive and loved the sons of Usna. When he was in Skye these legends became particularly real: 'Should the mists cover the moors the feeling of loneliness grows—one begins to believe in the old legends of the "Sithe" or the "Fairy Folk"; or when the curlews' dreary call "Dalua, Dalua, Dalua", is heard far away, a strange uneasiness seizes one, all the old Celtic tales of mysterious beings that haunt the wild places become possible.'[7]

Collie would often weave his own stories around these legends and late at night, around a camp fire under the stars or deep in the recesses of his armchair, with the dim light picking out his strange objects, he would talk to his friends, no one quite knowing how much he was believing himself. Friends thought it wise to dose his stories with salt on some occasions but as one of them said: 'His unusual eyes with the iris both pale blue and sandy brown gave him an air of mystery and association.'[8]

One story he told with obvious relish concerned the sea caves which surround the shores of Donegal. Only on the calmest of days can a boat be taken into them and on one such day Collie persuaded his boatmen to take him in to hunt seal. It was a mysterious place made unearthly by the murmurings of wind and water meeting the cavern walls. For over 300 yards a tunnel stretched deep into the cliffs and the daylight slowly faded. The tunnel widened into a vast chamber from where numerous other tunnels branched out into the bowels of the mountain, their entrances gloomy and dark as the candle light fluttered over them. A thousand feet of rock lay between them and the sun. The boatmen laughed quietly, oppressed by the atmosphere, and talk was of sea pigs and mermaids and of a great beast which fed on human flesh and lived somewhere over the far side of the cave, out of the flickering reach of their lights. Suddenly,

> large waves, tortured in some narrow passages, sent a terrific boom with multitudinous echoes reverberating through the caverns; at the same time a most curious phenomenon, half sound, half vibration of the air occurred. It seemed as though the whole body of the air in the cave pulsated, producing a swishing sound. . . . Probably the cave had been converted into a gigantic organ pipe, and the note was so low down in the scale that the vibrations were about one per second. Unfortunately I suggested that it was the great beast, and that finished the expedition. Our boatmen were at once terrified, shouting to each other, pushing and half-rowing the boat in a frenzy of fear.[9]

On the other hand, Collie believed emphatically in the Loch Ness monster. Professor Stewart, a friend of Collie's, had actually watched an animal in the water for over 15 minutes. His daughter was with him and they drew a picture, which showed the characteristic humps, and sent it to Collie who always maintained that something the scientists had failed to explain lived deep in the dark waters of the loch.

But when Collie was confronted with his one and only mountain ghost he seems not to have relished its company. The story of the Big Grey Man of Ben Macdui—Am Fear Glas Mor—has been told many times. In 1925, at the annual dinner of the Cairngorm Club, Collie, its Honorary President, was asked to speak. He related a strange event that had occurred to him in 1891, when alone on the Cairngorms' highest mountain, Ben Macdhui.

> One day at Eastertime I was climbing Ben Macdhui. It was very misty and I was only able to see a few yards from me when not very far from the summit, I suddenly heard footsteps on the snow behind me. Confident that some man was following me, I waited for him to join me, but the moment I stopped the footsteps also stopped. When I started on my way again, once more I heard the footsteps clearly. More than ever convinced that some man was on my track, I turned and ran back for some distance, but found no-one. Once again I started on my way to the summit and once again I heard footsteps which stopped whenever I stopped. When at last I reached the summit the footsteps did not stop but came nearer and nearer until they came right up to me. At that

> instant I was seized with an intolerable fright and I ran my hardest down the mountainside. No power on earth will ever take me up Ben Macdhui again.[10]

and it never did.

Collie's story might well have gone down as a good after dinner speech and no more, if it were not for its publication in the press. This resulted in a flood of correspondence in such august bodies as *The Times*. It seemed that Collie's experience was not unique; many others believed that the mountain was haunted and described similar experiences. Alexander Kellas and his brother Henry had once climbed the mountain and were resting near the summit. As Kellas looked around to his brother he saw an extraordinarily tall man walking by the summit cairn. The cairn was ten feet high and the man the same height. Henry Kellas, however, saw nothing. This story was told to a local man who replied, in a most matter of fact way, 'Oh aye, that would have been the Ferla Mor he would have been seeing.' Other locals refused even to discuss the matter but some admitted to hearing stories of a ghost on the mountain. The number of 'sightings' increased rapidly after Collie's story but Collie never mentioned seeing anything. His whole experience was based upon a noise and an unmistakable feeling of terror. Collie was quite ready to admit that 'there are places that one dreads, when one trembles and is afraid, one knows not why and fears stand in the way'.[11] Ben Macdhui was one of them.

There were many sceptics who were prepared to wager that Collie had drunk too much. Others believed he was irritated at being asked to speak at short notice and made the whole thing up. Yet Collie was a man of responsibility and integrity and this was also true of Kellas and other distinguished gentlemen, like Professor Sherrif of Southampton University, who also experienced the Grey Man. Collie enjoyed a joke and did embroider stories but this was quite a different thing. His niece heard the story from him many times and was quite clear that 'Uncle Nor believed in it completely'. Collie remained emphatic—something beyond the wit of man haunted that mountain.

It was not only the mystery of the mountains that fascinated Collie. Some of his objects were thousands of years old and must also have been imbued with wonderful powers. There was one object in particular, a stone Mayan God, with a most malevolent look, rescued by Collie from a friend who used it most ignominiously as an umbrella stand. The figure had a hollow in front in which to put offerings and Collie would burn incense there. (His niece was terrified it might be left on her hands!) Collie was a very bad bridge player and on one occasion his partner complained bitterly about the games they kept losing. On returning to Gower Street Collie stood in front of the God and asked it to teach his friend a lesson; but, he was careful to add, nothing too drastic. The following morning saw the friend with a broken ankle sustained on his front door steps and Collie appeased. Again, how much of this he believed we do not know but he certainly thought 'there was someting in it' and the accident seemed to fit completely.

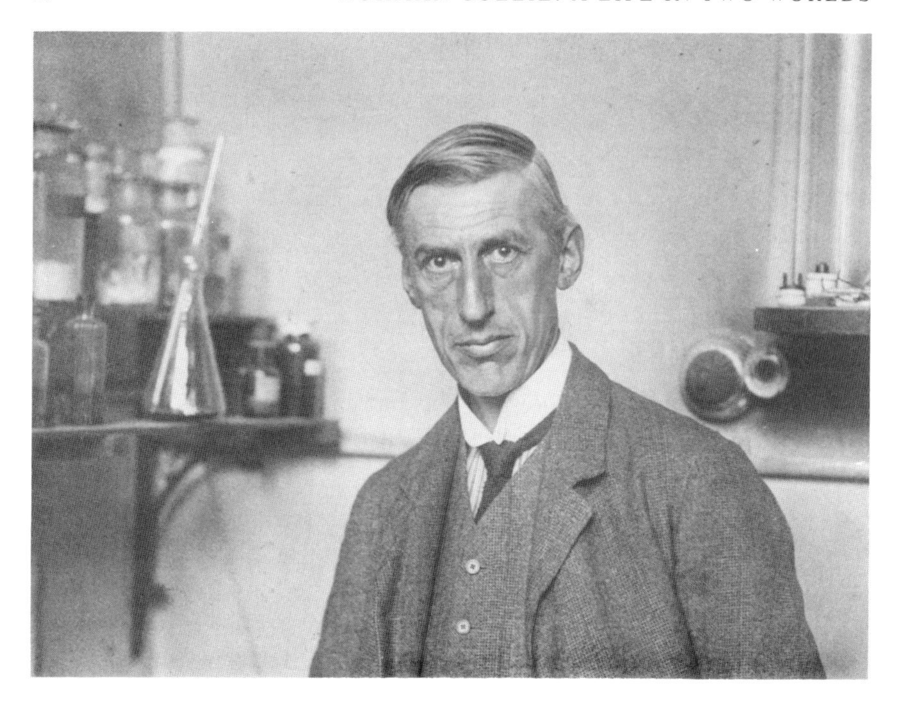

31 Collie in laboratories at University College, London. Date unknown.
Photo from Mrs Benstead, with permission.

It may have been this interest in magic that attracted him to Aleister Crowley, the mountaineer who was also a magician (and much else besides). Collie, and Sir Martin Conway of all people, proposed him for the Alpine Club in 1895. Collie warned Crowley of the probable rejection of his application, and of course, the Alpine Club being what it was, Collie was proved right. The AC must have felt they had had a narrow escape as they watched Crowley establish his reputation of evil and bestiality as the 'Great Beast 666'.

However, it was as a scientist, in the labs of University College, that the rational side of Collie had to take over and these last years of the nineteenth century were very important for him.

Because of Mummery's death, Collie did not get back to University College until mid-term. Ramsay and Travers had to take over his teaching commitments resulting in a halt on most of the research work on the gases. Collie's medical students were being particularly unruly. They would have resented being turned over to a junior and made this known. Ramsay, therefore, made them his responsibility, but it was a task he did not relish.

When Collie did eventually get back to London it was the end of November 1895. Ramsay wanted him to continue the work on the properties of helium and argon, for they had to determine whether the gases were mixtures of different atomic weight or homogeneous substances.

One important factor came to light during the work on these two gases—the almost certain knowledge that other gases must exist. The reason for this confident assertion rested on a knowledge of the Periodic Table of the Elements. If elements are arranged in tabular form according to their atomic weight they fall naturally into such groups that elements, similar to one another in chemical behaviour appear in the same column. When Ramsay and Collie slotted helium and argon into Group 8 they knew that another gas must lie between them. They could also say that it should be a gas with a boiling point higher than helium yet lower than argon and be inactive in resisting combination with other elements.

But it was one thing to know this and quite another to prove it. Two years were to pass before neon was finally isolated. The laboratory became a hive of feverish activity. Many different minerals were heated and their gases examined. The spectra of helium and argon were examined time and time again but no unknown lines denoting minute quantities of a new gas were discovered. Ramsay and Travers went off to the Pyrenees and Iceland to collect samples of gas from hot springs but these too yielded no new constituent.

A clue then came to light, although it was not regarded as a very hopeful one. When argon was systematically diffused it divided into two portions, one very slightly heavier than the other. As the difference was so minute the scientists thought it must be due to experimental error. However, they could not afford to leave any chance uninvestigated. There then began a laborious process of liquefaction and distillation which would separate small quantities of light and heavy constituents more perfectly than any other. They had to practise first with a litre of liquid air before risking the 15 litres of argon they had so painstakingly acquired. By chance they examined the dregs of this liquid air after it had almost all been boiled away during the practice experiment. Incredibly they saw not only the argon spectrum but two brilliant lines.

It was obviously a new gas but they could tell from its density that it was not the gas they were seeking but another one altogether. This gas, discovered on 30 May 1898, was named krypton—the hidden one.

The 15 litres of argon were now liquefied. The first portions of the gas which were boiled off this liquid were examined with a spectroscope on 8 June and a very beautiful sight was seen: a complicated spectrum composed of many red, orange and yellow lines. The density of this new element would enable it to fit in with argon and helium in the Periodic Table—they had found the unknown gas. Ramsay's son wanted it called novum but Ramsay felt they had better go to the Greek and it was called neon, or new. Another two years were to pass before an investigation of its properties was complete.

It has been necessary to deal with the history of neon because of its effect on Collie. When Ramsay and Travers finally isolated neon Collie was no longer on the staff at University College, having left two years before; yet Collie always maintained, in private, that he discovered neon. The mystery of this has never been solved but these are the facts.

32 A group in the laboratory of University College, London, 1896. Ramsay second from left, Travers third from right, Kellas first on right. *With permission from Edward Arnold and Co.*

Collie had been trying to leave University College since 1894. He was certainly happy there but he knew that as Assistant Professor he could not further his career except by getting Ramsay's job. It was not likely that Ramsay would leave the college (he did in fact stay there for the rest of his working life) and so Collie set about finding a full Professorship.

In May 1894 he applied to the Mason College, Birmingham, to replace Professor Tilden as Professor of Chemistry and Metallurgy. He was only 34 and despite excellent references from many distinguished chemists he failed to obtain the position. At Easter 1896 Collie had a tentative offer of a post at Oxford. So confident was he of getting the job that Ramsay was interviewing successors but for some reason he did not get this position either. However, in September 1896 he was appointed Professor to the Pharmaceutical Society in Bloomsbury Square, London, minutes away from University College. At the same time, Kellas also left Ramsay to become a lecturer at the Middlesex Hospital Medical School, also very near the labs.

These changes in the rare gas team occurred at a crucial time. During the years 1896–8 while the slow work of isolating neon was in progress Collie was no longer in Ramsay's laboratory, though he did visit the department frequently during 1897 because he was very interested in the gas work.

Collie told his niece many times, and close friends such as Geoffrey Winthrop Young, that he discovered neon. He was quite emphatic about it saying it could be put on his tombstone. His niece recalls how he told her that he ran around to Ramsay's home hot foot to tell him of the discovery, Ramsay being ill in bed at the time.

Because of these private conversations, nearly every non-scientific obituary notice about Collie states that he discovered neon but was not credited with the discovery. But we know from the dozens of articles that have been written about neon that Ramsay and Travers isolated the gas and their names are always given as the actual discoverers. Collie's name is not mentioned in a significant way in the original *Royal Society* paper where the discovery was communicated to the scientific world.

In 1928 Collie wrote a history of the Chemistry Department and gave fulsome credit to Ramsay for neon's discovery and when Collie was asked to furnish details for his own obituary notice, a common occurrence among professional people, he did not mention neon. What he did mention was the failure of the scientific world to recognise that he was responsible for the construction of the first neon lamp. Collie's niece was particularly emphatic that she was not confusing the discovery of the gas with the development of this lamp which came much later.

Given the integrity of both Ramsay and Collie, their close relationship and Collie's failure to mention his discovery in any written communication, there must be a plausible explanation that remains as elusive as the gas itself. For instance, it may have been Collie who established that another gas existed between helium and argon in the Periodic Table and in a sense this would be 'discovering' neon. But whether Collie gave Ramsay a vital clue or isolated the substance by chance, who can tell? Neither explanation is really plausible, given the nature of the experiments involved, but it is clear that Collie was working with gases while at the Pharmaceutical Society, although he published no papers about his work. Probably the answer will never be known but considering Collie's total lack of self-advertisement, and the circumstantial evidence, his involvement with the discovery of neon must surely have some element of truth.

Shortly after neon, xenon was found, bringing to an end the isolation of the five noble gases. Professor Letts and Collie wrote of the skill with which

Ramsay found xenon. 'Difficulties were overcome by magnificent technique ... can any praise be adequate for the discoverer who detects and isolates one part of a substance in about 170 million parts of the medium in which it occurs? Yet that is what Ramsay had done when he isolated xenon from the air.'[12]

These years of work were undoubtedly Ramsay's finest scientific achievement, worthy of the Nobel Prize he received in 1904 for 'the discovery of one whole missing group of elements in the periodic system of Mendeléeff'.

It was not just the search for the gases which occupied the department during these last years of the nineteenth century. The discovery of X-rays was to have very important consequences for University College, and for Collie in particular.

In January 1896, Röntgen, a German physicist, discovered X-rays. This caused great professional and public excitement. Those, like Collie, who were skilled glass-blowers spent a lot of time making and experimenting with what were called Crookes tubes. These tubes were very efficient generators of X-rays and demonstrations were given at the Chemical Society. Travers was irritated at the 'waste of time' caused by the enthusiasm of students and staff for this new scientific 'game'. Collie, however, saw the fantastic potential. It was during one of the public demonstrations at the Chemical Society that he suggested a photograph be taken of one of his fingers, in which he believed there was a piece of lead that had got there when a toy pistol exploded in his hand when he was a child. The photograph was taken during

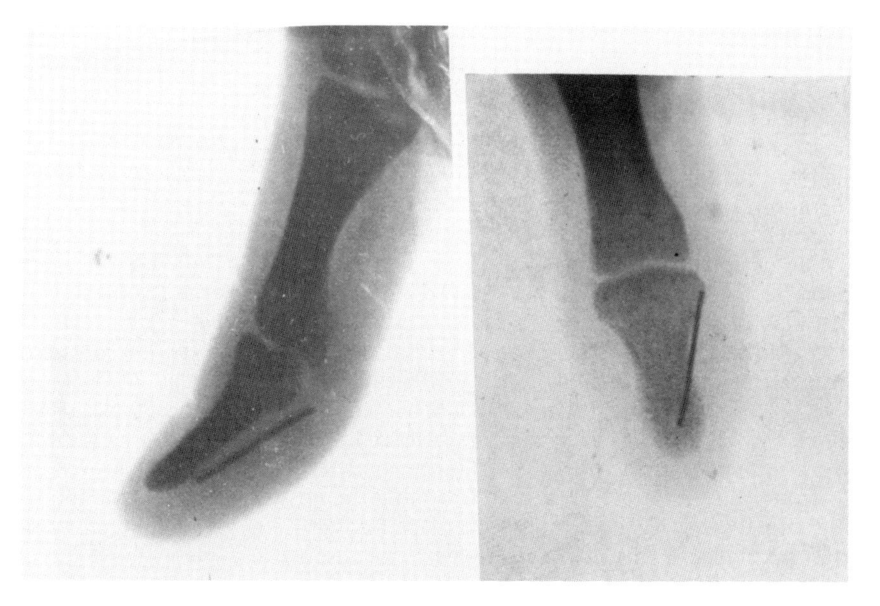

33 First X-ray for surgical purposes. Taken by Collie in 1896. *Photo from University College archives, with permission.*

the lecture and the small piece of lead showed up very plainly. (It became fashionable after this for the bones of the hand to be shown at scientific conversaziones.) Collie wrote of the consequences of this photograph: 'As a result the people at University College Hospital came to me about a woman who said she had a bit of needle in her thumb, would my X-ray show it? The accompanying photo is the result—*this was therefore the first X-ray photo used for surgical purposes.*'[13]

The chemistry department became well-known as a result of this. Shortly afterwards they were involved in a legal case. A trial was in progress at one of the London courts where an actress was suing a theatre for damages sustained when she fell through a trap door. The theatre denied liability and said she was not injured but a surgeon disagreed. To convince the jury he wanted an X-ray photograph taken of both her feet. Collie agreed to do this but whether it helped the actress win the case we do not know.

Shortly after this Collie left University College. He was then at the Pharmaceutical Society for six years, a period he thoroughly enjoyed. During that time he was able to manage four trips to the Canadian Rocky Mountains, as well as one trip to the Lofoten Islands in Norway. It was to be a different picture after he returned to University College in 1902.

That Collie was able to work once more at University College from this time was due to a complete re-organisation of the department as a result of the University of London Act. The university had over the years become a purely examining body with no involvement in teaching and research in the Colleges. It now assumed responsibility for both. The London County Council gave its support which put an end to the chemistry department's worries about money. It also meant that the chemistry department could now afford two professors. Ramsay was appointed Director of the Chemical Laboratories and Collie became the first Professor of Organic Chemistry. He was delighted to be back. One of his old students was appointed his assistant and he wrote, 'We found a new Collie, a master of organic chemistry, a brilliant experimentalist and a true philosopher.'[14]

Chapter 9

To the Great Lone Land

> Something hidden. Go and find it. Go and look behind the Ranges—
> Something lost behind the Ranges. Lost and waiting for you, Go! (Rudyard Kipling *The Explorers*)

In 1829 Dr Alexander Collie, Norman Collie's grand-uncle, set sail on *HMS Sulphur* bound for Freemantle, Western Australia. On arrival, an expedition was mounted to explore the south-west coast. During this trip one of the rivers was named the Collie and upon its banks the town of Collie later arose.

Norman Collie, continuing the family spirit of exploration, embarked in July 1897 from Liverpool, for a largely unmapped area of Canada—the Rocky Mountain range. One mountain 'with much strong individuality of feature worthy of its name'[1] was to be called Mt Collie.

Canada in 1897 was still a country whose mountain areas were unknown. The Rockies, one of her many mountain ranges, were as virgin as the Himalaya. No one had seen her ice fields or knew the heights of her mountains. The valleys, lying along beautiful rivers where the motorcar now speeds, were thick with luxuriant, impenetrable forest.

In the 1850s the nomadic buffalo-hunting Plains tribes still roamed free from the Canadian frontier to the Rocky Mountains and from the Saskatchewan River to the border of Texas. It was only during the 1860s that the Indian became seriously threatened in Canada as the white man extended through the country. But there was nothing like the brutality of the American system that drove the Indians forcibly into reservations. Canada had always been more tolerant and many Indians such as Sitting Bull, after Custer's Last Stand, found refuge there. When Collie visited the country the story of the near extinction of the Indian was barely history.

Some tribes like the Stoney and Kootenay had lived to the east of the Rockies, coming up to the mountain edges to hunt or trade with the trappers, but they did not inhabit the forests and few Indian names adorned the mountains or passes. The valleys had once had rough trails blazed through them by trappers and Indians but by 1897 they had long closed up, for game was scarce and the Indian had been confined to the reservations. The land was quiet and during Collie's first trip it was harder to travel through western Canada than it had been 40 years before.

It is difficult to place Collie and his sophisticated London life into the same era as cowboys and indians and the coming of the gold rush. He arrived in

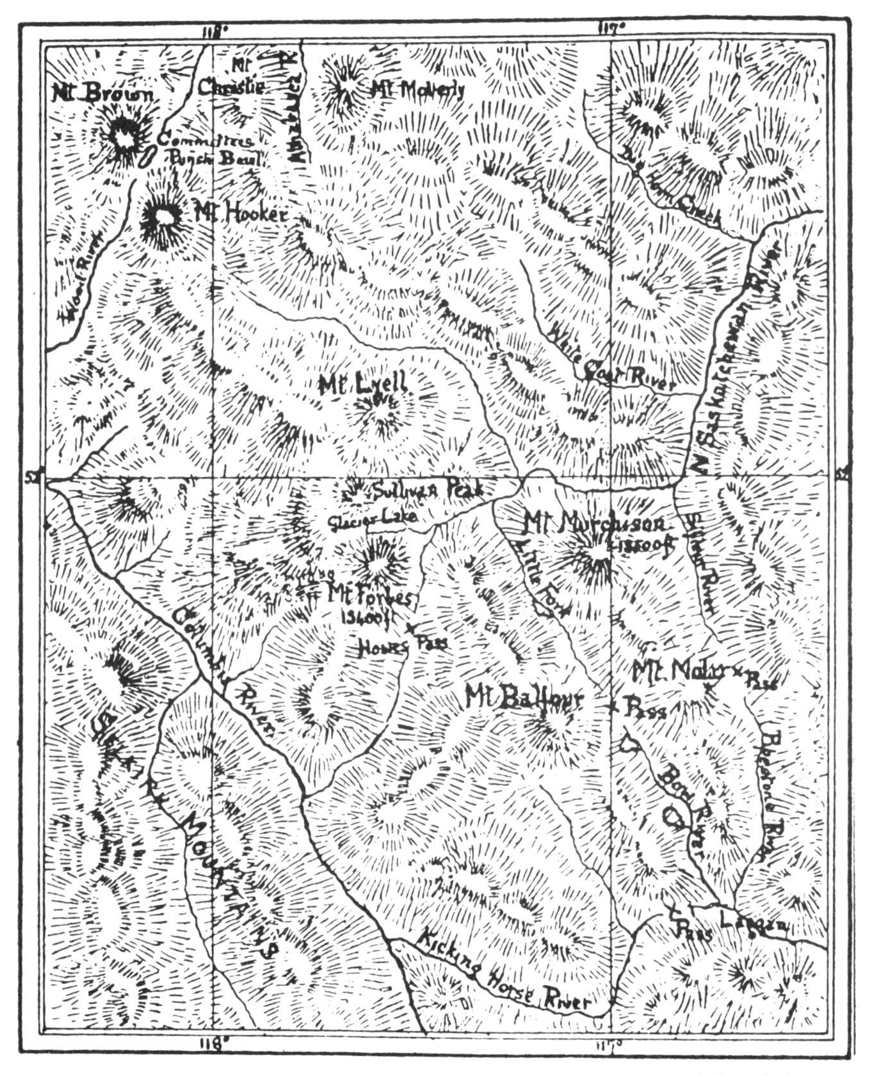

Map 3 Map by Collie of Canadian Rockies showing how little of the country had been explored in 1896. *Permission of the Alpine Club.*

Canada as the Indian had been beaten and was to witness, from afar, the mad rush to the Klondike gold fields. He saw the skies glowing orange from the forest fires raging along the Edmonton Trail. Here prospectors fought a nightmare journey down the Mackenzie River almost to the Arctic Circle. Of the 2,000 or so who set out from Edmonton, only 500 arrived. Collie climbed and explored through the brief gold rush years. The hardships he had to contend with were great even for an experienced man but the gold prospector was often an amateur at living in the wilds. Collie had great pity for these people whom he felt had 'been despatched to their death and ruin through the lies of the transport agents and storekeepers'.

Collie was only able to obtain a rudimentary knowledge of parts of western Canada from previous expeditions. The most important exploration into the mountain area had been carried out by Captain Palliser in 1857 on behalf of the British Government. Palliser's accounts of his travels presented to the Houses of Parliament were the best source Collie had. One member of that expedition had been a Dr Hector, naturalist, geologist and 'first-rate mapper'. It was Hector who gave the best descriptions and it was upon his map that Collie had largely to rely. One other early expedition of note was that in 1827 of the botanist David Douglas, after whom the Douglas Fir is named.

By 1886 the Canadian Pacific Railway (CPR) had opened. This linked the Atlantic and Pacific Oceans and facilitated access to the mountains either side of it, as it ran across the country from east to west. The Selkirks first received the attention of the mountaineers in the late 1880s, including such men as the Reverend William Green from Britain who was rapidly followed by members of the Appalachian Mountain Club of Boston. The Americans spent several seasons exploring and climbing around the two CPR stations of Laggan and Field.

In 1893 Professor Coleman of Toronto journeyed to the Athabasca River from the east in search of two mountains, Brown and Hooker, reputed to be 16,000 feet high. On the crude maps that existed they were entered as Canada's highest mountains; David Douglas had discovered them 60 years before but they had not been seen since. Also during the early 1890s Walter Wilcox explored south of the railway line as far as Mt Assiniboine and north of the railway to the Saskatchewan and Athabasca rivers.

By 1897, therefore, the area lying approximately 100 miles north and south of the railway had been explored but on the whole this exploration was confined to the valleys, low passes and mountains within easy reach of the railway. Very few peaks had been ascended and no mountaineer had ventured into the main chain. This was a situation that was to change rapidly in the next decade. Mountaineering took off in western Canada during the 1890s and once again Collie was in at the beginning.

The Appalachian Mountain Club (AMC) of Boston had asked the Alpine Club if some of its members would like to join them in a climbing holiday in the Rockies. One of their members, Philip Abbot, had been killed the previous year on Mt Lefroy and his death, the first in Rocky mountain climbing, precipitated the invitation: Lefroy had to be taken. Collie, looking for new challenges, accepted the offer. Professor Dixon of Manchester and George Baker, a wealthy man known for his expeditions to the Caucasus, accompanied him. They asked the Swiss guide Peter Sarbach to go with them. He was the first guide to come to the Rockies and was brought along to strengthen the climbing team rather than in his capacity as guide. He had also climbed with Abbot in the Alps.

In July 1897 they arrived at Glacier House in the heart of the Selkirk Mountains where they were asked if they were 'off to the Klondike'. According to Dixon, Collie's first appearance on the platform caused quite a stir. 'Newly shod, well-greaved and very beautiful. The ladies spied him. Even his almost Indian sang-froid could not stand up against the curiosity of these travelling Eves. Next moment his person reclined in a low chair, the centre of an admiring circle, while two fair dames, each supporting on high one of his neatly bandaged legs, tested with dainty fingers the sharpness of his Mummery screws.'[2] Collie may have expected Indians, but not this!

One of the Americans was Charles Fay, a Professor of modern languages, who was to play a prominent part in the history of Rocky Mountain climbing. Later he became the first President of the American Alpine Club. Various combinations of these gentlemen did some warm-up climbs in the Selkirks but their aim was to go eastwards to Lefroy.

At Laggan they were joined by Charles Thompson, another energetic American pioneer, who was to become a great friend of Collie—a friendship which began in a crevasse. From Laggan the climbers went to Lake Louise, the starting point for their attack on Lefroy.

On 3 August, the anniversary of Abbot's death, the party set out from the chalet at Lake Louise in the starlight of an early morning. The beauty of this mountain land sent Collie away into the land of daydream. They rowed slowly across the lake through 'some forgotten land, a land of old romance, where high above, perched on the almost inaccessible crags, is the castle of the lord of the valley, a land where knights in armour rescue fair ladies from imprisonment, and roam abroad in search of perilous adventures.'[3] Collie was soon returned to earth when the shoreline was reached and he encountered for the first time the sort of country typical of the area. The land of romance turned into a Hades where swamps and thickets of dead wood made all thoughts of fair ladies rapidly disappear.

As the dawn broke they were on the ice of the Victoria glacier heading for the Death Trap, a wide passage of snow that passes between Lefroy and Mt Victoria and down which avalanches thunder from both mountains. A long grind brought them to the Abbot Pass. Their route lay up the west face of the mountain. The climbing was not difficult but rotten rock, the probable cause of Abbot's death, made them very wary. Snow, ice and rock ledges eventually led them to the rocky cliff where Abbot had fallen. The climbers avoided this by cutting steps in the snow to the side. The summit was reached at 11 a.m. and by mercury barometer the height was about 11,000 feet. Collie wanted to climb Victoria as well and on 5 August he led a party to its summit.

Fay was very impressed by Collie's endurance as he made tracks for them all. 'Stride on Oh Collie' he remarked, 'we are right after you.'

These two climbs, although enjoyable, did not lure Collie into remaining in the area. Surrounded as he was by mountains which could afford him the pleasure of many first ascents, he decided instead that the 'call of the wilds was stronger than the love of climbing mountains'. He wanted more of a challenge and his decision to make 1897 a purely mountaineering holiday and 'not to trouble myself with exploration', soon changed when he found 'that the maps, such as they were, covered only a very small portion of the ground I proposed to go through, and as no knowledge whatever of the snowfields and peaks seemed to exist, it at once became obvious that exploration might very well be combined with mountaineering'.[4]

Some of the AMC members agreed to join Collie's party on a journey of exploration up the Bow Valley. Their objective was to find Mt Balfour, which was marked on Dr Hector's map. Before journeying into the wilds it was necessary to hire an 'outfit' consisting of men, horses and provisions. The hiring of an outfit was vital to these early travellers. The trailmen, familiar with the terrain, were analogous to Alpine guides and a good one was worth his weight in gold.

They hired their outfit from Tom Wilson of Banff, the first white man to discover Lake Louise, when he was employed by the CPR survey in 1881. He was to provide for Collie's first expeditions and the two men became friends, corresponding with one another until Tom's death in 1933. The leader of the outfit was Bill Peyto, a man who looked as if he had just stepped out of the Wild West, which in a sense he had. He was a good shot and always slept with a loaded rifle on the trail in case the Kootenay Indians attacked, though this may have been wishful thinking. But he was a colourful man who set bear traps for intruders in his cabin and once brought a wild lynx into a crowded bar. An Englishman, Bill had signed on with Wilson first as a packer, later as a guide. The stories of his varied life meant that evenings around the camp fire were never dull.

Collie soon became an experienced trail man able to cope with the problems of difficult terrain, the unpredictability of Indian horses and the physical exhaustion of axe-cutting, but in 1897 he was still a new boy. 'As one looks back', Collie wrote, 'one blushes for the utter incompetence shown.'

To begin with they would never have tied everything onto their ponies, if it had not been for a man at the Laggan railway station who showed them how to tie a diamond hitch. Roping packs was a skilful business and this knot vital to success. (When Noel Odell made his first visit to the Rockies in 1927 Collie's chief piece of advice was the importance of learning how to 'throw a diamond hitch'.)

The men fared no better on the trail. Peyto and his men had gone on ahead to blaze the way and at first it was not difficult to follow them. But soon the trail disappeared amongst the masses of fallen timber. Hours were spent leading the animals around impossible parts of the trail and cutting their way through the tangled undergrowth. When they at last broke through the timber into open ground they were surrounded by swamps or 'muskegs'. Following sticks in the ground, not in fact left by Peyto but by the railway surveyors some years before, they were soon hopelessly lost and buried in a swamp. The ponies sunk to their bellies and as the moon rose they were all still there. Professor Fay pushed on to find Peyto, soon bringing him back. The ponies had to stay where they were for the night with a dog left to guard them against grizzly bears. This embarrassing situation was not one that Collie enjoyed. After his many caustic comments on the 'mountaineers' in the Alps he could not have been proud of his position as an 'explorer' in the Rockies.

The following morning the push up the Bow Valley began. They had no idea how far they would have to go before striking into the mountains, having only a hazy idea from Hector's map where Balfour lay. Nearly two days' journey brought them to the Upper Bow Lake where they camped. From here they ascended an ice-fall that descends from the higher snowfields towards the lake. Coming out onto the upper snowfield they saw Balfour—or at least they thought they did.

It was not a difficult mountain to climb by the route they chose up the eastern arête but on the summit the real Balfour could be seen four miles away to the south. Between them lay a deep gap. The pioneers were not really bothered by this. After all, the mountain they were on was certainly virgin, dozens more surrounded them and the climb had been most enjoyable. They named the rogue mountain Mt Gordon after the Earl of Aberdeen. Also from the summit Collie saw a beautiful mountain that stood out from its companions. At the time he thought it was Mt Murchison, described and named by Dr Hector. It was in fact Mt Forbes and Collie was so captivated by its presence that he decided that one day he would make the first ascent.

The men descended Gordon but the day was still young. Perhaps the ascent of a peak they could see westwards across the snowfield would finish the day well. It may have been Mt Collie that they now set out for, and in the light of what was about to occur, very aptly named. The men were unroped as they moved across the glacier in its direction when suddenly Charles Thompson fell head first into a crevasse. Every second was vital. The intense cold would soon kill him even if the fall had not. Dixon recalls how they stood peering into the hole and how one tense sentence was spoken, 'Someone must go down.' The men looked at each other, it was no enviable descent. Sarbach and Baker were both large men, but Dixon at 11 stone said he would go. Collie, however, with quiet deliberation that commanded no dissent announced, 'I am nine stone six.' Rapidly he was roped up and lowered down. He thought he had gone the length of one 80-foot rope but actually those above had tied two together and it was not until he had run out almost 160 feet that he found Thompson who was wedged into the crevasse where it narrowed. That he was still alive after such a fall was something of a miracle. Presumably the heavy sack he was carrying slowed him down and broke the fall.

Thompson was face downwards, covered in snow and his head was three feet lower than his feet. He managed to tell Collie that he was unhurt but the frightened men above soon heard Collie calling out that he could not reach him. It was a very difficult situation because Collie was jammed between two slippery walls of ice and was only able to move his arms. He was scared Thompson would faint before he could get him out but how he was to do that was the problem that faced him.

Shouting up for a rope, which was hastily lowered to him, Collie threw it to Thompson's hand which was waving blindly about trying to catch it. This was no good, for when Thompson did eventually manage to grab the rope it immediately slipped out of his hand when Collie pulled on it. His next idea was to make a lasso. Putting both his arms above his head he tied a noose and lassoed Thompson's arm. Collie then shouted to those above to pull their hardest. He was doubtful if this would do any good at all and might well break his arm. It was really a last chance for if Thompson did not budge he would soon die. The seconds crawled by, then inch by inch Thompson began to move. Continuous pulling eventually got him into an upright position but the situation was still critical because Collie could not get a rope around his body. It looked as if it would have to be that arm again. By a terrific effort Collie was just able to tie 'the best and tightest jamming knot I could think

34 The summit of Mount Collie, from *Appalachia*, IX. *Permission of Appalachia.*

of around his arm, just above the elbow. A shout to the rest of the party and Thompson went rapidly upwards till he disappeared round the bulge of ice forty feet or more above. I can well remember the feeling of dread that came over me lest the rope should slip or his arm give way under the strain, and he should come thundering down on top of me; but he got out all right, and a moment later I followed. . . . ;we were both of us nearly frozen and wet to the skin, for ice-cold water was slowly dripping the whole time onto us; and in my desire to be as little encumbered as possible, I had gone down into the crevasse very scantily clad in a flannel shirt and knickerbockers.'[5]

Collie told Baker afterwards that when he had been left alone in the crevasse he heard a curious noise that puzzled him at first until he realised it was the beating of his heart. What Peyto thought of these crazy mountaineers on top of the episode in the swamp is not recorded.

The party returned to the Lower Bow Lake and here Dixon left them and the Americans returned homewards. Collie, Baker and Sarbach were left with the outfit. It had been their intention to push southwards for their remaining five weeks holiday to Mt Assiniboine, the 'Matterhorn of the Rockies'. However, the view from Gordon of the large northern peaks had made Collie change his mind. After an unsuccessful attempt on the real Mt Balfour, the three men travelled back to Banff to re-outfit for another expedition northwards. In particular Collie was in search of the magnificent peak he had seen towards the north from Gordon and which he still believed was Hector's Mt Murchison.

Peyto was quite prepared to take his raw hands on again. Wilson fitted them up with all they would need, plus a cook, and was able to draw them a very rough map, for he had once been in this area. On 17 August they once again set off up the Bow Valley but this time Peyto kept with them.

The trail was as bad as ever. There was so much fallen timber that it was quite possible for one to walk for a mile just along tree trunks. On many occasions they were as much as 12 feet above the ground. The lower part of the valley had been burnt when the railway was being built and every new storm brought down hundreds of rotting trees. It was the ponies that provided the biggest headache for while a man may climb, the horses had to have a trail cut for them. While this was being done the horses, growing impatient, would often lunge off into the wood to get caught up in a thicket from where it was difficult to cut them out. Another hardship was the insect life for the weather was very hot and mosquitoes bothered them incessantly. Tempers were short and while Collie does not exactly say so it would seem that an argument developed when Peyto declared an early camp for the day. Later, after a meal and rest he explained the situation. They must go easy on the horses who were heavily laden. Only when they were 'broken in' and had lighter loads could the days be longer. He did not want to ruin them in the first days of their month on the trail. Peyto and the 'dudes' still had to learn the capabilities of each other. Collie admitted wholeheartedly that Peyto turned out to be magnificent. On many occasions he was looking after the ponies, smearing their sore backs with fat, long after the others had settled

down for the night. On the other hand Peyto came to respect Collie for his rapid learning of the 'ways of the west' and his gentlemanly behaviour on the trail.

It took three days of slog to reach the head of the Bow Valley but the beauty of it made the hardship worthwhile. The Upper Bow Lake was full of trout which furnished a first-rate supper that evening. They spent a day here, for Baker was continuing a plane-table survey begun by one of the AMC men the week before. From this camp on 20 August they climbed a 9,000-foot peak which they did not name and were able to see the country down Bear Creek to the north and south. This helped Baker considerably and he was able to add many new points to his survey.

The party broke camp and crossed the Bow Pass, where a highway now runs, at nearly 7,000 feet descending into Bear Creek Valley, whose river was a fork of the Saskatchewan.

The pass was a pleasant change from the valley. Wide areas of grassland opened out with small lakes and clusters of pine, making idyllic camping. A large lake north-west of the pass was named after Peyto and half way down the valley they named three lakes the Waterfowl Lakes.

By 23 August they had reached the main Saskatchewan, travelling through wild and forbidding country. Due to the weather the river was in full flood from the melted snow pouring down from the mountains but the outfit had to cross it. It was not so much the depth that was a problem but the currents and moving boulders that covered the river bed, and according to Collie this crossing was reputed to be one of the worst. Anxiously they watched as Peyto coaxed his mare across. The ponies followed their leader and tense moments passed as the expedition's entire food supply of flour and bacon lurched perilously across the swollen river. One fall and a horse and man would be swept away, probably for good. Collie's mare, an old grey, carried him majestically across and on this occasion no mishaps occurred.

Travelling westwards up the main Saskatchewan valley they decided a climb was called for. They chose a mountain to the south which they named Sarbach. In common with many of the peaks in the area it was a crumbling mass of rock. Its one redeeming feature was an exposed summit ridge. Cloud obscured the view and they were unable to see their large peak. However, to the north-west they saw Mt Lyell, named by Hector after the geologist. To the west a large glacier wound down the hill and it was thought 'Mt Murchison' must lie in that direction.

On 27 August they arrived at the foot of the valley leading to this glacier. To the north they saw their peak and an attempt on it was planned. It was not until they returned to England and looked at the Palliser reports that they discovered that their mountain was in fact Mt Forbes.

facing page
35 The bad ground through which the party had to hack a trail in the Bush Valley, 1900. The figure is 12 ft from the ground.
Photo by H E M Stutfield from Collie's slide collection, with permission of the Alpine Club.

Forbes was a splendid mountain that they believed was higher than it is. They were certainly anxious to claim it. Unfortunately, as many mountaineers know, just at the moment when a peak is within grasp the weather changes: the heat gave way to snow. All they could do was look up at this mountain, a mixture of 'the Weisshorn and the Dent Blanche' as it rose straight up from its base. The only feasible route seemed to be up the south-west ridge to a sharp arête with broken rock towers. Below the summit the arête was heavily snow corniced and looked far from easy. Once the weather cleared they felt certain of success. Meanwhile, a little exploring up the other valley where the great glacier lay would pass the time.

36 Forbes group of mountains. *Photo by Collie, from his slide collection, with permission of the Alpine Club.*

Two ponies were loaded and after a day's walk they reached the glacier which they called Freshfield. At the top of the glacier an enormous ice field opened up and from it they could see three peaks. These they named Walker, Freshfield and Pilkington after the last three presidents of the Alpine Club. The weather, now perfect, encouraged them to attempt Mt Freshfield. The effort was only half-hearted; Baker, busy with his survey, being the only one to put in a full day's work. At about 10,000 feet, Collie, informing his friends that not only would they miss dinner but they would certainly have to bivouac on the glacier, should the attempt be persisted in, convinced all but Sarbach that a return was necessary. No one minded very much for attention was fixed on Forbes.

One important outcome of this attempt on Freshfield was Collie's decision to return to the Rockies the following year. While Baker had been surveying,

Collie had climbed around a rock rib to see what lay northwards. There he saw a giant of a mountain with a striking western face. This surely must be either Mt Brown or Mt Hooker, seen only once before by Douglas who named them, and entered in all the history books as Canada's highest mountains. Their capture would be a great prize.

On return to camp, preparations were got under way for the attempt on Forbes. On 1 September, after the usual difficulties of terrain, they camped at the base of the mountain. But the weather had turned wretched again. A brave attempt was made up the mountain slopes through the forest but wet snow and dripping trees forced a rapid return for they were soaked through. The weather had settled down for a spell of snow as often happens in this part of the country before an Indian summer sets in. The friends, not wanting to be snowed in with low food supplies decided to abandon Forbes and break camp. Time was now drawing in, for Collie had to return to the Pharmaceutical Society and his new responsibilities there before the end of the month, but their journey back to civilisation was not destined to be easy.

Due to the deteriorating weather they decided not to re-trace their route but with all haste to make for the north branch of the Kicking Horse River and follow it down to Field station. This was easier said than done. They had no problems until they had crossed the Howse Pass and begun the journey southwards through Blaeberry Creek. Wilson had been this way in 1887 and they later discovered that he had to abandon his horses in the dense forests that now surrounded them. It looked as if Collie's party would have to do the same. First, they lost the trail, then the forests got thicker and soon the streams were widening every mile. Peyto had gone ahead but soon returned declaring that it would take a week to clear the fallen timber that lay along the river bank. There was also a forest fire raging lower down that the rain had failed to quench. It was Peyto's opinion that Blaeberry Creek should be abandoned and his clients had to agree with him. However, a return to their original route would take time that the low state of their food supplies would not allow.

In order to obtain a clearer view of their surroundings Collie climbed a rock peak near to Blaeberry Creek and from the summit he saw a depression in the chain on the east side. He thought this might lead to the north branch of the Kicking Horse River. As Collie bluntly announced to the outfit, it was their last chance, for ten days' travel separated them from their old route and their food was almost finished.

A trail for the horses was not going to be easy to make. The climb up to the depression was steep with loose moss and dirt providing an uncertain footing for the animals. Luckily the horses were now fit and loads light but there was no fodder for them that night. The following day they successfully crossed the pass, named by Collie after Baker, and by 9 September the outfit was back at Field. When they reached Banff, Collie made enquiries about previous expeditions to the area and discovered that apart from Tom Wilson no one knew anything of the country they had just explored.

On the boat to England Collie went over in his mind plans for a return the following year. It was the lure of the unknown, the fact that hundreds of miles of land lay unexplored that drew him back. Before visiting Canada again, however, Collie needed to know more of the history of the Rocky Mountains. He sought out old journals and dusty tomes compiled from the work of past surveyors. In particular he wanted to find an account of Douglas's original journey, but was unsuccessful. He was able to purchase a copy of Palliser's reports, 'worth their weight in gold', and after studying them, he and Baker presented them to Tom Wilson. From these reports Collie discovered that Dr Hector had preceded them in many areas. Collie wrote to Wilson, 'Hector's journeys were usually twenty miles or more a day and he climbed hills as well as provisioning the camps with sheep whilst he was doing it. We don't do such things now in the Rockies.'[6] The reason being that in Hector's day trapper and Indian trails existed and game such as Bighorn sheep was plentiful.

One problem above all bothered Collie. Was the high peak he had seen from the slopes of Freshfield either Mt Brown or Mt Hooker? 'The two mountains standing on either side of the Athabasca Pass, and long reputed to be the loftiest summits, not only in North America, but possibly of the entire American continent. The Athabasca Pass forms the watershed between the two great river systems of the Athabasca and Columbia, whose waters flow out at either end of a small mountain tarn rejoicing in the name of "The Committee's Punch Bowl". West and east of the tarn, forming the Titanic pillars of this natural gateway to the north, were said to be the two great peaks, Mt Brown and Mt Hooker.'[7]

When Douglas had climbed one of these mountains its height had been estimated by the Hudson Bay Company astronomer as 16,000 feet. But, in 1893 when Professor Coleman, one of the earliest Rocky Mountain explorers, had located and climbed Mt Brown, he estimated its height as 9,000 feet. Coleman was convinced that he had not mistaken the mountain he had climbed. In that case who was right? It seemed inconceivable that anybody was wrong for Coleman and the astronomer were both reputable scientists who were unlikely to make such mistakes in calculation. Without an account of the original journey made by Douglas it was difficult for Collie to ascertain whether he had in fact climbed a different mountain to that climbed by Coleman. Collie was determined to return that summer and investigate. The spirit of exploration had caught him: could he 'rehabilitate the outraged majesty of Mt Brown'?

Professor Fay was also to return to the Rockies in 1898. He wanted to attempt Forbes. Collie was irritated at this for he regarded Forbes as 'his'. He wrote to Thompson, 'I don't think he will do much unless he has a Swiss guide to show him the way', and later, 'Fay and Michael are at present trying to engage Sarbach to try Mt Forbes. I wish them luck, without Sarbach they have no chance at all. I don't know about mountaineering etiquette out in America but over on this side of the duck pond it would have been considered the right thing to first write to Baker and me and find out what we intended to do.'[8]

Part of Collie's annoyance hinged on the fact that he had just had to cancel his plans for a return to the Rockies. Captain Bruce was returning from India on leave and Collie, while on Nanga Parbat, had promised to spend the first leave he got in England with him. Collie was fearful that as 'Fay has the field clear' Forbes would be climbed before he got out there again.

But suddenly Collie's luck was once more with him. Bruce had his leave cancelled due to the loss of officer material in the frontier wars. Collie must have been secretly pleased and he wrote a very enthusiastic letter to Thompson, adding that he wanted his plans kept secret: 'My programme is an ambitious one. Murchison from the Pipestone to begin with, then Forbes, and then we shall force our way north to Brown and Hooker by the north branch of the Saskatchewan. ... I hope we shan't put Fay's nose out of joint but you say he is going also for Forbes. ... However we shall see. ...[9]

Collie took no guide in 1898. Instead he was accompanied by two men who, like Mummery and Hastings in the Alps, were to become his most constant companions on many Canadian mountains.

Hugh Millington Stutfield was a wealthy man who retired early from the stock-exchange. He was a first-rate shot, an accomplishment that was to save his party from starvation on at least one occasion. Always a keen traveller, he had visited Spain and Morocco.

Hermann Woolley was a pharmaceutical chemist, head of a large drugs firm in Manchester, who was 13 years older than Collie. An amateur boxer and good all-round athlete his even temper was famous. One friend wrote, 'Although he climbed with some strongly opinionated comrades none ever quarrelled with him or wore out his good temper.'[10]

The three men started from Liverpool in mid-July. Baker had passed on the survey to Collie and the maps Collie was eventually to make from his explorations were the basis for all subsequent maps of the area. Again Wilson set up their outfit and Bill Peyto led the men. They took 13 horses but these were reduced to 12 almost at once when one broke a leg in the timber. Collie was not altogether disappointed to lose the unlucky thirteenth. Three dogs and unwieldy bundles of tents, survey equipment and cameras made up the 'train'.

On this occasion they travelled not up the Bow Valley but to the Saskatchewan River via the Pipestone and Siffleur Creeks. They were making for Forbes but on the way wanted to find the real Mt Murchison and climb it.

'For many weeks it would be good-bye to civilization and its conventions and boredoms; its feather-beds and table-d'hôtes; its tail hats, frock coats and stick-up collars. The wilderness lay between us and dull Respectability; we could wear what we liked, and enjoy the ineffable delights of being as disreputable as we pleased.'[11] They did not however, foresake their collars, ties or watch chains, as the photographs of their trip show.

Woolley and Stutfield took a day or two to get used to the rigours of life on the trail under Peyto. The usual heat, muskegs, mosquitoes and timber conspired to make life uncomfortable but the two newcomers soon settled down. On the third day out they made their camp an hour below the Pipestone Pass. Unfortunately their idyllic camp drew the attentions of the

37 Canada—party being eaten by mosquitoes adopt novel methods of protection. *Photo from Collie's slide collection, with permission of the Alpine Club.*

'bulldogs', great horse flies with pincers that broke the skin. These mustered with the mosquitoes to attack. Smoke failed to rout them and the men adopted novel methods of attire in attempts to keep the insects at bay. Nothing really worked and misery was complete when a violent storm soon had the river rushing through their teepee.

August 3 saw them continuing the climb up the Pipestone Pass, a grind of over 8,000 feet. Collie ascended a small peak that rose out of the pass in order to search for Murchison. Hector had drawn a rough map of the area and Collie, to the north-west, saw what could be the mountain. Even from where he was he could see that its great height had been exaggerated. Descending the pass they made their way through the Siffleur Valley over 'alps bright with red painters brush and big yellow daisies'. The trail soon improved and 15 miles were rapidly covered. Once they had crossed the Siffleur river the trail once more deteriorated but signs that this had once been a popular trail were in evidence. Now and again they found old notches on trees cut by some long gone trapper and on one occasion they picked up a sodden copy of Hamlet dropped by a hunter or prospector. Teepee poles of old Indian camping grounds were also seen. It was uncanny to find these relics of the trapper and the Indian and to see their trails returning to the wilderness. Not once on this journey or that of 1900 did Collie meet anyone on the trail, for the scarcity of game and the control of the Indian had wiped out their ways of life.

Once the main Saskatchewan Valley was reached they turned due west following the river. Up the valley a glacier-covered mountain was named by Collie Peak Wilson. Down the valley smoke clouds blew and the air became hot and heavy from fires raging miles away on the Edmonton Trail. Talk that night turned to the question of escape should the Saskatchewan Valley catch fire. Stutfield and Woolley, taking the talk to heart, slept with their boots on.

In the morning the ponies, up until now behaving well, decided to go for a bathe. Before the men could stop them they jumped into the river, wallowed about and then swam out to a small island. Peyto coaxed them back but the animals were fully laden and by the time they had swum back to the shore all the flour, sugar and bacon was well sodden. Hours were spent drying the mess. On top of this the trail turned into a bog and they were forced high up into the woods with the usual complications of fallen timber. One of their old camping grounds in Bear Creek was eventually reached but it had taken them two days longer than the previous year when they travelled up the Bow Valley.

From this camp they went in search of Mt Murchison and found it on the east side of the creek. For some reason they decided not to spend time climbing it at present; perhaps its decline from 13,000 to an estimated 11,000 feet may have had something to do with it. Instead they decided to go straight on in the direction of Hooker and Brown up the north fork of the Saskatchewan. Forbes they also left unclimbed hoping to attempt it on the return journey. Presumably Professor Fay was not in the vicinity or Collie would not have left the mountain.

As the horses were now needed to ride they cached a load of provisions at Bear Creek. A good Indian trail lay up the east side of the river but they could not get across. The river was in full flood and quite a sight as the waters careered madly past. A way up the west bank would have to be forced instead. Peyto and his hands began cutting the trail. From 12 to 16 August a long battle with the wilderness began. Collie feared many times that Peyto would refuse to go on as he and his men made heroic efforts to cut three or four miles a day. It was very aggravating to see a good trail the other side of the swollen torrent. While such labours were in progress Stutfield hunted game, to no avail. The forests were almost denuded of sizeable animals, shot or trapped out of existence. There was no control on the killing of what game was left and the Indians left their reservations on any pretext to hunt.

Eventually the harsh work began to get the men down. Peyto declared it was madness to persevere and unless they could ford the river the trip must be abandoned. Collie soothed him with whisky and within an hour Peyto was offering to try the river. Carefully his mare Pet edged her way in and was soon up to her back in water. She never put a foot wrong and soon the other ponies were following her demurely across. From then on life was easier and 18 days out of Banff they reached Athabasca Peak. 'Our blood was stirred within us', wrote Collie, at the prospect of being once more on the snow and ice. As they believed the big peaks they were in search of could not be far off they badly needed to climb a mountain to get their bearings. But food was also running very low, so low that only five days' supply was left on which to do a fortnight's climbing and return to Bear Creek. Stutfield reluctantly agreed to forsake the climb and set out to hunt anything from ptarmigan to grizzly but having seen nothing to hunt for three weeks he was far from hopeful. Collie and Woolley were left to climb a mountain.

Mt Athabasca was the obvious choice and its first ascent was probably the finest climb Collie had of all his trips in the Rockies. Ascending a small glacier they soon hit the north-east arête and for a short time they had some good climbing before the limestone rock turned loose and dangerous. A glacier to the west looked safer and they left the ridge for it. Easy climbing led them up to a great basin just beneath the summit. From here a choice of routes could be taken. Either they could traverse under some overhanging ice cliffs to their right to the northern arête or by cutting up an ice slope on the left regain the north-east ridge. They chose the latter. With Woolley leading, the ridge was reached but it turned out to be a steep and narrow arête of ice. At first they were able to kick steps but soon the ice axe was chipping away in the still air. Two hours of hard work brought them to a small platform beneath the precipitous rocks that lay near the summit. These looked too difficult but a narrow chimney was discovered at the base. This was their last chance for either they climbed it or abandoned the mountain. It was very cold and the limestone rock was so loose that great caution was needed. Edging their way upwards to regain the ridge they were disappointed to find the summit was still not within reach: a wall of overhanging rock 15 feet high almost halted them. Defeat was unthinkable with victory so near.

Collie could not remember how they climbed it but climb it they did. At 5.15 p.m. they reached the top.

The view that lay before them 'in the evening light was one that does not often fall to the lot of modern mountaineers', wrote Collie. 'A new world was spread at our feet; to the westward stretched a vast ice-field probably never before seen by human eye, and surrounded by entirely unknown, unnamed, and unclimbed peaks. From its vast expanse of snows the Saskatchewan glacier takes its rise, and it also supplies the head-waters of the Athabasca; while far away to the west, bending over in those unknown valleys glowing with the evening light, the level snows stretched, to finally melt and flow down more than one channel into the Columbia River, and thence to the Pacific Ocean.'[12] They had discovered the 100 miles of the Columbia ice field, today a ski-mountaineer's paradise. From it rise two of the three highest mountains in the Rockies.

Excitedly the friends looked about them. Could they see the mighty Mt Brown? To the west Collie saw the chisel-shaped mountain, covered with glaciers and snow that he had seen from Freshfield. Surely this was Brown for just to the north-east another magnificent peak arose: this must be Hooker, Brown's companion. Rapidly Collie drew lines in all directions on his plane-table survey towards these peaks. He hurried as fast as he could for night was approaching and the cold was intense. Woolley stoically waited for over an hour, as Collie frantically worked. He was sure he had solved the mystery of the mountains, now all they had to do was climb them.

Daylight was almost gone as they left the summit nearly 12,000 feet high. It was a dangerous descent with loose rock and poor visiblity but the glacier was reached as the darkness enveloped them. Not until almost midnight did they stumble into camp where Peyto was worrying for their safety. Stutfield had tried to reassure him but as Collie and his friends had to learn the ways of the trail man, so Peyto had to learn those of the mountaineer. Supper that night was a splendid occasion with two celebrations, for not only had a mountain been climbed, but Stutfield, contrary to all expectations, had shot three very large bighorn sheep. Starvation was a thing of the past and the conquest of the mighty mountains awaited them.

All thoughts turned now in the direction of the ice field seen from Athabasca's summit and from whose snow Mount Brown surely arose.

The following evening they bivouacked on the right bank of the Athabasca Glacier. Two of Peyto's men accompanied them and like Lor Khan were amazed at what they saw. Neither had been near a glacier before. The night was stormy but the men knew that it would be a long day if the mountain they had seen was to be climbed. Consequently they left their bivouac at 1.30 a.m.

The glacier was heavily crevassed and the going slow. Collie felt they could almost be threading their way through 'the ice-maze of the Col du Géant'. The Athabasca Glacier descends from her upper snow-fields in three ice-falls, the highest being the most crevassed and these crevasses were quite a sight. 'Huge chasms of immense depth yawned beneath us on every side, branching out below into mysterious caverns and long winding grottoes, their sides tinged with that strangely beautiful glacial blue, and festooned with enormous icicles.'[13]

Five hours later they emerged onto the ice. It was a stupendous sight. They were standing on the edge of an enormous ice field, bigger than anything in the Alps, which stretched mile after mile 'like a snow-covered prairie'. Their amazement may be likened to Livingstone's first sight of the Victoria Falls, for the knowledge that they were the first to gaze upon it increased their awe. To the north they saw the mountain they were seeking. Two other fine peaks, one of rock and one of snow, rose above them and they named them The Twins.

For hours they tramped across that world of snow but the mountain came no nearer. By noon they were forced to give up but not before they had made extensive notes of what they could see. Collie's survey was going to be exciting.

Thunder clouds now began to gather and the mystery of their surroundings was complete as they retraced their steps. On the return journey they could not resist attempting an unusual white dome of a mountain. Stutfield, feeling the need for a summit beneath his feet, suggested they climb it. He had been disappointed at not climbing Athabasca, so they all humoured him and turned towards The Dome. A very hot and tiring climb through heavy snow brought them to the summit at 3.15 p.m. 'Although we did not know it', wrote Collie, 'we were standing on probably the only peak in North America the snows of which, when melted, find their ways into three oceans—the Pacific, the Arctic, and the Atlantic; for the glaciers from this peak feed the Columbia, the Athabasca and the Saskatchewan rivers.'[14]

Back at their camp they discussed the findings of the last two days. Collie reluctantly had to agree that the topography of their mountain land did not correspond to that surrounding Brown and Hooker. Although they had seen two magnificant mountains, they were not the supposed monarchs of the Rockies. The friends decided to name their Mt Brown, Mt Columbia, the ice field, the Columbia ice field, and the mountain's companion, Mt Alberta. Although they were disappointed they need not have been for Mt Columbia is the Rockies' second highest mountain—a fact of which they were totally unaware at the time.

The friends discussed their next move. Brown and Hooker must lie further north-westwards and by now they must have been wondering whether they were as high as they had been made out to be. At 16,000 feet apiece surely they would have been sighted by now? On 24 August the decision was taken to move half the outfit over the Wilcox Pass into the main Athabasca Valley in order to find the Athabasca Pass and the Committee's Punch Bowl. As Collie ruefully remarked, 'We imagined they might be only two or three days' journey distant: we now know that it would have taken us at least a fortnight to get there.'[15] The rest of the camp was to stay where it was.

Accordingly they set out north-westwards up the eastern branch of the Athabasca river where the trail men panned for gold. They could see three fine peaks. The central and highest summit was named by Collie after Woolley and it was not climbed until 1925. Another was named after Stutfield and this simple snow climb was first done in 1927. The peak to the north-west they christened Diadem. They were hoping to find some valley that would take them to the bottom of Mts Columbia and Alberta but they soon saw that such a trip was not possible in the time they had and reluctantly the hunt for Brown and Hooker was given up.

The time was approaching when Collie would have to think of returning to London so the outfit packed up and travelled back towards the cached provisions at Bear Creek. From this camp they made an attempt on Murchison but bad weather drove them back. Forbes they also had to leave unclimbed for the weather would not now permit an attempt. They moved on homewards, climbing one mountain on the way, Thompson Peak, lying just north of the top of the great ice-fall of the Upper Bow Glacier. On 8 September civilisation was reached again.

The mystery of Brown and Hooker was finally resolved when Collie got back to London. At last he managed to find an original account of Douglas's journey. Together with Coleman's story he pieced the mystery together. Both Douglas and Coleman had in fact climbed the same mountain but Mt Brown's height had been wrongly given by Douglas. He had mistaken the height of the Athabasca Pass and as a result the height of the mountain had been wrongly assessed. It was only about 9,000 feet as Coleman had said. It was a simple solution to a problem that had caused Collie to abandon Mt Forbes. However, if Collie had not done so the satisfaction of discovering the Columbia ice field, probably Collie's most enduring contribution to Canadian mountaineering history, would not have been his. The cause of Canadian geography was certainly helped by the mapping and surveying the party carried out and there was still Forbes. Fay had made no attempt on her and Collie still coveted the mountain. But Forbes would not move and Collie was certainly coming back.

Chapter 10

Explorers and Rivals

> No I would not change if I could. I saw the buffalo and the indian as he was—I saw towns and cities grow where I had pitched my tent—I saw the railways come into the country bringing preachers and men with white shirts, who built churches and jails—I have seen the coming of the electric cars and light; telephone, autos, flying machines and the radio, so if I finish up in an old man's home nothing can cheat me out of that part of my life. (Tom Wilson to Collie, March 1924, Glenbow, Alberta Institute archives)

During 1897 and 1898 Collie and his friends had explored parts of the eastern, central and north-western Rockies. They were the first to investigate the snow-fields and peaks of the interior of these mountains. Collie had penetrated to the heart of three of her great ice fields—the Wapta, the Freshfield and the Columbia, as well as finding two out of her three highest mountains—Columbia and North Twin. Yet Collie's biggest argument for returning to Canada was the lack of knowledge concerning the western side. 'What was there on the other side of Freshfield, the Lyell and the Columbia groups? Were there great glaciers and further outlying mountains? Did the valleys run straight to the Columbia, or, like those on the eastern side, lie parallel with the range? Were the bottoms of these valleys underneath the high mountains three, four, five or even six thousand feet about sea level, like those on the opposite side? and were there any passes over which an easy trail might be made?'[1]

From the summit of Athabasca, Collie had seen many fine peaks to the west. It would be an arduous task to climb such mountains as Columbia, Bryce and Alberta from base camps in the Athabasca or Saskatchewan Valleys. The idea grew between Collie and Stutfield that an approach to these mountains from the west would be far more practicable. The new ground they would cover on the way would make the holiday one of exploration as well. There was no room for Forbes in this plan and Collie hoped it would stay unclimbed for yet another year.

Accordingly the two friends returned to Canada in 1900. Collie had spent 1899 in the Alps with Bruce, whose leave had come at last. Stutfield, with the leisure of wealth, had left for Canada a month before Collie. At Banff, he had previously made enquiries about getting to the mountains via the western valley of the Columbia. No one could tell him anything about the valley which lay 100 miles westward. So Stutfield travelled on to Donald, the starting point for a journey up that valley. Here he had the luck to meet a prospector who told him that there was a trail down the banks of the Columbia River which had served the gold mine at Big Bend. There was also a fair trail up the left bank of the Wood River. Of the country lying towards the mountains he knew no more than anyone else. Most of the old-timers that Stutfield spoke to agreed that the western valleys were harder to penetrate than those of the east. Existing maps also gave little guidance and after their journey Collie was able to show that most of them were grossly inaccurate in any case.

Stutfield wanted to approach the mountains from the north-west via the Wood River. At least they would be certain of a trail for some of the way and would possibly see Brown and Hooker. Their reduced height, which certainly made them nowhere near the highest mountains in the Rockies, had dimmed Collie's enthusiasm for them. He persuaded Stutfield that an approach up the Bush River would be so much shorter that it was worth trying. Many times he must have wished that Stutfield had overruled him. Only one old trapper could give them any information about the Bush River area. In his opinion it would be impossible to force a route through the timber and muskegs and the river itself was no paddling pool. After much discussion, and aware that it was not going to be easy, the friends decided to 'tempt fate on the western side of the range and the Bush River route was the one decided on.'

Collie arrived at Donald on 30 July. Accompanying him was Sydney Spencer, known today perhaps for his route from the Nantillons Glacier up the Blaitiere by the Spencer Couloir. Woolley, unfortunately, could not spare the time and his quiet good humour was sorely missed. At Donald, Stutfield had the outfit all ready. The horses had been conveyed at great expense from Banff on the train. Bill Peyto and his horse were away at the Boer War and their head trailman was Fred Stephens, 'one of the best fellows it has been our good fortune to meet'. The outfit was just getting ready to move out when the first of many mishaps occurred. Charlie Bassett, their chief axeman, was mounting his Indian pony when it reared and fell back on him causing bad injuries. Collie and Stephens organised transport to the train which left immediately for the hospital at Banff. As a result the party started without their best axeman, a person who would have been worth every penny of his pay and more, on a trip such as theirs turned out to be.

The outfit travelled up the Columbia River to begin with but the trail did not follow the bank, ascending instead the valley of the Blackwater Creek four or five miles to the east. Two creeks, the Waitabit and the Bluewater, were soon passed and the first ten miles was rapidly covered. Camp that night was made in a grove of trees where already the scenery was quite different. Collie wrote: 'The tallest pines in the Bow or Saskatchewan valleys were but as puny saplings; and the luxuriant undergrowth, mingling its brilliant hues with those of the silver birches, hemlocks, and other smaller trees, lent a richness and variety to the foliage such as we had never before seen. Side by side with the spectacle of vigorous growth, afforded by the young trees and shrubs sprouting from the damp earth, was that of decay—a mournful array of fallen monarchs, sublime even in their ruin—trunks of immense girth that lay slowly rotting away, moss-grown masses of decomposing vegetation, whose life and sap had long since gone forth to nourish their youthful successors.'[2]

For two days they journeyed through this magnificent forest where the sky hardly penetrated the roof of leaves. Night, the air heavy with pine scent, brought the mysterious murmurings of the darkness telling of the wanderings of animal and forest sprite. When the forests thinned the familiar muskegs appeared. On the third day out they were able to see through the woods for the first time. To their right was a fine range of mountains that Collie named after Spencer, on their left they glimpsed the mountains of the Selkirks.

38 Collie (*far left*), Fred Stephens (*middle*) and Sydney Spencer (*right*) surveying, Canada 1900. *Photo by H E M Stutfield from Collie's slide collection, with permission of the Alpine Club.*

39 Bush River, Canada, 1900. Collie exhausted after trail cutting. *Photo by H E M Stutfield, from Collie's slide collection, with permission of the Alpine Club.*

Friday 3 August brought them to the banks of the Bush River. Here the trail stopped and their troubles began. Camp was on the edge of a wide marsh next to the river, now 100 yards wide, which flowed quickly between steep muddy banks. The weather had become hot and sultry and the mosquitoes made their first appearance: they were particularly vicious. The trail men had never seen so many or experienced such agony and the night was one of unending torment. At first light a retreat was suggested by Collie, back up the trail to a mountain spur six miles away. This was steep and heavily forested but divided them from the upper reaches of the Bush Valley. Over this spur they now hoped to find a way.

Two days were spent hacking a trail through a mile of woodland. The horses would never have got up the hillside heavily laden so Collie and his friends ferried the animal packs to the top of the spur. The work was exhausting. One moment trees had to be hacked, then boulders rolled aside or muskegs worked around. Devil's Club was everywhere. This plant, about five feet high, emitted a dank unwholesome smell and its poisonous thorns caused wounds to fester for days. On the ridge stood a large rock, named by Collie, Mt Pisgah, and from it he was able to survey their promised land. It did not look very welcoming.

> Certainly there were no narrow canyons or defiles that would require lengthy detours up precipitous hillsides, and the valley was long, flat and open; but we could see muskegs, streams and shingle flats all tangled together, looking like a skein of ravelled grey wool thrown down between the dull green hills; while the main river, winding first towards one hillside, then towards the other, sometimes branching, again reuniting, formed a veritable puzzle of interlacing channels, islands of pebbles, stretches of swamps and small lakes, all hopelessly intermingled. At other places the water would spread itself far and wide over the flat floor of this desolate valley, and we wondered how long it would be before we could win to the foot of a splendid snow peak that stood boldly up alone and solitary some 12 or 15 miles away. We hoped that this mountain was Mt Bryce, but, as it turned out later, we were destined to be disappointed.[3]

Collie had first seen and named Mt Bryce, after the then President of the Alpine Club, from the summit of Mt Athabasca when he discovered the Columbia ice field.

The next day the fight began to gain the summit ridge with the horses and to descend to the Bush River. They had no water so it was essential that the journey was completed in a day. Twelve hours of battle lay before them which left man and beast utterly exhausted. The ascent to the mountain spur, where they cached provisions, went without mishap although two jays 'croaked dismally on a neighbouring pine presaging future woe'. They followed the ridge before descending into a narrow cleft between perpendicular rocks. It was hard getting the outfit through here and out into the forest on the far side. The hill was very steep and muddy and the horses were unhappy. During the descent one of them went crazy with fright and stampeded off the trail into the forest. There was no time to go after him and the precious load of bacon he carried. Fred found him the next day thirsty, hungry and very contrite trapped in a thicket of wood. Later that day the swamps of the Bush River were reached.

Two days were spent in this miserable place, for it rained heavily. but the cached provisions had to be brought down from the ridge and ponies retrieved. Stutfield went in search of game and Collie, not wanting to be idle, picked up the axe. They were missing Bassett but the outfit found in Collie a good second best. His skill with the axe meant that the task of trail cutting was often reserved for his delectation alone. Stutfield remarked that Collie 'displayed that desperate energy which I have long ceased striving to emulate but there are limits to human endurance and we sorely needed another axeman'.[4]

On 11 August they started up the banks of the swollen Bush River. The horses had to be watched the whole time for they loved the water as much as they hated the trail. At any opportunity they would either plunge into the river or stampede back up the trail until they had deposited themselves or their packs deep in mud. Fred, despairing of progress along the river bank, thought they should try to ford the torrent, now about 200 yards wide, to see if the far bank was any better. He and Harry Lang, another trail man, went first and got about half way across when the rest of the horses decided to join the fun. Before they could be stopped nearly the entire outfit was following Fred. Collie and Stutfield watched anxiously from the shore. All seemed to be going well until Fred's horse tried to climb the far bank. It could not get a grip on the mud and fell backwards into the deep river. Fred, trapped by his foot in the stirrup, fought to free himself as the current swept horse and rider downstream. Several times they went under before Fred got clear of the horse and swam to the shore. Harry and the rest of the horses all got out safely. Fred shouted across to Collie to stay where he was. He and Harry then unloaded and tethered the horses, constructed a raft from the only available timber, a few water sodden logs, and then proceeded to ferry themselves back to the other bank. It was a perilous journey for the raft became unmanageable in the river and was sucked into a rapid. Harry fought to control the crazy vessel as it spun round and round but his pole, sticking in the river bed, pulled him in. His heavy boots soon dragged him under. Fred, with great presence of mind, crawled along the raft and managed to stretch a pole to Harry when he surfaced. Desperately he grabbed it and hung on. The two men could do no more, for Fred was unable to help Harry onto the raft or control it. By pure chance they had swirled near enough to the bank for a rope to be thrown to Fred. Somehow he managed to hold Harry and the rope while Collie and Stutfield, wallowing in the shallows frantically guided the vessel and its half-drowned crew to the shore.

A cold and miserable night followed. Seven men, wet, cold and hungry, packed themselves into the only tent. Most of the food and equipment lay with the horses across the river. All through the dismal night, whilst the rain lashed down, the animals, the source of all their troubles, could be heard whinnying pitifully to one another.

Next morning, Fred, undaunted, set about building a proper raft. This time he used good dry pine and made oars. Alone he went across the river, drove over the horses and packed the raft with the provisions before rowing back again. Now they were once more together.

While this was in progress, Collie began cutting trail up the bank again. Stutfield, deciding that wet clothes were worse than none, strode naked through the reeds, gun in hand, searching for geese. As Spencer sarcastically remarked that night at supper, the only goose in the reeds that day had been Stutfield!

The weather was now very gloomy and the sun hardly shone at all during the rest of the trip. Progress was slow and miserable for jungle and mud were seemingly endless. As they were edging their way along a narrow strip of muddy land between the river and a deep swamp two ponies suddenly sprang into the water. Immediately the current whisked them away. One mare unladen got out but another, encumbered with 250 pounds of bacon and flour, could not heave herself up the bank. Desperately the men struggled after her and when she appeared near the steep mud bank they clung to her bridle. All they could do was keep her head above water for it was impossible to haul her out without a rope. This was quickly unpacked from another pony and got around her neck. With all seven men pulling she was dragged half strangled onto the bank. Collie was worried about the food she carried. The provisions were vital and if they were ruined then so was the expedition. After consultation the food was declared edible but some attempt had to be made to dry it. Accordingly they camped and again it was a miserable affair in an abominable quagmire. The trail men, with the exception of Fred, now began to grumble. They continued to do so until Donald was reached again. Fred however was an oasis of humour and cheerfulness. Collie admired him very much and a friendship began on the trail that was to last all their lives.

One more bad day was to follow before life began marginally to improve. Their way lay over the shoulder of a hill. Collie and Fred spent the morning cutting trail before the outfit was packed up and the party moved on. It was possibly the worst day of the trip. Not only was the hillside steep but 'it seemed composed wholly of decayed tree trunks and other vegetable matter. In such places one may be walking along some colossal trunk that looks fairly solid outside but within is a mass of rotteness; and if you break through the outside crust you may suddenly find yourself up to your neck in soft pulp.'[5]

The descent was a nightmare, particularly for the horses because of the deep bog holes. Stutfield, hauling one of them out, suddenly found himself beneath an avalanche of ponies sliding down onto him. Unluckily he chose to fall into a patch of Devil's Club and his bottom was never quite the same again. All hell broke loose at this stage; horses flew madly in every direction, crashing through the forest in blind panic with the men chasing after them. Amid loud swearing the rest of the day was passed cutting them out of the wood.

By 16 August they had reached the head of the Bush River. Believing at this time that their maps were vaguely accurate, whereas in fact they were hopelessly wrong, they thought the mountain they could still see was Mt Bryce. Therefore the Columbia ice field and Mt Columbia must be very near indeed. On 18 August they ascended a mountain spur which lay between them and the north fork of the Bush River. Somehow the country was different from what they had expected. Collie and Stutfield forded the main river to investigate the valley of the southern branch of the Bush. A gorge was reached where a splendid array of wild strawberries and blaeberries delayed them but clambering up a rocky knoll in the wood they had a clear view up the valley of the north fork. At its head rose Mt Columbia, the chief objective of their trip, but to their dismay it was possibly 15 miles away from where it ought to be if the Bush River were properly located on the maps. Obviously it was not.

Gloom descended on them all. Fred, who had explored the north fork, reported it impassable. His arm had become black and swollen from the bites of black flies. For 22 days they had been on the trail and had got nowhere. Collie, Stutfield and Spencer decided to take another look at their surroundings in order to decide what to do next. They climbed a peak that lay in the angle of the north fork and the main valley of the Bush. Near the summit Stutfield, feeling unwell, turned back. The others climbed on and as they rounded a corner surprised a he-goat which leapt away from them. They named their mountain Goat Peak in his honour. The view from the summit clarified things. Ten miles away up the north fork lay Mt Bryce and beyond that Mt Columbia. Due east was a peak later to be called Mt Alexander. They were 12 miles south of where they thought they were, the maps having placed the head of the Bush River much too far south. The mountain they kept catching glimpses of on the trail was not Bryce at all but an unknown mountain. As it was visible most of the way up the Bush River they later named it Bush Peak. To the right of Bush Peak rose Forbes, whilst far away at the head of the south fork was the Freshfield group.

Back at camp the dismal conclusion was reached that Columbia, lying so far up the dense valley, every mile of which would have to be hacked out with an axe, would probably not be climbed that year. But one could always try!

They decided therefore to cache provisions and, travelling as light as possible, go up the north fork in its direction. The way soon became difficult and as it was impossible to cross the river Fred thought up a bold plan. They should strike up above the timber line in a desperate last effort. A hard day followed. Evening found them camped about 700 feet below the summit of Goat Peak. It was impossible however to work around the mountain for steep rock barred the horses' way. A day was spent on the summit surveying and mapping whilst Stutfield hunted. He managed to kill a goat weighing 150 pounds which unfortunately fell down a precipice when it was shot. The men's recovery of their supper from its perilous situation afforded them the most exciting climb they were to have on the whole trip.

The prospect of getting any mountaineering done was now getting fainter and fainter. It had started to snow and sleet and altogether a week was passed at this high camp for they had not the heart to fight their way forward any more. Although it was cold and wet anything was a relief from the heat and mosquitoes of the valley. Collie rather enjoyed the rest, snug in his one-man Mummery tent. The trail men, however, wanted to get home. Reluctantly the others agreed, and the distant mountains were bidden farewell.

It was a sad journey homewards along their trail. Not one decent mountain had been climbed. Collie hoped that 'geographical science would be proportionately grateful' for the way they had spent their summer holiday: the Royal Geographical Society of London certainly was. Collie's map was published by them and the following year he was appointed, perhaps in grateful recognition, to its august Council.

Sundry peaks in the vicinity of Donald and Banff were climbed in the few days remaining, with Collie and Fred making the first ascent of Mt Edith. But too soon the 'bacon was cooked for the last time under the silent pines' and it was time to catch the Number 1 homewards.

Collie did not get out to the Rockies in 1901, going to the Lofoten Islands instead. By that year important steps were being made in opening up the Rockies to the tourist, as well as the mountaineer. The process that was to make parts of these mountains a holiday paradise had begun.

The Canadian Pacific Railway (CPR) started this popularisation. The mountain section of the railway had not been an economic success. In order to recuperate they heavily advertised the attractions of the mountains through which their railway ran. Most of the hotels were built and maintained by the CPR and the company brought over Swiss guides to stay in them. As a result one could have accommodation and a guide to take one on a climbing trip just as in Switzerland. In 1900, only three years after Collie had fought his way down the Bow Valley, a pony path had been cut by the CPR.

One of the advertising techniques used was the importation of Edward Whymper, conqueror of the Matterhorn. This did not please Collie. He wrote to Thompson,

> I don't know whether you have heard that the great Whymper is about to attack the Rockies during 1901–2–3. He has got the two finest Swiss guides Klucker and Pollinger and two others and will go to Banff and polish off all the peaks. I am dreadfully sorry for it will all be done for advertisement. Why the devil he won't leave them alone I don't know. He will simply go and gobble up the whole lot. As a hunting ground for amateurs the country was big enough and to spare but when a professional team lets itself loose—well all I can say is damm the man! I certainly can't get over there again next summer but if I could I would try my level best to spoil some of his game for him. There is one thing, however, he can't do any exploring for its all done now. If the CPR don't take care they will over-do it. Why I am so mad about it is that it is not done for sport at all or because Whymper has any real liking for the hills. From beginning to end it is *dollars*.[6]

Collie also believed that Whymper would 'attack Mt Assiniboine and certainly should get up it—What an advertisement there will be! All the CPR organs will be blowing away like mad about it, however he hasn't got there yet.'[7]

Collie disliked Whymper for one very good reason. When Mummery was making his first brilliant ascents in the Alps many criticised his style of climbing as 'foolhardy'. Whymper was not only one of these but he was also jealous of him. Mummery's climbs had a quality comparable to the early Whymper ascents and Mummery he saw as a rival. Collie must have known about the problems Mummery experienced when trying to break into the exclusive world of the Alpine Club and how he was blackballed on his first application. Collie could have no love for a man who was capable of writing about his friend, albeit privately, that he 'did not agree' that Mummery's death was a tremendous loss to the Alpine world.[8]

However, Collie was wrong about Whymper. He was not the man he had been in 1865. Whether the tragedy on the Matterhorn, when four of his companions were killed, affected his desire for the summits who can tell. But in 1900 he was 61 years old and his guides were bitterly disappointed in the man. Klucker wrote, 'It gradually became apparent to us that Whymper was merely there by way of propaganda for the CPR because we were never more than two days' march from the railway line. My eager wish to push forward and climb Assiniboine—a magnificent mountain . . . was not considered. We likewise advised an attack on Mt Columbia and Mt Robson. . . . In vain; the reply was: "I have no orders to do that".'[9] Whymper did however make the first ascent of Mt Collie—irony indeed!

Collie disliked not only the bagging of peaks by interlopers like Whymper but also the vulgarisation of the 'American Alps', as the Rockies were sometimes called. In particular the ignorance of some travellers reminded him only

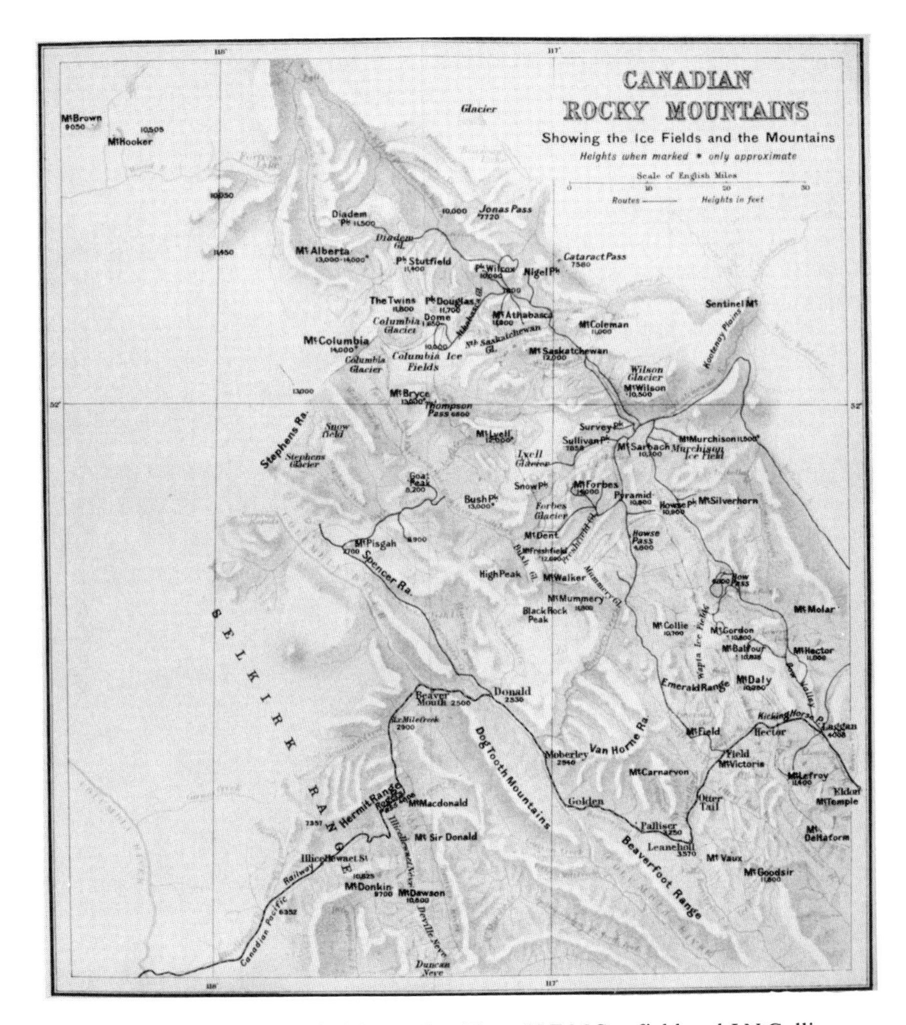

Map 4 Canadian Rocky Mountains. From H E M Stutfield and J N Collie. Climbing on the Himalaya and other Mountain Ranges, *permission from Longmans Green and Co.*

too well of similar people who cluttered up Alpine hotels. Stutfield returning homeward by train from Glacier House found one of the passengers 'was an American lady, who had ideas concerning the mountains. The crevasses on the Great Glacier, she maintained, were all artificial, they didn't even look natural she said; and it was no good trying to humbug her into believing that they were. It appears that not a few people from the States think that the glacier was put there by the CPR as an ornament—like fountains in the middle of a lawn; and one citizen of the Great Republic asked the manageress of the hotel if it was there when she arrived!'[10]

It was probably because Collie feared that the mountains he had taken such pains to discover would all have been climbed before he had a chance at them that he returned to Canada in 1902. There was still Forbes, believed by Collie to be perhaps the highest peak in the Canadian Rockies, possibly over 13,000 feet or even 14,000 feet high. He was quite wrong, for Forbes is only 11,852 feet, but it was still a magnificent mountain and the monarch of the region. Collie had been waiting since 1897 to climb her. However, the Reverend James Outram also had designs upon Forbes. Collie, unwilling to establish a race to the mountain, suggested they meet at its base and climb it together.

Outram was a good climber who was roaming through the Rockies each season with a party of guides from the CPR and with them polishing off a great many more peaks than Whymper. Collie resented him just as much. Outram, like Whymper, had played no part in the early exhausting exploratory work yet he was managing to make the first ascents of many first-class mountains discovered by others. Collie felt, perhaps unrealistically, that those who had done the exploration should have the first chance at the mountains. The least Outram could do would be to find out which mountains the pioneers particularly wanted to claim and leave those alone. Outram made the mistake of asking a friend of Collie's to propose him for the Alpine Club. On Collie's advice the friend declined and Collie was doubtful if he would ever vote for him should he be put up in the future. Collie was disappointed that Outram had climbed the spectacular Mt Assiniboine because he felt Walter Wilcox, who attempted the peak in 1901, should have been 'the first man there'.

In 1902 Collie was very anxious to climb mountains, as opposed to exploring. To Thompson he wrote. 'The Rockies are booming like anything now and next year many more will be no longer virgin summits. Stutfield is very keen to go out again, for climbing alone. ... I should very much like to have a try at Forbes or Freshfield or Bryce and Columbia but I guess many other people will be wanting to do the same thing.'[11]

Outram had suggested that he and Collie go on a complete expedition together. Collie declined the invitation, only agreeing to meet him at Forbes. He still had the idea of going northwards to Columbia and by keeping this secret he hoped to keep 'as many scalps away from Outram as possible'.

It was in this exceedingly competitive spirit that, together with Stutfield and Woolley, he left for Canada in July 1902.

The country Collie had mapped during his three previous visits amounted to about 3,000 square miles but obviously dozens of geographical details needed to be cleared up. Whilst Collie intended to concentrate mainly on mountaineering, he could not resist the opportunity to fill in areas of his map that were still blank. During his previous visits many of the views from summits had been obscured by the smoke of forest fires and there were still many glaciers, ice-falls, rivers and valleys about which little was known. Moreover, the heights of many mountains were doubtful. The friends hoped to see the valleys on the south-west side of the Freshfield range, to investigate the untrodden Lyell ice field and view the complicated series of snow peaks rising from her, and to see if an easy pass existed between the Forbes and Freshfield groups of mountains.

With memories of the Bush River trip in his mind Collie decided that on this expedition luxury would be paramount. He had written to Fred Stephens, who was to outfit for them, that he wanted all quantities of food doubled. A 1,000 pounds weight of 'necessaries' was to be taken in advance to Bear Creek some 50 miles away and cached. Good tents were to be taken and Collie, to the disgust of the trail men, took a camp bed! The friends were planning a six-week trip and wanted to be well-prepared for battle with Outram. This may have been why they engaged a Swiss guide, Hans Kaufman, from the CPR. He and his brother Christian, who was with

40 Collie and the camp bed, Canada 1902. *Photo from Collie's slide collection, with permission of the Alpine Club.*

Outram's outfit, were excellent men and Collie hoped that the strength of their climbing party would be greatly increased by his addition. G M Weed, an American climber, made up the mountaineers. Fred Stephens came along and brought trail men and a cook.

Apart from the loss of half their luggage by the railway company no mishaps marred the beginning of the trip. They were able to borrow many articles, one of which was a 'magnificent bedroom mattress'. This, together with Collie's bed, gave the trail men many an opportunity for sarcasm but the unwieldly train eventually tottered out of Laggan in the direction of Bear Creek.

What a pleasure it was to amble down the Bow Valley on this occasion. The miles of timber now lay either side of the pony track, reminding them of their tribulation in 1897. After three hours they found their advanced camp set up and ready with two additional men, Dave Tewksbury and Clarence Murray. Dave was a lumberman and an artist with the axe.

The journey to Bear Creek passed without incident. Collie recalled how different it all was from the Bush Valley trip for the weather was fine, the food plentiful and even the mosquitoes not too bad. As for the horses, they were a complete contrast to those of the previous trip. Not one of them tried to drown herself 'or swam about in the rivers merely for the fun of wetting our baggage. Everything, in short, seemed to combine to make our pilgrimmage the pleasant picnic we had intended it to be.'[12]

The old Bear Creek camping ground was soon reached. This time Mt Murchison, which had figured largely in Collie's thoughts on previous trips, was not to be by-passed but snapped up at once. Before they began the ascent, Collie was found routing around among the trees, compass in hand, apparently talking to himself. His abstract air was suddenly changed to one of joy as he scrabbled in the earth at the foot of a large pine. From its depths he produced two bottles, one of whisky and one of brandy, that he had cached there in 1897. Toasts being drunk, they sallied forth for Murchison.

The men believed that the summit of this mountain, which was composed of numerous pinnacles, probably lay too far east for it to be climbed in one day from Bear Creek. Therefore they set off to reconnoitre the mountain. One of Murchison's pinnacles overhung their valley and after a climb of seven hours they were on its top. They found themselves on the summit of one of two peaks of equal height but their clinometer made theirs the highest. They had chosen, quite by chance, the highest pinnacle of Murchison, the ascent of which was their first virgin summit of the holiday. Murchison however, 'had to suffer the degradation which sooner or later is the lot of most mountains in this region; and to be classed henceforth among the fraudulent or semi-fabulous mountain monsters which have so long imposed upon the makers of maps'. So far from it being 15,781 or 13,500 feet, as Hector imagined, Collie only made it 11,300 feet above sea level. This was to come down even further—Murchison is now assessed at 10,936 feet high.

The time had now come to journey to the Freshfield mountains and Forbes. Outram had been away in the north-west for two weeks and the friends wondered apprehensively what scalps he had won. When they arrived at his camp on Glacier Lake he was still away. Shortly, however, Outram's wagon train could be seen crossing the river fresh from new conquests. It was a great disappointment for Collie to hear from Outram that his party had just made the first ascent of Mt Columbia and Mt Lyell. Mt Columbia's ascent, in particular, was a blow.

As agreed in London, the two parties now joined up but before ascending Forbes they decided to warm up first on Mt Freshfield. They were a large party which they split into two, each being led by one of the Kaufman brothers. The trail Peyto had cut to Freshfield in 1897 was still passable and an easy journey took them to the snout of the Freshfield glacier. Here they made camp. Again they could tell that the height of the mountain had been overestimated. Collie thought that the smoke haze in 1898 and the bad weather of 1900 had caused them to overestimate most of the mountains they had not climbed or seen close up.

On 4 August the party began the ascent. They followed a similar route to that taken by Collie, Baker and Sarbach in 1897. Collie was anxious that the weather should hold for there was much he wanted to see from the summit. They experienced no problems up the steep snow slope on to the higher ice plateau for the glacier was in good condition. Only on the top section of the east ridge did several large crags of rock with difficult faces give trouble.

41 How the horses crossed the Canadian rivers, 1910. Men on shore making raft. *Photo from Collie's slide collection, with permission of the Alpine Club.*

They kept to the ridge but the rock was not firm. Hans Kaufman led Collie's team strongly all the way to the snow cornice near the summit. Collie was delighted with the summit view, for he could see that a low pass did exist between the Lyell and Freshfield ice fields and they named this Bush Pass. The west side of the mountain, a blank on Collie's map, as was the complicated geography of the south fork of the Bush Valley, was spread before them. Collie wrote. 'There is a great, if undefinable, pleasure in standing on a high mountain summit in a country but imperfectly known; so many uncertainties vanish in a moment, often with the comment "I thought so"; whilst a host of new possibilities and further queries take their place.'[13] They could also see that Forbes, like Freshfield, would have to come down in height. The view in some ways compensated Collie for the loss of Columbia, gleaming away in the west.

During 6 and 7 August, trail was cut along the left bank of the canyon leading up to the base of Forbes. Hot sun was melting her snows and they heard the avalanches thunder down the eastern precipices. Forbes was a magnificent looking pyramid of a peak but the route they chose, the south-west ridge, is a long, demanding and occasionally loose climb, not often done today. The party bivouacked on the southern slopes of the mountain where 'Forbes, grim and majestic, stood sentinel over us'. Since it was 9 August, Coronation Day, a fine peak to the south was named Coronation Peak.

The guides woke the party at dawn. A walk up a small snow-covered glacier soon brought them to the south-west arête. From here the climbing was hard for it was steeper than they had anticipated and holds not so abundant. Collie found Forbes more beautiful at a distance than close up. Higher up the ridge became more difficult and exposed. They inched along, one moment astride the ridge, then clinging to the sides for there was no opportunity to avoid it. The climbers likened this part to the Zinal side of the Rothorn but the rock was not so good. Hans Kaufman at one point had a lucky escape when a chunk of rock came away in his hands. He only fell a few feet and managed to grab the edge of the arête in time. The ridge, according to Woolley, seemed only held together by frozen snow. Soon, however, the difficulties were overcome and a short snow slope led them to the summit.

Again the view cleared up many problems particularly concerning the country lying between Forbes and Bush Peak. The party descended the north-west face down steep snow where steps had to be cut for 1,500 feet. At 8 p.m. their bivouac site was reached.

The following morning Collie, Outram and Weed set out to explore Bush Pass. After a lazy start the rest of the party tramped back to the camp where they met Fred Stephens, greatly worried for their safety, about to set out on a rescue mission, ice axe in hand. Fred thought poorly of mountain climbing for the sake of it.

In the next two days the Collie and Outram parties went their separate ways. Outram to ascend ten new peaks, including Mt Bryce, and four new passes, Collie and his party to ascend Howse Peak before moving on to Glacier Lake near the Lyell ice field.

At Glacier Lake they found a fierce forest fire ravaging this beautiful area, which is today the most popular base camp for climbing Lyell and the Forbes group of mountains. Collie was quite sure Outram had started it by failing to dampen his fire and parts of Glacier Lake were ruined for years to come. It would have been impossible to travel through the burning forest so the men built a raft, The Glacier Belle, in order to ferry their supplies to the far end of the lake where they hoped to make a base camp. A large stretch of hillside cleared by avalanches protected them from the fire. The raft carried them slowly and safely up the lake. Dave Tewksbury was captain and for some hours they floated amongst the most stupendous scenery. When they landed they made camp in the forests from which a journey of exploration to the fourth great ice field of the Rockies was begun.

42 The Reverend James Outram (*left*) after the ascent of Mt Forbes. *From Collie's slide collection, with permission of the Alpine Club.*

43 How the men crossed the Canadian rivers. 'The Glacier Belle' with Dave Tewksbury as captain on Glacier Lake, 19 August 1902. Stutfield on the shore. *Photo from Collie's slide collection, with permission of the Alpine Club.*

Collie enjoyed this trip to the Lyell ice field. It was good to be able to wander through the snows with no sense of urgency and to map and explore an area probably visited before only by Outram. The upper Lyell glacier, like the Columbia ice field, was a big snowfield. The view of Forbes from here was a startling one. She no longer appeared a 'slender, elegant pyramid, as from the hill above Glacier Lake; but an unshapely monster, grand and terrible under the rapidly darkening sky, and of most forbidding aspect'.[14]

They attempted Mt Lyell, 'a singularly uninteresting and unimposing mountain', or so they thought, mainly because Hans Kaufman and Woolley wanted to. However, deteriorating weather turned them back, much to Hans's disappointment. 'You will regret it' he said. Instead they ascended a small protuberance of snow below the level of the mist, from which to view the surrounding countryside. Glissading down, Collie knocked his pipe out of his mouth and, in trying to save it, fell rapidly head over heels to the bottom.

The friends decided to make a leisurely return to civilisation and to take in one or two peaks on the way. They climbed Mt Noyes near the Waterfowl Lakes where Collie saw the country to the east of Murchison for the first time. In the distance lay the Kootenay Plains now hardly visited by man but

44 Snow climbing on a Canadian mountain 1902. *From Collie's slide collection, with permission of the Alpine Club.*

45 Climbing Neptuak, Canada 1902. *From Collie's slide collection, with permission of the Alpine Club.*

46 Neptuak Peak from Neptuak Pass. *Photo by H E M Stutfield from Collie's slide collection at the Alpine Club.*

which a century ago were busy with the trappers and Indians trading at their annual fair. When they reached Laggan, a few days still remained so the whole outfit went south. They had their eyes on Neptuak, a mountain Woolley regarded as 'comparable to the Eiger from the Little Scheideck'.

They followed the north-west ridge. The going was easy enough to begin with but soon they were stopped by formidable slabby walls and towers of rock. To the left they looked down vast precipices facing Desolation Valley and to the right shale slopes and couloirs sheeted with ice were the home of rocks and icicles which fell frequently from above. They kept to the arête and the climb turned out to be 'the best of the trip'.

At last the time came to say goodbye to Hans and Fred. It would be many a long year before Collie was free to return to these mountains that he had come to love so much. As for Fred Stephens, who had done so much to make their expedition successful with his cheerfulness and hard work, Collie wrote, 'It was worth travelling to the Rockies only to spend a fleeting month in his company. May he continue to prosper, and may it not be long before we meet again.'[15] It was to be eight years before they did.

Chapter 11

The Land of the Midnight Sun

> There lay before us the long range of the Lofoddens, 70 or 80 miles distant, from near Bodö, like the jaw of a great shark, so many and so jagged were their points. (*Everest*—A Journey through Norway)

One can only assume that Collie's fight up the Bush River in 1900 dulled for him the charms of the Rocky Mountains, at least for a season, for in 1901 he went, with Hermann Woolley, to the Lofoten Islands which lie off the coast of Norway.

These islands were once under an ice sheet and in places the valleys are U-shaped in section, their polished walls formed by ice. The rocks are often glacier-worn up to heights of 2,000 feet and the valleys have little vegetation and few trees. Collie described the islands as 'worn down to the bone'. But the incredible beauty of water and jagged spikes of rock set against vast expanses of sky make up for the loss of gentler scenery. The islands are inside the Arctic Circle but washed by the Gulf Stream which keeps the surrounding waters free from ice. Because they are so far north it is permanently daytime during the summer months; the sun slowly circles the sky, bathing land and heavens in wonderful lights. This characteristic gives the islands their other name—The Land of the Midnight Sun. The climber can, if energy permits, scale the rocks for the whole 24 hours of every day. It is all together a wild, rugged and very beautiful land and nowhere else was to remind Collie so much of his beloved Skye, although the mountain forms are wilder and more extraordinary.

It was possible for Collie to say in a lecture at the Alpine Club the following year. 'What now is the knowledge of this Club of these mountains? I am afraid that it is not very extensive. Professor Bonney, in 1869 went there ... but after him I believe that the next party was that of Woolley, Hastings and Priestman in 1897.'[1]

Cecil Slingsby had in fact climbed the remarkable Svolvaergeita—Goats' Peak—hardly a mountain but a striking pinnacle of rock crowned with two rock 'horns' that rises out of the town of Svolvaer, for which feat he was made a freeman of the tiny fishing port. But the Lofoten were, as Collie said, rarely visited by the mountaineer.

In 1901 most of the Lofoten peaks were still virgin and even today many rock faces remain untouched. Collie was naturally attracted to this unexplored paradise of peaks set in a thousand seas. Although the climbers were slow to come this was not due to the character of the rock which is firm gabbro, gneiss and granite, resembling that of Skye and of the Chamonix aiguilles. There were other reasons for the absence of the mountaineer.

In Collie's day the journey, across the North Sea, took about a week. This could be most unpleasant if the weather was rough, as it often was. The mountains themselves have no large glaciers and so the exciting snow world of the Alps was missing at a time when rock climbing by itself was not the popular sport it is today. But the height of these peaks probably kept away the mountaineer most of all. None of them rise much above 4,000 feet and one could go to Skye for comparable climbing with half the bother. However, what these peaks lack in height they make up for in situation and in the excellence of their rock routes, as Collie was to discover.

Woolley had first visited these islands in 1897, the year Collie first explored Canada. One can imagine the discussions that took place between them on the merits of the two countries. Whilst Woolley accompanied Collie to Canada in 1898, it was not until three years later that he was able to woo Collie away from the Rockies.

Before they arrived at the islands the men joined Mrs Le Blond, first President of the Ladies' Alpine Club, and her husband in the Lyngen Fjord district. Here little climbing was done but at a sumptuous banquet in their tent Mrs Le Blond's husband was rescued by Woolley from a scourge of mosquitoes that suddenly attacked him. For a moment Collie must have seen shades of the Bush River. They only stayed a day or two for they had plans to meet Hastings and Howard Priestman on the mainland east of Lofoten. It was the first time Collie and Hastings had been on an expedition together since Nanga Parbat. Except for Collie, all the men had been to the Lofoten before.

On 2 August the friends took the boat to Svolvaer and from there crossed with their luggage in two boats to South Austvagoy Island near the head of the Ostnes Fjord, a peninsula immediately north-east of Svolvaer.

Their first expedition, by Collie and Woolley, was up one of the Langstrandtinder and is particularly notable for the view it gave Collie from the summit. As he was constantly to be attracted back to the Rockies by such mountains as Columbia and Forbes so it was the charms of the 'excessively savage looking peak in the background' that was to bring him again to the Lofoten. The peak was Rulten—two splendid summits separated by a deep gap, the east peak being the third highest summit in the islands. Woolley in 1897 had already attempted this mountain from the eastern side but failed in bad weather conditions. Collie, looking at the northern side, thought it was almost impossible but herein lay the challenge. From the summit Collie could also see Higraftind—Lofoten's second highest peak, and they both agreed that success was more likely there.

On 7 August they made their way by boat to Liland and began the ascent of Higraftind. From the shore, thickets of birch along the Lilandsdal Valley led them to the foot of a precipice which marks the upper part of Higraftind. Ascent was by the south-west ridge via a succession of ledges and rock gullies and the summit consisted of large standing stones with tremendous drops each side. Woolley was sent on alone because Collie wanted to photograph him proudly planting his ice axe on the top-most pinnacle. From Woolley's

47 Gjeitgaljartind, Lofoten. *Photo from Collie's slide collection, with permission of the Alpine Club.*

gesticulations it was obvious something was amiss. Collie, joining him, saw to his dismay that the real summit lay 20 feet away across a miniature Thearlaich Dubh Gap. Thirty feet of polished rock seemed to foretell failure on their side and the opposite wall was a series of overhanging blocks. By careful exploration they discovered a crack which enabled them to get into the gap but they could not get up the overhangs. Some time was spent attempting it before they decided to follow a ledge which ran around a corner. Edging along it they passed underneath the summit of the mountain and then an upward crack was found. Rapidly they climbed up this onto the summit. Collie wrote 'We lingered for a long time on the summit; but in a land where, at that time of the year, night never comes, what need was there to hurry?'[2]

Three days of pouring rain followed their success on Higraftind but all the men were waiting for the weather to clear in order to mount an assault on Rulten.

By 10 August the weather was warm and moist and the friends rowed in their boat to a small bay called Flaeskvik. It was agreed that the south-west arête of Rulten offered the best chance of success. The fairly easy ground up to the arête was nevertheless very steep, necessitating great care for

48 Summit of Gjeitgaljartind, 1901. Cairn built by E Hogrenning. Woolley nearest cairn. Others in party—Hogrenning, G Hastings, H Priestman *With permission of the Alpine Club.*

vegetation alternated with slabs of rock. Ultimately they climbed onto the south-west arête but the real difficulties had not yet begun. The ridge immediately steepened and in slimness Collie compared it to the Grépon. Collie was leading but it soon became apparent that a climb straight up the ridge was impossible; great slabs with only small cracks forced him to explore the sides for a suitable traverse. On the left, difficult slabs stopped him, and to the right a ledge, which he followed for a short distance along the mountain side, led him to smooth rocks 'bending over into space'. He thought of climbing straight up from here but decided against it. Later, on the descent, they were able to see that this too would have led them into a difficult situation. The attempt was abandoned about 800 feet below the summit. Collie wrote afterwards 'Rulten is undoubtedly a difficult peak; at present I have seen no way up it, but probably by a systematic attack, and by trying every side, a weak spot would be discovered.'[3]

Their camp site was overlooked by the rock pinnacles of Geitgaljartind, looking like a little Dru. They thought this grand peak deserved a little attention. The mountain has some excellent climbing on it including a sensational east ridge, and because of the many pinnacles much of the climbing is difficult and exposed.

49 Collie at the Lofoten camp, 1901. *Photo from Collie's slide collection, with permission of the Alpine Club.*

It took them a long time to leave camp on the morning of 14 August, for Hastings had to be dissuaded from salting and boiling a mighty leg of mutton declared by all but himself to be bad. Due to Hastings' domesticity their camp was well provided for. He had, with characteristic good humour, collected pots and pans from various houses on the island and together with the many bottles of wine that always accompanied Collie, the camp had assumed the appearance of a really 'first-class gipsy encampment'.

Due to the late start it was very hot work through the first 1,000 feet of birch scrub and ferns before the north-east ridge was reached. This proved an easy rock scramble to the summit. It was surprisingly easy all the way considering the impossible appearance of the mountain. They had all expected another Rulten.

Many more days were spent in this fashion; days broken up with fishing trips on the fjords, swimming and talking. Collie was sorry to leave and the following year he found it a difficult decision to make as to where to spend his holiday. Outram's campaign was the deciding factor that sent him again to Canada. However, in 1903 he went once more to Norway on possibly the most exciting trip of the three he made.

On that occasion he was accompanied by Cecil Slingsby and his son Will, together with Collie's friend Northall-Laurie. The principal objective of the trip was Rulten.

Arriving in Lofoten on 23 July they had before them four glorious weeks of pleasure. An elderly fisherman, Christian, was engaged to look after their camp and cook. Before Rulten the friends decided to get fit by visiting Moskenesöy, furthest west of all the islands and possibly the most striking. Here mountains rise straight from the sea with knife-edge ridges that overlook slabs of 1,000 feet in height where even a bird finds problems in perching.

It took a long time to find a space flat enough to accommodate the tents. Wood for cooking, never a problem in the Rockies, was a permanent one here. Collie wrote to Charles Thompson: 'Wood for cooking had all to be brought in ships for perhaps a hundred miles ... after the Rockies it is a great change to have to carefully buy small pieces of wood about a foot long by three inches thick at an exorbitant price ... I think wood is almost as dear as food in the Lofoten islands, and if biscuits were rather more inflammable they might be taken as a cheap substitute.'[4]

From the camp rose the island's highest mountain, Hermandalstind, which they had no problems in climbing. However, their attention was arrested by a very sharp rock tooth called Munken which resembled in many ways the

facing page
50 Slingsby in Norway. *Photo from Collie's slide collection, with permission of the Alpine Club.*
51 Mosadlen camp, Lofoten 1903. *Left to right:* Christian, Collie, Will Slingsby, W C Slingsby. *Photo from Collie's slide collection, with permission of the Alpine Club.*

Bhasteir Tooth in Skye. Collie was naturally anxious to climb it. Now 42 years old he was quite willing to bring young Will Slingsby up to the front when the problems began. Collie described the climb:

> No difficulty was found in getting as far as the base of the tooth, where the real climbing began. After carefully scanning the whole face with our glasses, it was evident that to start with the left-hand side of the western ridge would be the easiest side to attack, the ridge itself being too steep. For some distance we managed to climb from point to point, but the slabs got steeper and the pitches more difficult. I was leading, and ultimately found myself unable to climb further; a traverse some short distance out to the left showed nothing easier, whilst to the right I was only able to get as far as the nose of the ridge, which at this point was clean cut to a solid angle, almost perpendicular for at least forty to fifty feet. Across this solid angle, round on to the other, or southern face of the mountain, was a crack. If I could have climbed up so as to get my feet into this crack, which sloped inwards, it could have been used as a traverse for about six feet to a small shelf, from which there seemed an easier way up. There was, however, an alternative: using the crack to hold on to, I might make a hand traverse across that six feet, but there would be no support for my feet. The more I looked at it the less I liked it; perhaps I should find difficulty in getting back; moreover I could get no help from the rope; yet it seemed the only way out of our difficulties.
>
> Further investigations showed nothing better, and after being dangled at the end of an eighty-foot rope and taxing the patience of the party for a considerable space by having all the fun to myself, whilst they sat on a ledge, the conclusion arrived at was, it must be the traverse or nothing. Will Slingsby came as far as the nose, and looked round it at the traverse; he thereupon announced his intention of trying it. I saw that, by standing at the corner of the ridge, with the rope hitched through the crack, even if Will had to let go altogether whilst on the traverse, no harm could have come to him; he would be quite safe as long as I was there to hold the rope into the crack. The change of leaders was most successful; Will traversed along to the small shelf, where, hanging on by one hand, he cleared away from the shelf some moss and soil; he then pulled himself on to the shelf; thence clambering up a short distance further, he sat himself down on a spacious platform, and was ready to pilot the rest of the party across the nose of the mountain. Beyond that point the climbing became easier, and not long afterwards we reached the summit.[5]

By 6 August they all felt fit enough to renew the attack on Rulten. Hiring a boat they rowed to a small bay, Reknes, east of Rulten, and were able to camp at the foot of the peak. Collie had prophesied that the mountain would only fall after a systematic attack and that is what happened.

In 1901 he had been beaten back on the southern ridge so Collie and Laurie decided to reconnoitre the mountain before making any other attempts. They

facing page
52 Climbing Munken, Lofoten, 1903. Collie (first man), Will Slingsby and W C Slingsby. *Photo from Collie's slide collection, with permission of the Alpine Club.*

53 Rulten, Lofoten, 1904. *Photo from Collie's slide collection, with permission of the Alpine Club.*

went first to the northern side and climbed up the Snö Skar glacier. As they passed underneath the precipices that ran along the north side of the peak they were unable to find any possiblity of a route from the glacier onto the mountain's summit ridge. At the head of the glacier was a pass from which a ridge led straight up to the summit of Rulten 1,000 feet above. Composed of bare slabs it looked too difficult for them but Collie thought the western side was more hopeful. He descended a snow gully on the west side of the pass for some way and then by climbing a chimney was able to get onto the ridge some distance above the pass. Collie, looking at the west face from a sideways position, thought a route would be fairly easy to find once a snow patch some distance up had been reached. On return to camp Collie announced that 'the mountain was a fraud and that we could easily get to the top in less than an hour from the pass.'[6] In this, he greatly underestimated Rulten.

On 10 August the whole party set off for the western face. At lunchtime the pass was reached and the difficulties began at once. The first pitch involved a descent in order to traverse along the western face to the snow patch. Collie, as last man, experienced great unease on this descent where even such mediocre rope support as they had was missing. The traverse itself was nasty with a dangerous combination of grass and soil covering small footholds. When they got into the snow patch a wide gully opened up, seemingly to the mountain summit. By a combination of rock and ice work they proceeded to climb it. Some distance up another gully which looked easier branched off to the left and seemed to connect up with the ridge. For about 200 feet they followed it but found that they could neither get onto the ridge from it nor traverse out to rejoin the main gully. Collie for a moment thought he was on the Grépon, so similar did it all seem. They had no choice but to descend again to the main gully where they spent the next five hours fighting every inch of the way.

At an early stage Collie gave the lead up to Will Slingsby, who having proved himself on Munken, was again to show his ability. At one point the gully was blocked by a cave with an overhanging roof about 40 feet above. About 25 feet up a large block lay across the cave opening; if they were not to be stopped they had to reach it. Will wriggled his way up a wet crack at the back of the cave and then traversed across the wall until he got onto the block. Another traverse took him out onto the face from where he was able to ascend and then get back into the gully above the block. Eight hours after they had left the pass Will led them onto the summit of Rulten's west peak. But great disappointment awaited them—about a third of a mile away lay Rulten's east peak and it was quite obviously about 20 feet higher. The ridge that connected the two looked quite hopeless.

No more could be done that day. As it was it took them four hours to get back to the pass. It seemed unthinkable to abandon Rulten having spent so much time and thought on her, so it was inevitable that an attempt on the eastern peak should be made. Having already decided that it would be too difficult to climb the eastern peak via the gap between it and the western peak, three other options remained: the northern face which was one long precipice, the eastern ridge or a savage-looking gully lying between the two peaks on the south side of the mountain. They had seen into this gully the previous day and it looked difficult. Even if it was climbed they did not know whether they could get out of it onto the eastern peak. The eastern ridge itself was steep and from below looked exposed and unpleasant. After much discussion it was decided to attempt the gully which at least was filled with snow even though at a steep angle.

On 15 August they began the ascent up an enormous tongue of snow that had avalanched down the gully onto the glacier. At the top of the snow tongue it narrowed to the neck at the bottom of the gully but a bergschrund, about 20 feet wide, descending into gloomy depths barred the way. A snow bridge lay across this and one by one they carefully walked over it to the foot of the gully. Endless steps were cut and Collie, tiring of this exhausting work, repeatedly tried to find a way up the rock walls of the gully, always being forced back to the snow. Several hours of labour brought them within view of the top of the gully, still a long way above them. They could see that the gully only led to the gap between the east and west peaks. Reluctantly they turned back but did not feel as if they had been easily beaten. Collie and Slingsby both agreed that not even amoung the couloirs of the Mont Blanc aiguilles had they seen such rock slabs. The descent had to be undertaken faces to the snow all the way and fears of a rock avalanche did not heighten their excitement.

The next day they returned reluctantly to Svolvaer but the memories of Rulten and her unvanquished eastern peak did not leave them. Collie believed it would never be climbed but Slingsby persuaded him out of this pessimistic frame of mind. The upshot was that, strengthening their party with a Norwegian, they sailed back to Reknes.

Again everything was organised for an early start on the mountain. They began the ascent up the eastern ridge, ruled out before as too hard and exposed. After a short distance, however, it soon became apparent that the ridge was far from difficult. A very convenient gully ran right up the nose of the ridge and this enabled them to climb rapidly upwards. The last part of the ridge that had looked particularly hopeless they were able to avoid by descending onto the southern face and traversing it to the final peak. With great excitement they climbed to the summit, glad that at last 'this desperate mountain had been conquered'.

The ascent of Rulten's highest peak was undoubtedly the climax of their holiday. Lazy days followed around the camp but soon the disreputable life was once more packed up in boxes and it was homewards to the frock coats and another year of professional life in big cities.

54 From a Lofoten ridge. *Photo from Collie's slide collection, with permission of the Alpine Club.*

55 Surveying in Canada, 1911. Other party members were Yates, Mumm and Inderbinen. *Photo from Collie's slide collection, with permission of the Alpine Club.*

Collie's days of long expeditions were drawing in. The following year he returned to the Lofoten with a large party which included Cecil Slingsby, his son Will and young cousin Morris who was to become an excellent climber, learning his craft in the Himalaya. Morris was killed, as were two of his brothers and one of Slingsby's sons, in the Great War. Collie had also invited a colleague from University College and Woolley made up the party. Slingsby remarked that Collie and Woolley were his ideal companions for the Lofoten and even on difficult climbs nothing could perturb them. But this visit in 1904 was to be Collie's last to these islands.

In 1906 he went with Woolley to the Italian Alps but Collie confided in Charles Thompson; 'We did not do much big climbing but got up a few minor peaks. The fact of the matter is, Woolley is getting old.'[7] He was 60 at the time and most probably troubled by the rheumatism that was to end his climbing career.

From 1906 to 1910 Collie spent every summer in Scotland. He wrote to Charles Thompson that pressure of work was keeping him away from Canada and indeed from 1902 when he became a Professor at University College, the time he could spend away from the university was severely curtailed. It was impossible to stretch his holiday that little bit further and he often had to spend part of his summer holiday in the labs. Also his friends were either getting old, like Woolley and Slingsby, or others like Stutfield were actually retiring from climbing all together as family responsibilities took precedence. As Collie rather plaintively remarked, 'I am left with no one else to climb with now.'

However, in 1910 and 1911 Collie joined up with Arnold Mumm, another Rocky Mountain enthusiast, who was on Longstaff's successful Trisul expedition in 1907. Their first season was taken up with an attempt on the Rockies' highest peak, Mt Robson. Robson, or so it was thought, had been climbed in 1909 by the Reverend G B Kinney and party. Mumm, who had spent 1909 in Canada, had met Kinney on his descent from the mountain and heard from him an account of the first ascent he had just made. Mumm's party were disappointed because they had planned to make the first ascent themselves. Nevertheless they carried out a reconnaissance of the mountain in very bad weather and in 1910 Collie joined Mumm in an attempt to make the second ascent. Snow storms and rain drove them back so they journeyed northwards to the virgin country north of the Yellowhead Pass, which was also to be the scene of their explorations in 1911. Many years later, however, the Reverend Kinney admitted that his patriotic zeal to claim Robson for his own country and the Alpine Club of Canada had made him lie. He had not in fact reached the top and Robson was first climbed by the American MacCarthy and the Austrian guide Conrad Kain, in 1913.

Collie was thinking of returning to Canada in 1914 but the insecure European situation prevented him from doing so. By the time the war had finished in 1918 Collie was nearly 60. While this would not necessarily have prevented him from returning to the far flung places of his youth, inflation and the Depression certainly did.

Chapter 12

The Old Man

Just as on a ship the master is called the Old Man so it was in the organic laboratory for Collie was invariably known as the Old Man, a title of which he was very proud for he knew all that in it lay—unbounded respect, admiration and affection. (*Obituaries of Fellows of the Royal Society*, 4, 1942–4)

Unlike most of his friends and colleagues Collie did not marry and never came near to it. He did, however, envy his friends their marriages and wrote to Hastings that as far as he could see they were much better men for it. Because he was not distracted by the pressure of family life he was able to devote himself wholeheartedly to the mountains and to his career. Although his life as a scientist was busy and fulfilling, he still regarded the mountains as his first love. Nevertheless, it was University College that claimed him most of all during the years of middle-age and, because he did not have the time to travel far, all but put an end to his large expeditions.

There were many areas of organic chemistry in which Collie became involved during the years of his Professorship from 1902 until his retirement in 1928. But, of the two most exciting, the development of the neon lamp and the transmutation of the elements, one was to be taken up by others and the other was to be discredited.

Collie claimed that he developed the first neon lamp and his scientific colleagues recognised this in their tributes to him on his death. Unlike the question of his involvement with the discovery of neon, Collie did leave a description of how this lamp was made in a letter to another professor at University College. This letter began: 'There are two things worth recording in any obituary notice of yours truly: 1) the *first photograph* ever taken by means of X-ray of metal in the human body I was *responsible* for it. 2) I constructed what was in reality the *first neon lamp*.'[1]

Although this letter, in the University College archives, continues with a description of the X-ray photograph the page in which the lamp is described is missing. Again one can only surmise.

After neon was discovered there was no attempt by other scientists to reproduce Ramsay's experiments until ten years had elapsed. Possibly scientists regarded the technique of gas manipulation as being too difficult or thought of neon as no more than a scientific curiosity. It was, in any case, very difficult to provide neon in sufficiently large quantities for experimentation. During 1908 Collie was working with a very small quantity of neon lent to him by Ramsay. He noticed 'that as the gas escaped at atmospheric pressure from a Töpler pump, up through mercury into an inverted test-tube, each bubble glowed with a fire-red glow'.[2] Other experiments showed that if you sealed up neon in a glass tube with mercury and then shook the tube the glow was considerable. It was well-known that gases could be made to shine if shaken up with mercury but what impressed Collie about this experiment was the degree of brightness obtained from neon which far exceeded the brightness from any other gas under the same conditions. For example, a tube filled with helium at 100 mm pressure only gave a very faint bluish glow when shaken. At this stage Collie only had 5 cc of pure neon, almost the entire world's supply, and with no prospects of obtaining any more without considerable time and effort, his experiments had to cease. Luck was with him however, for whilst his experiments were in progress Georges Claude of the Paris Institute perfected his process for large-scale production of liquid air. Claude, on Collie's request, sent Ramsay 40 litres of a mixture of helium, neon and nitrogen that he had obtained during the liquefaction of air. From the mixture Collie and his colleague in the labs, H E Watson, were able to obtain almost pure neon by fractional absorption of the gases by charcoal cooled in liquid air. Collie recalled, with delight, how the world's supply of pure neon was no longer to be restricted to the two small tubes, inverted over mercury, which stood on Ramsay's mantlepiece.

Collie and Watson were now able to carry out a series of experiments with neon. At first Collie thought that a glow could always be obtained if mercury and neon were shaken together but this was not the case. He described the experiments in his paper 'Note on a Curious Property of Neon' reproduced in the *Proceedings of the Royal Society of Edinburgh*, May 1909. Collie filled many tubes, passing mild or violent discharges through them, and got varying degrees of light.

> Some [tubes] were produced that glowed at both ends but not in the middle, others would glow only in the middle, and some at only one end. This abnormal state seems fairly permanent if no further electrical charges are brought near the tubes. If the neon has the slightest trace of moisture in it, no glow can be obtained; minute traces of carbon monoxide also diminish the power of glowing in a marked manner, but spectroscopic traces of hydrogen do not seem to have much effect. There is no doubt however that the purer the neon the more brilliant is the glow and at the same time it is more difficult to destroy

> the glow by shaking or electrifying the tube. An experiment was made in a silica tube. With the neon at atmospheric pressure the glow was very much brighter than in a glass tube under the same circumstances.

Collie made a variety of discharge tubes which he filled with pure neon. He was fascinated by the colour of the electric discharge in neon and would demonstrate this publicly. His cousin Dorothy Winkworth attended a Royal Society soirée in 1909 and recalled the thrill of the audience when in the darkness the neon began to glow. Collie's friend Sir Herbert Jackson remarked, 'Collie, I truly believe that you are far more interested in the colours of the discharge than in the striking phenomena you are observing.'[3]

No trace of a lamp has ever been found at University College and it is unlikely that Collie's lamp ever got beyond the construction of tubes in his laboratory. As he said, he made, *what was in reality*, the first neon lamp. The use of gas for illumination was not a new idea. In 1897, to celebrate the Queen's Jubilee, an arrangement of vacuum tubes, filled with gas, was erected above a house in Kensington. At night these glowed Vivat Victoria Regina. The first public exhibition of neon lighting was at the Paris Motor Show in November 1910 but some time between 1908 and 1910 Collie had made his lamp. The potential of neon, whilst foreseen by Collie, was not exploited by him. Watson did make preliminary applications for a patent in 1911 but did not continue. The commercial companies then rapidly moved in and it was very quickly seen that neon lamps could be operated off domestic lighting mains. By the 1920s big companies like Osram had taken up neon lighting.

It was typical of Collie not to be interested in the marketing of a lamp and also typical that he should be uninterested in obtaining the credit. As one friend wrote, 'Publicity, the appeal to "profanum vulgus" was wholly distasteful to him.'[4] For Collie the quest was over once he had established the possibilities of neon; now it was time to move onto other mysteries.

Collie's next scientific journey was indeed a mystery and was to remain one for some years.

About 1910 Collie and Ramsay began work independently on a series of experiments that led them to the same conclusion but also caused a scientific furore—the transmutation of the elements. They believed that the rare gases and hydrogen disintegrated spontaneously into other elements like neon when under the influence of an electrical discharge.

In February 1913 Collie and H S Patterson read a paper before The Chemical Society, 'The presence of neon in hydrogen after the passage of the electric discharge through the latter at low pressures.' Patterson wrote,

> Collie found that when calcium fluoride was subjected to cathode rays a gas was obtained which contained traces of neon. Later it was shown that if the tube contained a trace of oxygen the product of treatment with cathode rays always contained neon whether calcium fluoride was present or not.[5]

Years later Patterson recalled this meeting:

> Ramsay gave his reasons for his faith in transmutation. Collie followed and gave a history of his own work with extraordinary skill and dramatic effect. He explained his early disposition to believe in the possibilities of atomic disintegration in the electric discharge and the work which he had done from experiments with fluorspar under the discharge to the use of powdered glass and then to simple tubes. The constant appearance of neon under these conditions led him to believe it came from nowhere. Ramsay got up and said he was glad to feel the burden of advancing transmutation as a fact no longer rested on him. According to Professor Arthur Smithells who chaired the meeting, the scene transcended that ever experienced at a scientific meeting. The applause when Collie had finished his masterly exposition was beyond anything I have ever heard.[6]

Collie's work did not convince everyone. Many thought that neon from the atmosphere must be leaking into the discharge tubes. There were other possible sources of error. No one could repeat his experiments and Collie himself moved on to other things. The matter rested with no conclusive proof either way until 1927 when it was shown that the neon supposed to be produced in these experiments really derived from the air. What was confusing Collie and Ramsay was the recent knowledge of radioactivity. Ramsay had been carrying out experiments with the radioactive substance radium. It was his work with this solid that led him to believe in transmutation. But radium is remarkable for its active spontaneous disintegration. Both men were still working in nineteenth-century darkness. Much would be revealed once the potential of radioactivity and the real structure of the atom was understood.

Collie's work with the noble gases accounted for only ten out of the 78 papers he published between 1879 and 1928. However, his interest and his researches with gases certainly formed a large part of his life's work; possibly the most interesting to the layman but not necessarily his most important. His paper of 1907, 'Derivatives of the multiple keten group', is probably his most important paper in organic chemistry but this has only become apparent in recent years. His contribution to biochemistry has been assessed as follows:

> Collie's ideas, as presented in this paper, have had great significance. Amongst the major classes of low-molecular weight compounds of importance in primary metabolism are included the fatty acids ... [they] are one of the major classes of fundamentally important biological compounds. Related to the fatty acids are the 'polyketides' [a term first used by Collie]. These are not primary metabolites, being of restricted occurrence. They are usually aromatic and/or policyclic compounds, produced in the main by micro-organisms and by fungi in particular. This class includes such medically important compounds as the tetracycline antibiotics, the macrocyclic lactone antibiotics such as erythromycin, and the more recently discovered anti-tumour anthracyclines.
>
> Many of these compounds are phenolic. Collie's key observation was that in the laboratory, compounds with structures identical with, or closely related

to those of known polyketides, could be produced by cyclisation—condensations of synthetic compounds composed of repeating ketomethylene units (poly β-keto compounds). In the laboratory, such compounds are prepared by sequential condensation of acetic acid. ...

Collie's great insight was to suggest that in nature too, polyketides are produced from acetate *via* poly-β-keto methylene compounds, in basically the same way.

Collie, unfortunately, had no way of testing experimentally his ideas, and so they lay fallow until the Australian chemist A J Birch and his colleague F W Donovan rediscovered Collie's hypothesis, giving their ideas in a publication in the *Australian Journal of Chemistry*, 6, 360 (1953). Birch was at first unaware of Collie's work. However, when it was pointed out to him he gave full credit in subsequent papers and reviews. Birch presented his ideas in terms of his 'Acetate Hypothesis'. This was basically the same as Collie's theory of fifty years previously, namely the idea that polyketides (a term adopted from Collie by Birch) are formed by condensation—cyclisation of poly β-keto-methylene precursors, and that the latter are formed in turn from acetate by multiple biological Claisen-type condensations. Birch and his co-workers subsequently proved, in a now classical series of experiments using radiotracer techniques, the correctness of the basic theory.

Although Collie was concerned with polyketides (usually phenolic in nature), it turns out that essentially the same process is used in fatty acid biosynthesis, with the essential difference that whereas often one oxygen atom from each molecule of the initial acetic acid persists in the product, typically as a phenolic hydroxyl group, during fatty acid biosynthesis, all of the oxygen, except that in the terminal position, is reductively eliminated. Collie's ideas were therefore of wider significance than he himself would have guessed.[7]

Professor Smiles of University College, an old student of Collie's and a close friend, gave a fuller account of his scientific work in the *Obituaries of Fellows of the Royal Society*, 4 (1942–4):

Collie took a very broad view of his subject, the relations of the various parts of it to one another, and of the whole to other branches of chemistry. He was no specialist, anything which savoured of narrowness was repugnant to his nature, but he was a true philosopher. It was this that made his lectures and his teaching so interesting, for there always appeared to be something intriguing beyond the horizon of what he was saying.

Collie always seemed to publish reluctantly, but anything which he did publish was nearly always of a fundamental character; for example, dimethyl-pyrone and the related compounds which led to his really comprehensive generalization on the polyketides. He was the first to suggest a labile formula for benzene which was familiarly known in the laboratory as the 'Collywobble'. Moreover, his investigation of naturally occurring compounds, necessarily in small quantities, led him to devise his semi-micro method of organic analysis long before the days of Pregl ...

The essential feature of his later work was a desire to bring together in one comprehensive scheme the manifold products of organized matter. He succeeded in providing a scheme by which this difficult problem might be approached, whilst in his experimental work he certainly attained this object by uniting pyrone, coumarin, benzopyrone, pyridine, isoquinoline, naphthalene and the aromatic series through the fundamental polyacetic acids. This endeavour to construct an harmonious picture of many of nature's chemical features is in keeping with Collie's character and his artistic sense; he perforce could not be satisfied with leaving these features as fragments scattered through the general scheme of synthetic organic chemistry; he sought a common origin for them.

Collie's space formula for benzene (1897–1916) is witness to his mechanical skill and clear thinking in three dimensions. In this model (now in the Science Museum) the six carbon atoms were arranged at the corners of a regular octahedron and it was assumed that each could rotate about its centre and was endowed with power of movement relatively to the centre of gravity of the system. With these assumptions Collie was able to show the passing of the nucleus through the phases of the Kikulé formula and the condition indicated by the 'centric' formula. At the same time he found interpretation of Crum Brown and Gibson's rules of substitution. Here again Collie's fundamental attitude is manifest; he sought to harmonize the chief theories of the benzene nucleus and, while showing that they could be referred to a common origin, he demonstrated the validity of both.

Collie continued his transmutation experiments until 1914 and was, according to Ramsay, having little success. Ramsay went back to his work with radium. Little was then known about the body's reaction to constant exposure from radioactive material and Ramsay, who had retired in 1912, developed cancer of the nose from his constant contact with it. In July 1916 he died. Collie was not at the funeral but he did attend the unveiling of the Ramsay Memorial in Westminster Abbey which was a grand affair. Ramsay's plaque was placed beneath that to Sir Joseph Hooker. Just before his death, University College had hung a portrait of Ramsay by Mark Milbanke. At the unveiling, Collie, as chairman of the organising committee, referred to Ramsay as 'the greatest experimentalist I have ever seen'. Morris Travers cryptically remarked, 'he was a great deal more than that'.[8]

When Ramsay retired, Collie took over as Director of the chemical laboratories. One of his first tasks was the supervision of the building of a new chemical laboratory in Gower Place. From about 1920 until his retirement in 1928 Collie was not the man of former years at least not according to some of his students. One of his students, who knew nothing of his earlier work with Ramsay, wrote of him:

> I first saw Collie in 1921 when he was 62. He looked, walked and spoke like a much older man. ... He did more lecturing than most modern professors—a 2nd and 3rd year course on organic chemistry. The former read like a text book. His delivery was dull. They lasted last two terms one on alkaloids and one on terpenes ... these were his own choice and I found out later that he was out of date on those. Only once did I see Collie in a teaching lab, walking silently through. He was just a rather ghostly figure with a dull voice ... accepted by the students as an act of God.

It is a comment in marked contrast to the testimonials from his students in previous years, many of whom regarded him as a 'born teacher' whose talks were a 'revelation and inspiration to his students'. In the students' *Union Magazine* for 1908 they wrote:

> The subject of our dissertation for this number is 'The Old Man'. On most occasions he looks lean and hungry. . . . At all times he preserves a philosophic calm, whilst his corridor moments are positively reflective; in this connection, however, he was once observed to be somewhat moved; it is a long story and very much mixed up with a potash stick swimming in a metal balance pan. His smile is like the summer sun, rare and to be revelled in. What is once, and once only, to be mistaken for a smile, is neither rare not to be revelled in; it is inseparably connected with a small yield or a broken flask, the yield or the flask, as the case may be, belonging exclusively to oneself. If he has ever broken a flask or experienced a small yield, it must have been very much on the quiet. In his spare moments he is wont to christen mountain peaks, and play racquets with a distinguished Arts professor. A cigarette to him is like a wafer to a hungry man; he once smoked one; he was then filling his pipe. The appellation 'The Old Man' may not mean what it says, but it certainly says what it means to those who know him.[9]

In the year he retired Collie became external examiner at Durham University. A former pupil wrote, 'Sadly he was quite useless, and out of date even on straightforward lecture material. He did not come back for the usual 2nd and 3rd years.'

In 1928 Collie was asked to retire from University College and given the honour of Emeritus Professor. He did not retire willingly. He regarded it as forced upon him and his pension as 'inadequate', which troubled him for, as he wrote to Tom Wilson at Banff, it meant he could not travel far. Friends in the American Alpine Club managed to get him a free rail ticket on the Canadian Pacific Railway during the early 1930s and guaranteed to give him free accommodation in their clubhouse. For some reason he declined the invitation making the excuse that he was committed to Skye. Collie's friend, 'the distinguished Arts professor' W P Ker, who held the Chair of English at University College for 33 years, was also asked to retire. He wrote to Collie, 'After all I had done for the University of London they did that.' This was very much how Collie felt but he hung on just too long. With his home next door to the university and no family life to distract him it is understandable that he should do so. But, he was still haunting the labs up until 1933 when he was 74.

Chapter 13

Sligachan

> Collie is still up in Skye like an eagle in his eyrie but I hope he will get tired of that lonely vigil and come back to London. (F G Donnan, 1939, *Donnan and Masson Papers*, UC archives)

Most men carry out their best work in youth and middle-age; Collie was no exception. But in the years when he was seen, at least by some of his students, as a man very much on the edge of things, he was concentrating a great deal of energy in other directions.

He waged a vigorous campaign to get geography admitted as a research subject in the Faculty of Science at University College, calling on the might of the Royal Geographical Society to help him. Centuries of prejudice in favour of the Classics made it an uphill battle to get adequate teaching and research facilities for all science-based subjects in British universities, as Collie himself discovered. Cambridge led the way in establishing a geographical tripos. London University followed soon after, in the 1920s, due to the barrage of convincing evidence marshalled by Collie, the geographical associations and other universities.

In 1919 Collie became President of the Alpine Club, a position he cherished. During his presidency, in 1921, a joint committee of the Alpine Club and the Royal Geographical Society was set up organise expeditions to Mount Everest, the first to take place that year. This committee was made up of some of the most eminent men in the mountaineering and geographical worlds. The secretary of the Royal Geographical Society, Arthur Hinks, was made responsible for the daily administration of the committee but he was a domineering and pedantic man and there was constant friction between him and other members. He had a paranoid dislike of the press and publicity and did not want the newspapers anywhere near the expedition or its members. However, money was needed to finance the expedition and the committee decided to make financial agreements with the press for exclusive

release of photographs and expedition telegrams. Hinks did all he could to prevent this, which seems extraordinary when one considers what part publicity plays in modern expeditions. To Collie such narrowness of mind would have been an anathema and with characteristic humour he annoyed Hinks. He had an idea, now common to all expeditions big or small, but then a very novel suggestion, that the committee should approach industry for sponsorship. Collie's scheme, however, was far too outrageous for Hinks to swallow, as indeed it was intended to be. Collie wrote to him: 'I have a grand new idea that I am sure will commend itself to you, it is the following:
Go to Lord Leverhulme and say, give us £10,000 and we will take a large cake of Sunlight Soap and a flag also with Sunlight Soap emblazoned on it, and we will plant them on top of Everest, then he will be able to say:
1 Sunlight Soap beats the record—29,002 tablets sold hourly.
2 Sunlight Soap towers aloft and dominates the kingdoms of the earth.
3 Avoid worry—use Sunlight Soap and for Ever-rest.'
Hinks did not reply.[1]

The Everest Committee sent three expeditions to Everest in 1921, 1922 and 1924. The first, in 1921, was to concern itself with reconnaissance. Alexander Kellas, Collie's colleague from University College days, joined the expedition in India. He had been many times to the Himalaya and was regarded as an expert on the effects of high altitude on the human body. Kellas died on the approach march, probably from the effects of an illness he had been suffering during his previous trip in Sikkim. Major Bruce led the 1922 expedition on which seven porters died, and in 1924 the brilliant young climber George Leigh-Mallory disappeared on Everest with Andrew Irvine in a mountain mystery that caught the public's imagination much as Mummery's death had done.

Collie put the committee in a quandary when he offered himself as leader of the 1921 expedition. He may well have been trying to irritate Hinks again but, whilst he must have realised no one would take his suggestion seriously (he was 62 at the time), there is little doubt that he would have loved to return to India. The 1921 expedition was concerned with reconnaissance and Collie was quite emphatic that the mountain should not be attempted until it had been thoroughly explored from all sides. His age would not necessarily have debarred him from a reconnaissance expedition, after all, the leader of the 1922 expedition was Bruce and he was 56, but he was persuaded to withdraw. An expedition concentrating on exploration and containing Kellas and his physiological experiments must have had a great deal of appeal for him.

It was the mountains that captivated Collie to the very end of his life. Winthrop Young wrote: 'Most of us, as the years pass, find our exclusive devotion to mountains becomes divided, at least, as between them and other and more human ties. Of all the wholehearted mountaineers I have known, Collie alone remained to the end wholly and passionately absorbed in the mountain world.'[2]

Winthrop Young also assessed the contribution made to mountaineering during the previous era by such men as Collie, Slingsby, Mummery and Sir Martin Conway:

> Together they constituted a new prophetic brotherhood, representing a fresh approach to mountaineering and incorporating a body of novel doctrine in their writings. The two main elements of this teaching were, first, the enlargement of the mountaineering idea to cover all distant ranges and the development of suitable climbing technique; and secondly, the energetic implanting and promotion of climbing in our own islands, so as to provide for our mountaineering that local root and native nurture, without which no British institution or interest can survive. There had been mountaineers before them in both these fields; but in their activities as a group, and in their writings, the two movements first came to a collective consciousness and found effective expression.[3]

For almost 30 years up to his death in 1942 Collie spent virtually every summer in Skye. Up to 1915 he and his friend Colin Phillip would rent Glen Brittle House on the south-west side of the Cuillin.

> There one found Collie at his best, a charming host, always ready to gratify his guests' desires whether these lay in climbing, fishing or shooting. Although he was a first-rate shot, as one found when shooting over dogs on the grouse moors, he refused to take part in deer-stalking. One of the terms of the lease of Glen Brittle House was that a definite number of stags were to be shot each season, and Collie invariably invited friends to undertake this. One day I asked him why he himself would never shoot a stag and he replied, 'Too high up the scale, my friend'.[4]

At Glen Brittle Collie held open house, transferring his dinner parties and hospitality there from Gower Street. No one was turned away and if beds ran out then there was the smoking room floor. Whenever Collie was in residence John Mackenzie was invariably with him and they led their guests up many a climb. Colin Phillip, who was a painter of some note, taught Collie to paint and he produced dozens of pictures of Skye and of the Canadian Rockies where, as in the telling of his nightly ghost stories, artistic licence was employed with the scenery manipulated to suit the picture.

As he grew older Collie shifted his base back to the Sligachan Inn where his favourite after-dinner retreat was the old corrugated iron smoking room. Here, round-eyed young climbers and old friends would be entertained with Collie's stories and tales of long ago, or a chosen few would maybe be invited to his bedroom, with its wonderful view down Glen Sligachan, to see his paintings.

When he retired from University College he came to Skye for even longer periods, arriving in May and staying until the autumn. Although his students thought him elderly and frail (his grey hair and unusually pale face completed the picture) this was far from the truth. He remained agile, fit and healthy until three weeks before his death. In their 60s he and Mackenzie were still

facing page
56 Collie crossing Sligachan River. *Photo from Collie's collection, probably around 1900.*

climbing. Collie wrote to Winthrop Young, 'John is magnificent and although he is over sixty he performed gymnastic feats of pulling himself up that are usually considered possible to be performed only by young men.'[5] Cecil Slingsby at 70 was also enjoying the delights of being hauled up into 'aaful' places.

When they were not climbing and walking the friends were fishing. At the age of nine Collie had surprised the family at Glassel by bringing home eight trout one day. Few could match his record of 1930 when he caught 1,442 fish—salmon, sea trout and loch river trout. Michael Low whose father knew Collie well, went with his family to Skye every summer between 1928 and 1933. He recalled two stories about Collie and his fishing. One summer there had been no rain for weeks, 'the sun shone all day and the rocks of the Cuillin were almost too hot to touch. There was next to no water in the river and no one had caught a fish for weeks. My mother said to Collie that she was sorry that we would be leaving without a taste of one of his salmon. On our last night there was a twelve pound salmon with the best portion on our table. Collie knew where every fish was in the river but we never dared to ask how this one was caught. On the other occasion I was going out of the hotel with my trout rod and Collie asked where I was going. I told him my idea was to fish the small loch above the hotel from the boat. He suggested I would do better on the Shepherd's pool on the river so I took his advice. After a barren two hours thrashing the river I decided to try the small loch and there of course was Norman Collie in the boat pulling them in and a bag of five ½-¾ pound brown trout.'[6]

Mackenzie and his brother Murdo would come to Sligachan every day. Murdo, being younger, would take visitors up Bruach na Frithe, while Collie and Mackenzie would take a boat and spend lazy days on the Storr Loch. If they tired of this there was always small game—grouse, woodsnipe, woodcock and wild duck. Mackenzie was entered in the fishing catch records of the inn as 'Mr Morton', to disguise the fact that he was actually a local and not to discourage other guests from trying! So used to the name did he become that many referred to him as Morton.

Collie and Mackenzie were a familiar sight around the inn. Mackenzie short and fierce looking with his long, white beard. Collie tall and gaunt with bright, brown eyes looking out over his large pipe. In 1933 tragedy struck. John died and Collie was never to fully recover from his death. Their friendship was almost like a marriage and certainly a marriage of two minds. Collie mourned him for the remaining nine years of his life. He had a headstone of rock erected over Mackenzie's grave with the simple words engraved upon it: 'To the memory of John Mackenzie Cuillin guide died 20 July 1933 aged 76.' One friend wrote of their friendship: 'It was a pleasant and stimulating sight to see Collie and his friend and gillie, John Mackenzie, pacing up and down in front of Sligachan, two old men, one a distinguished scholar, the other a simple peasant, smoking their pipes and seldom speaking because their intimacy was such that it needed no words for its expression. These two men did not presume on each other. But they had a friendship that not even death, in my belief, could destroy.'[7] Another believed that Mackenzie 'worshipped the ground on which Collie stood'.[8]

Yet Mackenzie's death was only another in a long line. All Collie's friends of his youth were dying—Woolley in 1920, Slingsby in 1923, Stutfield in 1929; and Collie was also to outlive Bruce, Hastings and Solly.

Many who knew Collie at this time remarked on the change that came over him. Always something of a recluse, he would now avoid all strangers, becoming more than a little eccentric. Now and again a climber arriving at the inn would be favoured with his company and he always wanted to know what climbs had been done. Many thought him very lonely and although one's first impression was of a 'solitary unfriendly man living in a world of memories' he gradually unbent and even in old age had the power to captivate. Young climbers meeting him in the 1930s thought it a great privilege to talk with this pioneer of mountaineering. They would see him passing along the road in the yellow Sligachan Rolls en route for the Storr, or in the chair in the outer vestibule of the inn known as 'Collie's Corner', where he would sit for hours, pipe in mouth, gazing out at Glamaig or down Loch Sligachan to the Red Cuillin. One young climber, Hugh Welsh, saw him there often and wrote, 'I often wondered what he thought of as he gazed out with far-reaching and listening eyes. Sometimes when spoken to he seemed to return from a great distance as if he had been living over again some of his early exploits.'[9]

Perhaps Collie was recalling the summer of 1899 when he had discovered the Cioch. That was the summer when Bruce came home on leave with gurkha Harkbir. Collie had taken them both off to the Alps where Harkbir had his first experience of the European mountains. They wandered from one centre to another, briefly meeting with O G Jones a few days before he was killed on the Dent Blanche, and making ascents of Mont Blanc and Monte Rosa, before Collie took them all off to Skye where Harkbir showed them how to deal with mountains. Bruce and Collie had been 'pulled up' many a climb on Alasdair by this natural mountaineer. Rumour had it that Harkbir had made an extraordinary run from the Sligachan Inn to the summit of Glamaig, and back again, in one and a quarter hours. The estate owner, Macleod of Macleod, refused to believe this and a heated argument ensued between him and some local gillies. Bruce offered to end the discussion by asking Harkbir to repeat the run—a distance of two miles with an ascent of 2,600 feet. He was perfectly game and beat his first record by 20 minutes. What a sight it must have been to see the disbelieving face of Macleod change to one of astonishment as the bare-footed gurkha careered back down the mountain.

Or perhaps Collie was silently laughing over the words that the Austrian mountaineer Julius Kugy had written about him when they met at the Aiguille du Midi hut, again during 1899. Kugy had offered tea to Collie and Bruce and 'managed to bring a brief smile to Collie's stern, dark countenance, which strikes me as a greater achievement than the day's ascent of Mont Blanc'.[10] Yes, he had met some fine and interesting men in his time like that

57 Alps 1899, Harkbir, Woolley and Bruce. *Photo by Collie from his slide collection, with permission of the Alpine Club.*

exceptional young Englishman Gino Watkins. So impressed was he by that man's qualities that it seemed natural to offer him a grant on behalf of the Royal Geographical Society after only a few minutes conversation. Gino had repaid the trust a dozen times in his famous arctic journeys before he was drowned in Greenland. Then of course there were the Rockies. He had memories enough and to spare for those days. He was still telling the yarns he heard around the camp fire and they were much better than the ones he was getting in return. 'The smell of the pinewoods and the muskegs—and all the good old times. I can see the Pinto and the Grey and remember the mosquitoes and the bulldog flies and hear Peyto telling us all sorts of things over the camp fire. My! but I wish I was twenty years younger again! We had the cream of the wanderings at the end of last century, and have lots to sit and think about in a comfortable chair.'[11]

One pouring morning, Collie was sitting in the vestibule dreaming such dreams when 'two ladies approached, clad in oilskins and sou'westers and armed with umbrellas. To their query "Oh, Doctor what kind of a day will it be?" he gave no answer but gazed out through the streaming window. A second venture was responded to by his withdrawing his pipe and without taking his gaze away replying, "Can't you use your eyes?" '[12]

Collie was in Skye in 1939 when war was declared. The hotel emptied at once but Collie decided to stay put. All through the bombings of 1940 and 1941, when University College was in part razed to the ground and the Ramsay Memorial Laboratory destroyed, he kept a lonely vigil in the inn worrying about his treasures and writing constant letters to London regarding them. His home was not bombed, although several houses in Gower Street were totally demolished.

He never returned to his London home, and University College, now restored, owns the house in which he had rented rooms.

Though he may well have intended to settle eventually in Skye, the war made the decision for him. Skye in wartime was much further from the centre of things than it had been in peace and the exile, even here, told on him. He believed, rightly, as it turned out, that he would not live to see the liberation of the world from 'the foul beast of Europe'. He kept in touch with his friends, many of whom he was never to see again, and one of his last letters was to Winthrop Young who had asked him for his views on the new age and techniques in mountaineering. Collie replied: 'It's growth I think was due to many causes. More people took to guideless climbing, more books were written about climbing in various parts of the world. Slingsby on Norway, Bruce on India etc. Also every year it became easier to get to various ranges of mountains with hundreds of unclimbed high peaks. The loss of Mummery on Nanga Parbat and Mallory also helped, just as Whymper's ascent of the Matterhorn did.'[13]

One of the last people to see Collie was Richard Hillary, a young RAF pilot who was spending a leave in Skye. Hillary had suffered terrible burns when his plane crashed into the North Sea but he had fought his way back to life, only to die in another crash shortly after he wrote these words. 'We were alone in the inn, save for one old man who had returned there to die. His hair was white but his face and bearing were still those of a great mountaineer, though he must have been a great age. He never spoke, but appeared regularly at meals to take his place at a table, tight-pressed against the windows, alone with his wine and his memories. We thought him rather fine.' Hillary and a friend spent a day in the mountains but fell into a river on the descent. 'Over dinner we told the landlord of our novel descent. His sole comment was "Humph" but the old man at the window turned and smiled at us. I think he approved.'[14]

58 Collie outside Sligachan Hotel in Skye in 1942, two months before his death. *Photo from Mrs Susan Benstead, with permission.*

In October 1942 Collie fell while fishing in Loch Storr and received a drenching, as a result of which he became ill. He was plagued by neuritis, lumbago and sciatica and the Portree doctor prescribed morphia tablets but there was a rapid deterioration. He managed to write to one of his friends at University College saying he was in terrible pain. This was not to last and he died on the first of November. In vain his friends tried to get permits to Skye, but due to the war the island was now a restricted area and only one friend from London was able to attend the funeral. The national newspapers carried very short obituaries, possibly because of the paper shortage, which

Norman Collie's grave with John Mackenzie's grave behind. At the Free Presbyterian Church of Struan, Island of Skye. *Photo by Donald Mill.*

upset his friends who felt he deserved much more recognition. Consequently, an appreciation of his life and work appeared the following January, in *The Times*.[15]

Collie, at his own request, was buried near John Mackenzie in the beautiful lichen-covered churchyard of Struan. A gabbro boulder is his headstone, a wild sea loch and a Skye river his nearby companions. You could almost believe the friends haunt the lonely hills around, for if ever two men left their spirits amongst the mountains, it was John Mackenzie and Norman Collie.

Appendix I

Recorded First Ascents of Norman Collie

Many of the cliffs where Collie first put up routes are still regarded as classic rock-climbing areas but many of his lines have been improved upon by the discovery of better and more direct variations. Others have sunk back into obscurity and disuse. However, they have all been included in the following list because they make an interesting picture of one man's contribution to the history of mountaineering. It is a picture that can never be complete for Collie, like so many early climbers, achieved far more than we will ever know about, a striking example being the almost complete absence of any details about his rock climbing in Ireland—a country he visited many times and upon whose mountain cliffs he was one of the first to tread.

Skye

1888	Am Basteir—The Bhasteir Tooth—SW Ridge with Mackenzie.
1890	Sgurr nan Gillean—Gully between Third and Fourth Pinnacles—alone.
1890	Sgurr Mhic Choinnich—Collie's Ledge—with Mackenzie.
1891	The Thearlaich-Dubh Gap—with Mackenzie and W W King.
1896	Sgurr a'Mhadaidh—NW Buttress—companions unknown.
1896	Sgurr Alasdair—NW Face—Collie's Climb—with W W Naismith and E B Howell.
1896	Sgurr a'Ghreadaidh—SE Ridge—Collie's Route—with E B Howell.
1896	Sgurr nan Gillean—NE Face of First Pinnacle—with W W Naismith and E B Howell.
1896	Sgurr Coire an Lochain—N to S (route unknown) with Mackenzie, W W Naismith and E B Howell.
1906	Sron na Ciche—The Cioch—Collie's Route—with Mackenzie.
1906	Sron na Ciche—Western Gully—with Mackenzie.

1906	Sron na Ciche—The Flake—with Mackenzie.
1906	Sgurr Dearg—Window Buttress—with Mackenzie.
1907	Sron na Ciche—Eastern Buttress—Zig Zag—with Mackenzie.
1907	Sron na Ciche—Western Buttress—Amphitheatre Arête—with Mackenzie.
1907	Coire Lagan—Western Buttress—route unknown—with Mackenzie.

Scottish Mainland

11 Sept 1891	Aonach Dubh—N Face—route unknown—alone.
1891	Buachaille Etive Mor—Great Gully—alone.
24 March 1894	Buachaille Etive Mor—Collie's Climb—with G Solly and J Collier.
March 1894	Bidean nam Bian—Collie's Pinnacle—short side—with G Solly and J Collier.
26 March 1894	Bidean nam Bian—Central Gully—alone.
29 March 1894	Ben Nevis—Tower Ridge by the Western Traverse—with G Solly and J Collier.
April 1894	Aonach Dubh—East Wall Climb—with G Hastings.
April 1894	Stob Coire nan Lochan—NE Face—route unknown—with G Hastings.
April 1984	Stob Coire nam Beith—route unknown on NW top of Bidean—with G Hastings.
12 April 1895	Ben Nevis—Castle Ridge—with W W Naismith, G Thompson and M W Travers.
1897	Beinn Eighe—Coire Mhic Fearchair—The Triple Buttress—Collie's Route (final section explored first on top rope)—companions unknown.
?	Sgurr a'Chaorachain—SE Face—A'Chioch—companions unknown.
?	Stack Polly-Western Butteress—S side—route unknown—companions unknown.

Lake District

27 Dec 1891	Wastwater—Great Gully on the Screes—with G Hastings and J W Robinson.
15 April 1892	Buckbarrow—Rowan Tree Gully—with W Brunskill, G B Gibbs and W W King.
15 April 1892	Buckbarrow—Left Face Climb—with W Brunskill and W W King.
23 April 1892	Great Gable—Naples Needle—The Lingmell Crack—with O G Jones and Mrs Comeline.
27 Dec 1892	Scawfell—Moss Ghyll—Collie's Exit—with G Hastings and J W Robinson.

The Alps

18 Aug 1892	Aiguille du Grépon—first traverse—N Ridge and SW Ridge—with G Hastings, A F Mummery and H Pasteur.

25 July 1893	Dent du Requin—Mummery Variant—with G Hastings, A F Mummery and W C Slingsby.
7 Aug 1893	Col des Deux Aigles—SW Face—with G Hastings, A F Mummery and W C Slingsby.
7 Aug 1893	Aiguille du Plan—Route Mummery—with G Hastings, A F Mummery and W C Slingsby.
14 Aug 1893	Grand Combin—Variation up to Isler's Shoulder—with G Hastings and W C Slingsby.
3 Aug 1894	Col des Courtes Argentière Face—with G Hastings and A F Mummery.
4/5 Aug 1894	Mont Blanc—first guideless via Old Brenva Route—with G Hastings and A F Mummery.

Himalaya

2 Aug 1895	Butesharon Pass—with A F Mummery, G Hastings, C G Bruce and Ragobir.
11 Aug 1895	Diamirai Peak—with A F Mummery, Ragobir and Lor Khan.

Lofoten

4 Aug 1901	Higraftind—3,810 ft—SW Ridge—with G Hastings, H Priestman, H Woolley and E Hogrenning.
14 Aug 1901	Geitgaljartind—3,555 ft—NE Ridge—with G Hastings, H Priestman, H Woolley and E Hogrenning.
1901	Langstrandtinder—routes unknown on two peaks in this range—with H Woolley.
2 Aug 1903	Ertenhelltind—E Ridge—with D Northall-Laurie, W C Slingsby and W Slingsby.
10 Aug 1903	Rulten—3,485 ft—W Side—with W Slingsby and W C Slingsby.
14 Aug 1903	Midtre Langstrandtind—N Face—with D Northall-Laurie, W C Slingsby and W Slingsby.
17 Aug 1903	Rulten—E Side—with D Northall-Laurie, W C Slingsby and W Slingsby.
29 Aug 1903	Hermandalstind—3,391 ft—N Ridge—with D Northall-Laurie, W C Slingsby and W Slingsby.
30 Aug 1903	Munken—2,640 ft—N Ridge—with D Northall-Laurie, W C Slingsby and W Slingsby.
5 Aug 1904	Kjaendalsnaebbe—E Side—with E C C Baly, W C Slingsby and M Slingsby.
17 Aug 1904	Ostind—2,232 ft—SW Face—with E C C Baly, W C Slingsby, M Slingsby, H Woolley and W Slingsby.
19 Aug 1904	Klokketinder—Tretinder—N Face and W Ridge—with E C C Baly, W C Slingsby, M Slingsby and W Slingsby.
21 Aug 1904	Hermandalstind—N Face—with E C C Baly, W C Slingsby, M Slingsby, W Slingsby and H Woolley.
22 Aug 1904	Bishopshuen—1,971 ft—E Side S Ridge—with E C C Baly, W C Slingsby, M Slingsby and W Slingsby.

29 Aug 1904	Store Langstrandtind— NW Face—with E C C Baly, W C Slingsby and H Woolley.

Candian Rocky Mountains

(All first ascents of the mountain)

2 Aug 1897	Mt Lefroy—11,230 ft—with H B Dixon, C E Fay, P Sarbach, A Michael, J R Vanderlip, C L Noyes, C Thompson and H C Parker.
5 Aug 1897	Mt Victoria—11,365 ft—SE Arête—with C E Fay, A Michael and P Sarbach.
Aug 1897	Mt Gordon—10,510 ft—with G P Baker, H B Dixon, C E Fay, A Michael, C L Noyes, H C Parker, C Thompson and P Sarbach.
Aug 1897	Unnamed—9,750 ft—2½ miles SSE of Peyto Lake—with G P Baker and P Sarbach.
Aug 1897	Mt Sarbach—10,350—with G P Baker and P Sarbach.
22 Aug 1898	Mt Athabasca—11,452 ft—N Ridge—with H Woolley.
23 Aug 1898	Snow Dome—11,322 ft—with H Stutfield and H Woolley.
Aug 1898	Diadem Peak—11,060 ft—SE Ridge—with H Stutfield and H Woolley.
Sept 1898	Mt Thompson—10,050—SW Slopes—with H Stutfield and H Woolley.
Sept 1900	Mt Edith—8,380 ft—W Face to N Peak—with F Stephens.
Aug 1902	Mt Murchison—10,936 ft—NW Peak—with H Stutfield, G M Weed and H Kaufman.
4 Aug 1902	Mt Freshfield—10,945 ft—E Ridge—with J Outram, H Stutfield, G M Weed, H Woolley, H Kaufman and C Kaufman.
8 Aug 1902	Mt Forbes—11,852 ft—SW Ridge—with J Outram, H Stutfield, G M Weed, H Woolley, C Kaufman and H Kaufman.
Aug 1902	Howse Peak—10,793 ft—WNW Ridge—with H Stutfield, G M Weed, H Woolley and H Kaufman.
Aug 1902	Mt Noyes—10,120 ft—with H. Stutfield, G M Weed and H Woolley.
Aug 1902	Neptuak Mountain—10,620 ft—NW Ridge—with H Stutfield, G M Weed, H Woolley and H Kaufman.
Aug 1910	Mumm Peak—9,718 ft—with A L Mumm and M Inderbinen.
Aug 1910	Mt Phillips (Resolution)—10,660 ft—E Slope—with A L Mumm, M Inderbinen and J Yates.
Aug 1911	Mt Bess—10,550 ft—SW Ridge—with A L Mumm, M Inderbinen and J Yates.
Aug 1911	Barricade Mountain—10,210 ft—NW Peak—with A L Mumm, M Inderbinen and J Yates.
Aug 1911	Hoodoo Peak (Monte Cristo)—9,000 ft—W Face—with A L Mumm, M Inderbinen and J Yates.

Appendix II

Scientific Bibliography of Norman Collie

1879 On the celestine and baryto-celestine of Clifton (*Proc. Bristol Nat. Soc.* 2, 292-300. *Miner. Mag.* 2, 220-2)

1882 (with E A Letts) On the action of haloid compounds of hydro-carbon radicals on phosphide of sodium and on the salts of tetrabenzylphosphonium (Abstract). (*Proc. Roy. Soc. Edinb.* 11, 46-53)

1883 (with E A Letts) On the action of phosphide of sodium on haloid ethers and on the salts of tetrabenzyl phosphonium. (*Trans. Roy. Soc. Edinb.* 39, 181-215)

1884 Ueber die Einwirkung des Ammoniaks auf Acetessigsester. (*Liebigs Ann.* 226, 294-322)

1886 (with E A Letts) On the salts of tetrethylphosphonium and their decomposition by heat. (*Proc. Chem. Soc.* 2, 164-5; *Phil. Mag.* 22, 183-206)

1887 Ueber einige Condensationsproducte des Amidoacetessigsäther mit Salzsaüre. (Ber. dtsch. Chem. Ges. 20, 445-7)

1887 On the action of heat on the salts of triethylbenzylphosphonium. (*Phil. Mag.* 24, 27-37)

1888 (with E A Letts) Zur Kentniss der Tetrabenzylphosphonium Verbindungen. (*Ber. dtsch. Chem. Ges.* 21, 1602-3)

1888 (with T A Lawson) The action of heat on the salts of tetramethylammonium. (*J. Chem. Soc.* 53, 624-36)

1888 The action of heat on the salts of tetramethylphosphonium. (*J. Chem. Soc.* 53, 636-40)

1888 On a new method for the preparation of mixed tertiary phosphines. (*J. Chem. Soc.* 53, 714-16)

1889 On some Leadhills minerals. (*J. Chem. Soc.* 55, 91-6)

1889 Note on the fluoride of methyl. (*J. Chem. Soc.* 55, 110-13)

1889 Some compounds of tribenzylphosphine oxide. (*J. Chem. Soc.* 55, 223-7)

1890 (with S B Schryver) The action of heat on the clorides and hydroxides of mixed quaternary ammonium compounds. (*J. Chem. Soc.* 57, 767-82)

1891 The action of heat on ethylic β-amidocrotonate (Part 1). (*J. Chem. Soc.* 59, 172–9)
1891 On the constitution of dehydracetic acid. (*J. Chem. Soc.* 59, 179–89)
1891 The lactone of triacetic acid. (*J. Chem. Soc.* 59, 607–17)
1891 Some reactions of dehydracetic acid. (*J. Chem. Soc.* 59, 617–21)
1892 (with W S Myers) Production of pyridine derivatives from the lactone of triacetic acid. (*J. Chem. Soc.* 61, 721–8)
1892 Ueber die Constitution des Turpentins und des Camphers. (*Ber. dtsch. Chem. Ges.* 25, 1108–18)
1893 (with W S Myers) The formation of orcinol and other condensation products from dehydracetic acid. (*J. Chem. Soc.* 63, 122–8)
1893 The production of naphthalene derivatives from dehydracetic acid. (*J. Chem. Soc.* 63, 329–37)
1893 The fluorescein of camphoric anhydride. (*J. Chem. Soc.* 63, 961–4)
1894 (with H R Le Sueur) Salts of dehydracetic acid. (*J. Chem. Soc.* 65, 254–62)
1894 A new method of preparing carbon tetrabromide. (*J. Chem. Soc.* 66, 262–4)
1895 A new form of barometer. (*J. Chem. Soc.* 67, 128–32)
1895 Action of heat on ethylic β-amidocrotonate, Part II. (*J. Chem. Soc.* 67, 215–26)
1895 (with A P Sedgewick) Some oxypyridine derivatives. (*J. Chem. Soc.* 67, 399–413)
1895 (with W Ramsay and M W Travers) Helium, a constituent of certain minerals. (*J. Chem. Soc.* 67, 684–701)
1896 (with W Ramsay) On the behaviour of argon and helium when submitted to the electric discharge. (*Proc. Roy. Soc.* 59, 257–70)
1896 (with W Ramsay) Sur l'homogénéitié de l'argon et de l'helium. (*C. R. Acad. Sci. Paris*, 123, 214–16)
1896 (with N T M Wilsmore) The production of naphthalene and *iso*quinoline derivatives from dehydracetic acid. (*J. Chem. Soc.* 69, 293–304)
1897 Production of pyridine derivatives from ethylic β-amidocrotonate. (*J. Chem. Soc.* 71, 299–311)
1897 (with E Aston) Oxidation products of $\alpha\gamma$-dimethyl-α'-chloropyridine. (*J. Chem. Soc.* 71, 653–7)
1897 (with W Ramsay) Helium and argon, Part III. Experiments which show the inactivity on these elements. (*Proc. Roy. Soc.* 60, 53–6)
1897 (with W Ramsay) The homogeneity of helium and argon. (*Proc. Roy. Soc.* 60, 206–16)
1897 (with A Lapworth) Production of some nitro- and amido-hydroxypicolines. (*J. Chem. Soc.* 71, 835–45)
1897 A space formula for benzene. (*J. Chem. Soc.* 71, 1013–23)
1898 (with T Tickle) Production of some nitro- and amido-oxylutidines, Part I. (*J. Chem. Soc.* 73, 229–35)
1898 (with L Hall) Production of some nitro- and amido-oxylutidines, Part II. (*J. Chem. Soc.* 73, 235–41)
1898 (with C Frye) Note on the action of bromine on benzene. (*J. Chem. Soc.* 73, 241–3)
1898 (with W Lean) Production of some chloropyridine carboxylic acids. (*J. Chem. Soc.* 73, 588–92)
1899 (with T Tickle) The salts of dimethylpyrone and the quadrivalence of oxygen. (*J. Chem. Soc.* 75, 710–17)

1900 (with B D Steele) Dimethyldiacetylacetone, tetramethylpyrone and orcinol derivatives from diacetylacetone. (*J. Chem. Soc.* 77, 961–71)
1900 Dehydracetic acid. (*J. Chem. Soc.* 77, 971–7)
1900 (with B D Steele) Periodides of substituted oxonium derivatives. (*J. Chem. Soc.* 77, 1114–18)
1901 (with W Garsed) On the estimation of cocaine and on cocaine hydriodide periodide. (*J. Chem. Soc.* 79, 675–81)
1901 On the decomposition of carbon dioxide when submitted to electric discharge at low pressures. (*J. Chem. Soc.* 79, 1063–9)
1902 (with T Tickle) Some hydroxypyrone derivatives. (*J. Chem. Soc.* 81, 1104–7)
1903 Note on the effect of mercury vapour on the spectrum of helium. (*Proc. Roy. Soc.* 71, 25–7)
1904 The action of acetyl chloride on the sodium salts of diacetyl-acetone, and the constitution of pyrone compounds. (*J. Chem. Soc.* 85, 971–80)
1904 A method for the rapid ultimate analysis of certain organic compounds. (*J. Chem. Soc.* 85, 1111–16)
1904 Note on methyl fluoride. (*J. Chem. Soc.* 85, 1317–18)
1904 (with W Ramsay) The spectrum of the radium emanation. (*Proc. Roy. Soc.* 73, 470–6)
1905 (with E C C Baly) The ultra-violent absorption spectra of aromatic compounds, Part 1. Benzene and cetain mono-substituted derivatives. (*J. Chem. Soc.* 87, 1332–46)
1905 Syntheses by means of the silent electric discharge. (*J. Chem. Soc.* 87, 1540–8)
1907 (with T P Hilditch) An isomeric change of dehydracetic acid. (*J. Chem. Soc.* 91, 787–9)
1907 (with E R Chrystall) The production of orcinol derivatives from the sodium salt of ethyl acetoacetate by the action of heat. (*J. Chem. Soc.* 91, 1802–16)
1907 Derivatives of the multiple Keten group. (*J. Chem. Soc.* 91, 1806–13)
1909 A curious property of neon. (*Proc. Roy. Soc. A*, 82, 378–80)
1913 (with H S Patterson) The presence of neon in hydrogen after the passage of the electric discharge through the latter at low pressures. (*J. Chem. Soc.* 103, 419–26)
1913 (with H S Patterson) The presence of neon in hydrogen after the passage of the electric discharge through the latter at low pressure, Part II. (*Proc. Chem. Soc.* 29, 217–20)
1914 Note on the paper by T R Merton on 'Attempts to produce the rare gases by electric discharge'. (*Proc. Roy. Soc. A*, 90, 544–6)
1915 (with H S Patterson and J I O Masson) Production of neon and helium by the electric discharge. (*Proc. Roy. Soc. A*, 91, 30–45)
1915 (with F Reynolds) Removal of oxygen from diethylphosphine oxide. (*J. Chem. Soc.* 107, 367–9)
1915 (with G White) Some benzopyranol derivatives. (*J. Chem. Soc.* 107, 369–76)
1916 Space formula for benzene, Part II. (*J. Chem. Soc.* 109, 561–8)
1919 (with H E Watson) Spectrum of cadmium in the inactive gases. (*Proc. Roy. Soc. A*, 95, 115–20)
1920 Notes on krypton and zenon. (*Proc. Roy. Soc. A*, 97, 349–54)
1921 (with A A B Reilly) A new type of iodine compound. (*J. Chem. Soc.* 119, 1550–4)
1922 (with A A B Reilly) Diacetylacetone. (*J. Chem. Soc.* 121, 1984–7)

1922 Monograph on the copper-red glazes. (*Trans. Oriental Ceramic Soc.* 1921–2, 21–31)

1925 (with G Bishop) Nitro- and amino-ethoxylutidines. (*J. Chem. Soc.* 127, 962–4)

1925 Reactions of triethylphosphine. (*J. Chem. Soc.* 127, 964–5)

1927 (with L Klein) Action of bromine on dimethylpyrone. (*J. Chem. Soc.* 131, 2162–4)

1928 *A Century of Chemistry at University College.* (Privately printed by University College, London)

References

Chapter 1—The Early Years

1 Geoffrey Winthrop Young, 'Obituary of Norman Collie', *Himalayan Journal*, vol XIII, p 116.
2 J I O Masson to E C C Baly, Donnan Papers 8, University College London archives, D M S Watson Library.
3 Henry Winkworth, *The Life of Catherine Winkworth*, vol II, privately published. In the possession of Mrs S M Benstead.
4 Emma Winkworth, *The Life of Catherine Winkworth*, vol II.
5 Catherine Winkworth, *The Life of Catherine Winkworth*, vol II.
6 Selina Collie, *The Life of Catherine Winkworth*, vol II.
7 Selina Collie, *The Life of Catherine Winkworth*, vol II.
8 E A Letts, Application and testimonials in favour of J N Collie candidate for the Chair of Chemistry and Metallurgy in the Mason College, Birmingham, May 1894. Wellcome Institute London, archives, B3 (8).
9 Letter from J N Collie to Selina Collie 29 Dec 1879. Archives of the Canadian Rockies, Banff, Alberta.
10 E A Letts, Application and testimonials in favour of J N Collie candidate for the Chair of Chemistry and Metallurgy in the Mason College, Birmingham, May 1894. Wellcome Institute London, archives, B3 (8).
11 Letter from Selina Collie to J N Collie undated. Archives of the Canadian Rockies, Banff, Alberta.
12 Letter from J N Collie to Selina Collie Dec 1882. Archives of the Canadian Rockies, Banff, Alberta.
13 Letter from Selina Collie to J N Collie 15 May 1884. Archives of the Canadian Rockies, Banff, Alberta.
14 Letter from Selina Collie to J N Collie 16 May 1884. Archives of the Canadian Rockies, Banff, Alberta.
15 Letter from Mrs S M Benstead. In the author's possession.
16 Sir William Ramsay, Collie Correspondence AM/D/186. University College London archives, D M S Watson library.

Chapter 2—Island of Cloud

1 J N Collie, 'Island of Skye', *Alpine Journal*, vol 32, p 170.
2 J N Collie, 'Island of Skye', *AJ*, vol 32, p 174.
3 J N Collie, *Climbing on the Himalaya & Other Mountain Ranges*, David Douglas (Edinburgh 1902), p 212.
4 J N Collie, 'Obituary of John Mackenzie', *Scottish Mountaineering Club Journal*, vol 20, p 124.
5 J N Collie, 'On the height of some of the Black Cuchullins in Skye', *SMCJ*, vol 2, p 168.
6 W M Mackenzie, 'Climbers Guide to the Cuillin of Skye', *SMCJ* (1958), p 9.
7 J N Collie, 'The Island of Skye', *AJ*, vol 32, p 164.
8 A P Abraham, *Rock-climbing in Skye*, Longmans Green & Co (London 1908), p 1.
9 A P Abraham, *Rock-climbing in Skye*, p 123.
10 Letter from Bill Wood to the author. In the possession of the author.
11 J N Collie, 'The Island of Skye', *AJ*, vol 32, p 167.
12 J N Collie, 'The Island of Skye', *AJ*, vol 32, p 168.
13 J N Collie, 'The Island of Skye', *AJ*, vol 32, p 169.
14 Letter from J N Collie to William Douglas, July 1894. Scottish Mountaineering Club archives. Housed at the Music Library, Edinburgh.
15 Geoffrey Winthrop Young, 'Obituary of Norman Collie', *Himalayan Journal*, vol XIII, p 116.
16 J N Collie, 'A Reverie', *SMCJ*, vol 5 (Sept 1898), p 99.

Chapter 3—Wasdale

1 J N Collie, *Climbing on the Himalaya and other Mountain Ranges*, David Douglas (Edinburgh 1902), p 247.
2 J N Collie, Letter to William Douglas. SMC archives. Housed at the Music Library, Edinburgh.
3 R W Clark and E C Pyatt, *Mountaineering in Britain*, Phoenix House (London 1957), p 38.
4 W P Haskett Smith, *Climbing in the British Isles—England*, Longmans Green & Co (London 1894), p 17.
5 J N Collie, 'Reminiscences', *Fell & Rock Journal*, vol 7, p 215.
6 J N Collie, *Climbing on the Himalaya and Other Mountain Ranges*, p 259.

Chapter 4—Argon and Helium

1 Sir William Ramsay, Ramsay Papers, vol 15, 15 June 1887. University College London, archives. D M S Watson Library.
2 E C C Baly, *Obituaries of Fellows of the Royal Society* (London, 4, 1942–4), p 331.
3 E C C Baly, *Obituaries of Fellows of the Royal Society*, p 331.
4 J N Collie, 'A Reverie', *SMCJ*, vol 5, p 97.
5 Sir W A Tilden, *Sir William Ramsay*, Macmillan & Co Ltd (London 1918), p 141.
6 S Smiles, *Obituaries of Fellows of the Royal Society*, p 345.

Chapter 5—Undiscovered Scotland

1 Letter from J N Collie to William Douglas. SMC archives. Housed at the Music Library, Edinburgh.
2 W H Murray, *Mountaineering in Scotland*, J M Dent & Sons Ltd (London 1947), p 94.
3 W T Kilgour, *Twenty Years on Ben Nevis*, Alexander Gardner (Paisley 1905), p 143.
4 W T Kilgour, *Twenty Years on Ben Nevis*, p 139.
5 J N Collie, *Climbing on the Himalaya & Other Mountain Ranges*, David Douglas (Edinburgh 1902), p 287.
6 Letter from W W Naismith to William Douglas. SMC archives. Housed at the Music Library, Edinburgh.
7 Letter from J N Collie to William Douglas 1 January 1894, SMC archives. Housed at the Edinburgh Music Library.
8 Author unknown. *SMCJ*, vol 3, p 316.
9 Donald Bennett, *Scottish Mountain Climbs*, B T Batsford Ltd (London 1979).

Chapter 6—The Three Musketeers

1 A F Mummery, *My Climbs in the Alps & Caucasus*, Blackwell's Mountaineering Library (Oxford 1936), p 79.
2 C D Milner, *Mont Blanc & the Aiguilles*, Robert Hale Ltd (London 1955), p 80.
3 Miss L Bristow, 'Letters to her family', *AJ*, vol 53, p 373.
4 G Hastings, *'Over Mont Blanc, by the Brenva Route, without Guides'*, *AJ*, vol 18, p 540.
5 G Hastings, '*Over Mont Blanc, by the Brenva Route, without Guides*', *AJ*, vol 18, p 543.

Chapter 7—Diamir—King of Mountains

1 J N Collie, *Climbing on the Himalaya & Other Mountain Ranges*, David Douglas (Edinburgh 1902), p 2.
2 J N Collie, *Climbing on the Himalaya & Other Mountain Ranges*, p 1.
3 A F Mummery, *My Climbs in the Alps & Caucasus*, Blackwell's Mountaineering Library (Oxford 1936), p XVIII.
4 C G Bruce, 'The Passing of Mummery', *Himalayan Journal*, vol III.
5 C G Bruce, 'The Passing of Mummery', *Himalayan Journal*, vol III.
6 A F Mummery, *My Climbs in the Alps & Caucasus*, p XXI.
7 Author unknown, *AJ*, vol 17, p 567.
8 J N Collie to Geoffrey Winthrop Young 7 Nov 1903. Alpine Club archives. GWY correspondence C-F B.41.
9 Geoffrey Winthrop Young, *Himalayan Journal*, vol XIII, p 117.
10 J N Collie, *Climbing on the Himalayan & Other Mountain Ranges*, David Douglas (Edinburgh 1902), p 2.
11 J N Collie, *Climbing on the Himalaya & Other Mountain Ranges*, p 88.
12 A F Mummery, *My Climbs in the Alps & Caucasus*, p XXIII.

Chapter 8—Gower Street, Ghosts and Gases

1 Geoffrey Winthrop Young, *Himalayan Journal*, vol XIII, p 115.
2 Note from J I O Masson to E C C Baly, 22 November 1942. Donnan Papers 8, University College London archives, D M S Watson Library.
3 Geoffrey Winthrop Young, *Himlayan Journal*, vol XIII, p 115
4 Note from J I O Masson to E C C Baly, 22 November 1942 University College London archives, D M S Watson Library;
5 J N Collie, *Climbing on the Himalaya & Other Mountain Ranges*, David Douglas (Edinburgh 1902), p 271.
6 J N Collie, 'Dreams', *Cairngorm Club Journal*, vol 15, p 214.
7 J N Collie, 'The Island of Skye', *AJ*, vol 32, p 175.
8 Letters from Michael Low. In the possession of the author.
9 J N Collie, *Climbing on the Himalaya & Other Mountain Ranges*, p 234.
10 E C C Baly, *Obituaries of Fellows of the Royal Society* (London, 4, 1942-4), p 347.
11 J N Collie, 'Dreams', p 213.
12 J N Collie, *A Century of Chemistry at University College*, privately printed by University College, 1928, p 21.
13 J N Collie, Ramsay Papers, vol 15, iii. University College London, archives, D M S Watson Library.
14 E C C Baly, *Obituaries of Fellows of the Royal Society*, p 333.

Chapter 9—To the Great Lone Land

1 C Noyes, *Appalachia*, vol IX, p 22.
2 R L G Irving, *A History of British Mountaineering*, B T Batsford Ltd (London 1955), p 124.
3 H E M Stutfield and J N Collie, *Climbs & Explorations in the Canadian Rockies*, Longmans Green & Co (London 1903), p 17.
4 J N Collie, 'A Search for Mt Hooker and Mt Brown', *Geographical Journal*, vol XVIII, p 339.
5 H E M Stutfield and J N Collie, *Climbs & Explorations*, p 32.
6 J N Collie to Tom Wilson 22 March 1898. AW753A.F.3, Glenbow Alberta Institute, Calgary.
7 H E M Stutfield and J N Collie, *Climbs & Explorations*, p 68.
8 J N Collie to C Thompson 23 March 1898. Archives of the Canadian Rockies, Banff, Alberta from an original in the Thorington archives, Princeton University Library.
9 J N Collie to C Thompson 4 May 1898. Archives of the Canadian Rockies, Banff, Alberta from an original in the Thorington archives, Princeton University Library.
10 Charles Hopkinson, 'In Memoriam—Hermann Woolley', *AJ* (1920), p 261.
11 H E M Stutfield and J N Collie, *Climbs & Explorations*, p 74.
12 H E M Stutfield and J N Collie, *Climbs & Explorations*, p 107.
13 H E M Stutfield and J N Collie, *Climbs & Explorations*, p 118.
14 J N Collie, 'Climbing in the Canadian Rocky Mountains', *AJ*, vol 19, p 460.
15 H E M Stutfield and J N Collie, *Climbs & Explorations*, p 124.

Chapter 10—Explorers and Rivals

1 H E M Stutfield and J N Collie, *Climbs & Explorations in the Canadian Rockies*, Longmans Green & Co (London 1903), p 156.
2 H E M Stutfield and J N Collie, *Climbs & Explorations*, p 164.
3 J N Collie, 'Exploration in the Canadian Rocky Mountains', *Geographical Journal*, vol 17, p 258.
4 H E M Stutfield, *AJ*, vol 20, p 495.
5 H E M Stutfield and J N Collie, *Climbs & Explorations*, p 188.
6 Letter from J N Collie to C Thompson 21 March 1901. Archives of the Canadian Rockies, Banff, Alberta from the original in the Thorington archive, Princeton University Library.
7 Letter from J N Collie to C Thompson 30 May 1901. Archives of the Canadian Rockies, Banff, Alberta from the original in the Thorington archive, Princeton University Library.
8 W Unsworth, *Tiger in the Snow*, Victor Gollancz Ltd (London 1967), p 76.
9 C Klucker, *Adventures of an Alpine Guide*, John Murray (London 1932), p 179.
10 H E M Stutfield and J N Collie, *Climbs & Explorations*, p 221.
11 Letter from J N Collie to C Thompson 12 November 1901. Archives of the Canadian Rockies, Banff, Alberta from the original in the Thorington archive, Princeton University Library.
12 H E M Stutfield and J N Collie, *Climbs & Explorations*, p 243.
13 H E M Stutfield and J N Collie, *Climbs & Explorations*, p 269.
14 H E M Stutfield and J N Collie, *Climbs & Explorations*, p 299.
15 J N Collie, 'Further Explorations in the Canadian Rocky Mountains', *GJ*, vol 21, p 498.

Chapter 11—The Land of the Midnight Sun

1 J N Collie, 'The Lofoten Islands', *AJ*, vol 21, p 101.
2 J N Collie, 'The Lofoten Islands', p 97.
3 J N Collie, 'The Lofoten Islands', p 98.
4 Letter from J N Collie to C Thompson 2 November 1903. Archives of the Canadian Rockies, Banff, Alberta from the original in the Thorington archive, Princton University Library.
5 J N Collie, 'Lofoten', *AJ*, vol 22, p 7.
6 J N Collie, 'Lofoten', p 11.
7 Letter from J N Collie to C Thompson 23 January 1906. Archives of the Canadian Rockies, Banff, Alberta from the original in the Thorington archive, Princeton University Library.

Chapter 12—The Old Man

1 J N Collie, Ramsay Papers, vol 15, ii. University College London archives. D M S Watson Library.
2 J N Collie, 'Note on a Curious Property of Neon', *Proceedings of the Royal Society of Edinburgh* (1909), 378.
3 J Jackson, *Obituaries of Fellows of the Royal Society* (London, 4, 1942–4), 334.

4 J I O Masson, Donnan papers, University College London archives. D M S Watson Library.
5 H S Patterson, Ramsay Papers, vol 15.
6 H S Patterson, Ramsay Papers, vol 15.
7 Letter from Dr D H G Crout. In the possession of the author.
8 M Travers, Ramsay Papers.
9 Union Magazine 1908. In the possession of the author.

Chapter 13—Sligachan

1 W Unsworth, *Everest*, Allen Lane (London), p 34.
2 Geoffrey Winthrop Young, 'Obituary of Norman Collie', *AJ*, vol 54, p 62.
3 Geoffrey Winthrop Young, 'Mountain Prophets', *AJ*, vol 54, p 111.
4 E C C Baly, *Obituaries of Fellows of the Royal Society* (London, 4, 1942–4), p 347.
5 Letter from J N Collie to Geoffrey Winthrop Young 5 October 1919. Alpine Club archives. GWY correspondence C-F B.41.
6 Letters from Michael Low. In the possession of the author.
7 St John Ervine, *Obituaries of Fellows of the Royal Society*, p 347.
8 E C C Baly, *Obituaries of Fellows of the Royal Society*, p 347.
9 H D Welsh, *The Cairngorm Club Journal*, vol 15 (1942–3).
10 J Kugy, *Alpine Pilgrimage*, John Murray (London 1934), p 272.
11 Letter from J N Collie to Tom Wilson 9 January 1928. Glenbow Alberta Institute archives, Calgary, Alberta AW 753A F.3.
12 H D Welsh, *The Cairngorm Club Journal*, vol 15 (1942–3).
13 J N Collie to Geoffrey Winthrop Young 2 May 1942. Alpine Club archives. GWY correspondence C-F B.41.
14 Richard Hillary, *The Last Enemy*, Macmillan (London 1943), p 40.
15 *The Times*, 2 January 1943.

Index